People of God

People of God

José Comblin

Edited and Translated by
Phillip Berryman

ORBIS BOOKS

Maryknoll,   New York   10545

Founded in 1970, Orbis Books endeavors to publish works that enlighten the mind, nourish the spirit, and challenge the conscience. The publishing arm of the Maryknoll Fathers and Brothers, Orbis seeks to explore the global dimensions of the Christian faith and mission, to invite dialogue with diverse cultures and religious traditions, and to serve the cause of reconciliation and peace. The books published reflect the views of their authors and do not represent the official position of the Maryknoll Society. To learn more about Maryknoll and Orbis Books, please visit our website at www.maryknoll.org.

Translation copyright © 2004 by Orbis Books

Originally published in Brazil under the title *Povo de Deus*, copyright © 2002 by Paulus Editora, São Paulo, Brasil.

Published by Orbis Books, Maryknoll, NY 10545-0308.

Manufactured in the United States of America

Library of Congress Cataloging-in-Publication Data

Comblin, José, 1923-
   [Povo de Deus. English]
   People of God / José Comblin ; edited and translated by Phillip
Berryman.
        p. cm.
Includes bibliographical references and index.
   ISBN 1-57075-521-3 (pbk.)
   1. Church.   2. Catholic Church—Doctrines.   3. Vatican Council (2nd :
1962-1965)   I. Berryman, Phillip.   II. Title.
   BX1746.C539313 2004
   262'.7—dc22
                                    2003021864

Contents

Introduction

This book has been written in view of the next papacy. It expresses hope for a return to the principles of Vatican II. Not Vatican III—there can be no Vatican III without first returning to Vatican II.

Such a return is not simply to the texts of the council but to its underlying inspiration as found in John XXIII's speeches and especially his inaugural address (October 11, 1962), which increasingly seems to point the way not merely for the council but for future generations of Christians. John XXIII clearly indicated the need for a radical shift away from the direction taken by the church, since the Council of Trent, at least, or perhaps even since the fourteenth century.

First, contrary to the "prophets of doom" who had condemned modernity for centuries, John XXIII saw primarily the new opportunities offered by contemporary society. Second, he stated that the church now prefers "to use mercy rather than harshness," and hence the council should not issue condemnations or seek to add definitions to the deposit of faith. The problem now was not the deposit but its garb, so that the message could be understood and accepted by contemporary people. On the whole, the bishops sought to follow the direction set by the pope, although a minority failed to understand this new development in the direction of the church and prevented the council from being more consistent.

Many believe that the concept of "people of God" was Vatican II's main theological contribution, affecting all the council documents; it is certainly the best expression of the "spirit" of Vatican II. If we wished to sum up the council's contribution in a phrase we could say: it reminded the church that it is people of God.

But even during the council a backlash began to take shape, as the groundwork was laid for sabotaging the council after its conclusion. The euphoria aroused by Vatican II lasted only three or four years. What set off the reaction against the council was the great crisis of civilization that shook the entire First World in the 1960s: the "Paris May" (1968) was the symbol of this cultural revolution. What is now called "postmodernity" was set in motion, though it found theoretical expression only in the 1970s.

The crisis of Western civilization impacted the church, where change was in full swing. The council's adversaries took advantage of the confluence of events to blame the council for phenomena of crisis (e.g., in the priesthood) that were caused by a change in culture. The crisis showed how distant the church was from society and how little prepared it was to adapt the changes taking place there. It showed not that Vatican II was wrong, but that it had arrived late.

The turning inward that began during Paul VI's final years became even more pronounced with the program of "restoration" led by Cardinal Josef Ratzinger under Pope John Paul II. One sign of that program has been the virtual suppression of the very idea of "people of God" from official church documents in the past two decades.

Hence the aim of this book is to explore the theological and pastoral significance of the "people of God." The concept of "people of God," which was central to Vatican II, highlights the human reality of the church (chapter 1). Preconciliar notions of the church, which emphasized the hierarchy and made ecclesiology a "hierarchology" (Yves Congar), have provoked centuries of opposition ranging from medieval reform movements and heresies, through the Protestant reformation, to modern anticlericalism. The situation began to be addressed in the biblical, liturgical, and social action movements in the first half of the twentieth century (chapter 2). The theme of the "church of the poor," broached at Vatican II, has been carried out most thoroughly in Latin America (chapter 3).

While the backlash could not directly repudiate the theme of "people of God," it has sought to downgrade its importance and replace it with the more vague notion of "communion." That tactic of Cardinal Ratzinger became evident at the 1985 extraordinary synod (chapter 4).

The starting point for understanding "people of God" is the peoples of the earth: e.g., just as peoples have "heroes," the people of God has martyrs (chapter 5). The story of human history is the gradual emergence of peoples acting, and particularly a history of increasing freedom (even though the hierarchy has often opposed that freedom). The biblical theme of "covenant" has been secularized in the emergence of democracy (chapter 6). In Christian base communities, by standing with the poor, defending their rights, and enabling the poor to become active in society, the church in Latin America has sought to be people of God (chapter 7). The people of God lives among and within other peoples. In seeking to understand what the church receives from peoples, how it relates to them (inculturation), and what it gives them, we need to reexamine the church's historical experience (chapter 8). The church can assume a position of either "maintenance" attending to its own internal needs or "mission" going out to the broader society (as in the practice of the Latin American church in recent decades, e.g., standing up to human rights violations) (chapter 9). Taking the people of God seriously entails a reexamination of the role of the hierarchy, the liturgy, church governance, church teaching, and models of ministry (chapter 10).

This book is in continuity with several of my earlier books devoted to the work of the Holy Spirit through reflection on specifically Christian concepts, namely those of "action," "word," and "freedom."[1] The concept of "people" is likewise biblical, albeit related to broader cultural and philosophical currents.

We believe a return to Vatican II starts by rehabilitating the concept of "people of God" and returning it to its proper place in ecclesiology. This concept cannot of course explain all aspects of the church, but it expresses—and only it can express—something that is fundamental for the future of Christianity in the new humankind that is emerging in the Third World. That is precisely what this study is about.

Chapter 1

THE PEOPLE OF GOD AT VATICAN II

COUNCIL TEXTS

Toward the end of the Second Vatican Council, a group of the most prominent theological advisers to the bishops decided to start an international
journal named *Concilium*. As stated in the first issue's editorial, the intention was "to build on Vatican Council II." It was no accident that the first
article in that issue, "The Church as People of God," was written by Yves
Congar, who had struggled most to have that issue introduced into the council
framework.

It was then generally agreed that "people of God" was a kind of symbol
of the entire change that the council wished to imprint on the church. The
placement of the people of God as the second chapter of *Lumen Gentium*
(between chapters on the mystery of the church and the hierarchy) adopted
by the assembly after long discussions was one of the most significant decisions of the council and a great victory for the advocates of change, as Congar
emphasized:

> The expression People of God in itself has such depth of meaning and
> such dynamism that it is impossible to use it in reference to the reality
> that is the Church, without orienting our thoughts in certain perspec-
> tives. As for the place assigned to this chapter, everyone knows the often
> decisive doctrinal significance that may result from the order in which
> questions are arranged and of the place assigned to one of them.
>
> In the *Summa* of St. Thomas Aquinas, order and place contribute to
> the intelligibility of a given fact. In the schema *De Ecclesia* the sequence
> might have been: the Mystery of the Church, Hierarchy, the People of
> God in general. . . . But the sequence adopted was: Mystery of the
> Church, People of God, Hierarchy. Thus, the highest value was given
> to the quality of discipleship, the dignity attached to Christian existence
> as such. . . .
>
> Only time can tell what consequences will follow from the option

made when the chapter *De Populo Dei* was placed in the sequence that we have indicated. It is our conviction that these consequences will be considerable.[1]

Almost forty years later Congar's article remains relevant and could be a program for restoring the theology of the people of God after the current retreat from it.

Let us recall the most important texts from chapter 2 of *Lumen Gentium* on the people of God, starting with the most important:

Christ instituted this new covenant, the new covenant in his blood (see 1 Cor 11:25); he called a people together made up of Jews and Gentiles which would be one, not according to the flesh, but in the Spirit, and it would be the new people of God.

That messianic people has as its head Christ. . . .

This people possesses the dignity and freedom of the daughters and sons of God. . . . Its law is the new commandment to love as Christ loved us (see Jn 13:34). Its destiny is the kingdom of God . . . on earth.

Consequently, this messianic people, although it does not, in fact, include everybody, and at times may seem to be a little flock is, however, a most certain seed of unity, hope and salvation. . . . [It] enters into human history, though it transcends at once all times and all boundaries between peoples.

Christ the Lord, high priest taken from the midst of humankind (see Heb 5:1-5), made the new people "a kingdom of priests to his God and Father" (Rev 1:6, see 5:9-10).

The holy people of God shares also in Christ's prophetic office: it spreads abroad a living witness to him. . . .

It is not only through the sacraments and the ministries that the Holy Spirit makes the people holy, leads them and enriches them with his virtues. Allotting his gifts "at will to each individual" (1 Cor 12:11), he also distributes special graces among the faithful of every rank. . . .

All women and men are called to belong to the new people of God. This people therefore, whilst remaining one and unique, is to be spread throughout the whole world and to all ages in order that the design of God's will may be fulfilled.

All are called to this catholic unity of the people of God, which prefigures and promotes universal peace.

Finally, those who have not yet accepted the Gospel are related to the people of God in various ways.[2]

Understanding these texts properly means understanding what those who wrote them intended to say. Monsignor Gerard Philips, the secretary of the theological commission who organized *Lumen Gentium*, explains that the aim of chapter 2 was to show how the mystery of the church and its catholicity are attained in history. Congar says that the commission that drafted the text, after speaking of the Incarnation and the Trinity intended "(1) to show this Church also in the process of constructing itself in human history; (2) to show this Church expanding and reaching various categories of men who are unequally situated in relation to the fullness of life that is in Christ and of which the Church is the sacrament; (3) to explain what all the members of the People of God hold in common on the plane of the dignity of Christian existence, prior to any distinctions among them based on office or state."[3]

The council fathers were fully aware that chapter 2 was going contrary to accepted ecclesiology. What they did was no accident; they fully intended to bring about a profound change in ecclesiology by choosing the "people of God" theme, and they chose those words fully understanding their meaning. They were quite aware that for almost seven hundred years Catholic ecclesiology had so concentrated on the hierarchy that lay people seemed to be passive objects to be cared for by that hierarchy, and that is what they wanted to change.

The previous ecclesiology was based on the idea of *societas perfecta* and drew inspiration from the nominalist ideas according to which the crucial point of society is the powers governing it—thereby turning ecclesiology into a "hierarchology." The council fathers explicitly wanted to do away with this image and return to the church's origins, the biblical and patristic sources and the great thirteenth-century theologians.

The choice of "people of God" as a theme expressed this return to the sources. For the bishops, the ancient and truly traditional ecclesiology was based on the concept of people of God, not that of *societas perfecta*. Hence any effort to downplay the concept of people of God goes against the council's most explicit intentions. The option for the concept "people of God" expressed an intention to strike out toward something new; that was clear to both the majority, and to the minority who feared what was new in conciliar theology. This intention of the council, so strong and so clear, must be kept in mind in the face of criticisms, doubts, and attempts to blot this concept out of ecclesiology, as apparently happened at the 1985 synod. Which has precedence: the council or the synod?

As could have been predicted, the shift in ecclesiology also had effects in the church's everyday life. When the consequences appeared many were frightened and wanted to turn back, fearing changes in structures and behavior, such as are inevitable in any period of transition. Transitory problems cannot justify a rejection of the explicit intention of an ecumenical council. It will not do to say that the council would not have written it had it foreseen what has happened.

In a tragic misunderstanding, many blamed the council for the events of the late 1960s. The crisis of abandonment of the priesthood and religious life was the result of an explosion of Western culture, utterly independent of what was happening in the church. It is wrong and unjust to blame the council for such a dramatic development in the world. Indeed it is ridiculous to imagine that a council could have changed the direction of the world so as to prevent the explosion of 1968 and all the subsequent postmodernity.[4]

HUMAN REALITY OF THE CHURCH

Rather than a complete study of the theology of the people of God in Vatican II, about which much has been written, here, following Congar, we will recall the general lines on which there is practical consensus.[5] Chapter 1 of *Lumen Gentium* showed the divine reality of the church, that is, its relationship to the divine persons ("mystery of the church"). The council fathers then felt the need to highlight its human reality in chapter 2.

In *Lumen Gentium* 8 there is a strong analogy in the relationship between the mystery and visible historic reality in the church.

> . . . the visible society and the spiritual community, the earthly church and the church endowed with heavenly riches, are not to be thought of as two realities. On the contrary, they form one complex reality comprising a human and a divine element. For this reason the church is compared, in no mean analogy, to the mystery of the incarnate Word. As the assumed nature, inseparably united to him, serves the divine Word as a living instrument of salvation, so, in somewhat similar fashion, does the social structure of the church serve the Spirit of Christ who vivifies it, in the building up of the body (see Eph 4:16).

Vatican II accordingly extends to the church the doctrine that the Council of Chalcedon applied to Christ: two natures, each complete in its own order and substantially united.

Chalcedon's primary concern was to affirm the full human reality of Jesus in the face of Monophysitism. Indeed, it has always been more difficult to appreciate the humanity of Jesus than his divinity. Likewise, there has always been a strong tendency toward Monophysitism in the church, emphasizing its divine, invisible, and mysterious aspect, and downplaying its human aspect, as though it had no meaning or deserved no consideration. After the Council of Trent, theologians almost unanimously held the doctrine that there was a univocal identification between the theological dimension and the empirical dimension, between divine and human, mystery and social reality, as exemplified by Saint Ignatius Loyola: "*After any ruling, we must have a disposition willing and ready to obey in everything the true spouse of Christ our Lord, which is the holy mother hierarchical church.*"[6]

In this conception everything that comes from the hierarchy has divine value; it comes directly from God and obedience must be immediate, total, and unconditional—even the mind must recognize the truth of what comes from the hierarchy. This is a kind of Monophysitism in which the human reality of the church vanishes.

The church exists in history and everything it does is conditioned by history, even though in particular cases it has God's divine help. The hierarchy is made up of human beings who act with their entire human being, qualities, and limitations. Moreover, the hierarchy is an institution that is not exempt from the sociological laws applicable to all government and management—and more recently, we must add, to any bureaucracy, which has expanded greatly in the past century. It is not only the hierarchy, but the people of God that exists in history. It is not composed of passive individuals moved by the hierarchy, but of agents who are subject to what drives the evolution of peoples, culture, and humankind itself.

The persistence of this Monophysitism into the mid-twentieth century—even later in certain Catholic circles—has caused a radical reaction among some First World Catholics. Increasingly, a distinction is made between God's church, the people of God, the church as mystery, and the ever more discredited "official" or "institutional" church. The connection between them disappears. The "official church," i.e., the hierarchy, is simply rejected and its action is disqualified as completely foreign to the true church.[7]

The council provided the right response, but it arrived late, and its application has been even more delayed. The turn in recent years leads one to think that henceforth it will take a very long time to restore the credibility of the hierarchy.[8] Certainly throughout his pontificate Pope John Paul II has enjoyed great popularity, as have some bishops. This is, however, a media phenomenon, one of personality, style, and political activity. How John Paul II deals with the problems of the contemporary world is appreciated—even though often the teaching he defends, e.g., on sexuality, is rejected as irrational. In practice, what the pope and bishops say, particularly in the realm of sexuality, which so polarizes the attention of the contemporary world, is disregarded. Everything is disqualified in advance as antiquated, repugnant, and out of touch with people today. The appearances seem to validate those who radically separate the "official church" from the church of Jesus Christ, and it will not be easy to undo these appearances.

The hierarchy has been so sacralized and placed above the church that it has lost its human character and become a superhuman mediation—almost on the level of Christ himself. In a book on ecclesiology that was long considered one of the most significant of the twentieth century, *The Church of the Word Incarnate*, Charles Journet teaches that God instituted the hierarchy first, and that the church proceeds from the hierarchy, and is the result of its action. The first efficient cause of the church is the humanity of Christ; the second is the hierarchy, which founds the church through the sacraments.[9] The hierarchy is the active element and everything else comes from the hierarchy. The people of God simply receives the sacraments. What makes the church is receiving the sacraments from the hands of the hierarchy.

For Journet the great miracle and mystery is the hierarchy, which is in a sense above the church, above humankind, and enters into the mystery of God. Reducing the church to the hierarchy and sacralizing it go together. The people of God is not seen as founded directly by Christ. Journet ignores Pentecost and the gift of the spirit to the entire people, and states that whatever the people receives from God comes to it from the hierarchy.

The extreme form of such a theology, what Congar called "hierarchology," was offered by Aegidius Romanus in the thirteenth century. In his view, in some sense the church is the pope, because all the elements needed for its constitution are present in the pope. This is a caricature, but the caricature brings out what is included in this theology of the hierarchy, which the council sought to overcome once and for all. In such a hierarchology the human reality disappears; it is reduced to the sacraments, i.e., to symbolic realities. Consequently a spiritualized and dehumanized vision of the church becomes enshrined.

Journet's ecclesiology was based on the sacraments. It was intended as an alternative to an ecclesiology based on jurisdiction, that is, on the power of governance, whose most illustrious representative was Robert Bellarmine (d. 1621).[10] Comparing the church to civil societies, Bellarmine drew inspiration from the political theories of his time, when the absolutist theory of the state was coming to the fore: a state and a society are constituted by power. If the church is *societas perfecta*, it must consist essentially of a power, because the church is a society as complete as the kingdom of France or the republic of Venice. Actually Bellarmine's and Journet's theologies are both reductionist: they attribute no value to the action of the people.

The ecclesiology of Vatican II is intended as a radical reaction against these theologies that completely forget human reality and treat human beings as though they were objects in the hands of an almost divinized hierarchical power. If lay people are dehumanized, the clergy lives on high and from there guides lay people to salvation.

However, the fact is that the church takes on the full human reality, active human beings brought together as peoples. That human reality is not made up of purely passive individuals; Christians are not in the church solely to receive the sacraments or the dogmas of the faith. They are church in their whole life; acts of faith and charity are not separated from the rest of their life.

What the council wanted to affirm was precisely the full extent of the church's human reality in accordance with the analogy of the Council of Chalcedon. Obviously when the human fullness of the church is recognized, ministries change their meaning. Previous theologies placed ministries above the church; they were not at the service of the church but founders of the church. In the Vatican II vision, by contrast, ministries are really services because they act in the church. The church as a whole is founded by God directly with the sole human mediation of the human nature of Jesus, and the hierarchy is comprised of services within a church founded by God. This church has a fully human reality, and hence the ministries and hierarchy are also human realities with all the conditions thereby entailed. The mystery of the church becomes real, visible, and concrete in the human reality.

Whereas the church's human reality, so clearly manifested in the Bible and early Christianity, had been hidden or almost smothered by representations of a sacralized world in the Middle Ages and thereafter, the rediscovery of this human reality was the great discovery and affirmation of modernity—indeed the essence of modernity. In earlier ages the sacred realm hid the dimensions of the human reality: everything came from God or the gods. Human beings lived in dependence on sacred forces. Modernity saw the birth of autonomous "human reality" (politics, economics, language, art, thought, bodiliness, sex, freedom).[11]

Given this denial of its human reality, it is not surprising that theology had reduced the church to manifestations of the sacred: the sacraments, sacred doctrine, holy places, times, places, and people. For centuries it was forgotten that Jesus had performed his earthly work outside any sacralization, in the midst of human, profane, ordinary reality. Just as the new Christology has restored the humanity of Jesus, the concept of people of God includes restoring full human reality. That means all of history with its races, cultures, and peoples, and their development and interactions.

This concept of people of God represents a return to the Bible. It is a fundamental theme in the theology of Israel (what we call the Old Testament): all other themes in the theology of Israel are organized around the theme of the people of God. Israel was chosen by God to be his people. Hence its idea of God: God is the one who has called Israel. The law, worship, its placement in the midst of the peoples, politics, economics—everything comes from being people of God.[12] The theme is equally central in the New Testament,[13] which shows the birth of the church from the people of Israel. Indeed it can never be completely separated from Israel (Rom 9-11).

In proposing the biblical theme of people of God, Vatican II was not returning to the Old Testament, as some have said, because the entire New Testament is built explicitly or implicitly on the theme of the people of God.

The gospels show Jesus in the midst of God's people, acting within the people, a new Israel that begins with the disciples. Saint Paul's theology takes the "people of God" as a basic concept,[14] but so do other biblical books: "they will be his people and God himself will always be with them" (Rev 21:3). "But you are a chosen race, a royal priesthood, a holy nation, God's own people, in order that you may proclaim the mighty acts of him who called you out of darkness into his marvelous light. Once you were not a people, but now you are God's people . . ." (1 Pet 2:9-10).

This rooting of the church in Israel makes its concrete and historic nature more manifest. The people of Israel is set in the midst of the peoples, with all the characteristics of a people. The Bible continually stresses the relations between Israel and the other peoples of the earth. Being people of God does not mean that Israel ceases to be human—with all the values and all the sins of the peoples of the earth. The new people of God will be no less human and no less subject to the challenges of history, with its failures and victories, its virtues and vices, as shown by the prophets in the Old Testament. Indeed, prophets continually emerge within the new people as a reminder of the church's human character. Today there is little point in seeking to maintain an edifying vision of the church in its hierarchy, as though everything were successful and inspired by the Holy Spirit—as was done for centuries.

To some extent it can be said that the historicity of the church is more radical than that of Israel, which tended to remain somewhat isolated from other peoples and to sacralize its land, temple, priesthood, practices, laws. Even the diaspora did not integrate Jews into other peoples. In the New Testament, the people of God is not separated from other peoples, but lives in their midst and is not set apart by distance or by difference.

What distinguishes it is mission. In adopting the idea of people of God, the council made mission the church's raison d'être, thereby making it different from ancient Israel. The council renewed the theology of mission by restoring its wider meaning, which it had lost over the centuries. Mission had been something marginal that took place alongside the life of the church. Now mission to the nations of the world is seen as the historic movement that defines how the church is to exist. The new people of God enters the world as missionary.[15] Indeed the mission to the Gentiles was what prompted the separation between the church and ancient Israel (Rom 9-11).

The former theology of perfect society offered a static vision of the church unrelated to peoples and history, as an entity isolated and alone in the universe. The hierarchy seemed to be above the contingencies of the world and peoples, offering the same dogmas and sacraments to everyone around the world. There was no involvement with the outside world. Indeed, the church even gloried in its isolation. The church's nonhistoricity seemed to be one of its main notes.

Of course, in practice there were always involvements, but they were seen as defects and proof of the frailty of human nature. The aim was a church unmarked by the world, as Lacordaire said in his first Lenten sermon in Paris in 1833: the church *mole sua stat*—its mass keeps it immobile. The church may be surrounded by a world in agitation but it is like a great mass; nothing can move it. This vision may have delighted Catholics two hundred years ago—and some even today—but it is rejected by most of our contemporaries, even in traditionally Christian lands.

Through mission, the theology of the people of God makes the church something present in the midst of the peoples of the earth, moving, expanding continually by interacting with all the peoples of the earth. It gives to other peoples and receives from them. It is in history, in solidarity with the peoples of the world, participating in the evolution of humankind, in both sin and renewal. It depends on the resources in the world for its life, but may be distinguished by the means it uses. It shares the dramas, hopes, and dreams of the nations. Its vocation is to be a new leaven of freedom and love, even though it is often unfaithful to its calling.

The council sought to restore the eschatological perspective that had been retrieved by biblical studies. Eschatology enabled it to introduce the modern notion of time and history into theology. *Gaudium et Spes* is rooted in the restoration of the concept of people of God:

> The people of God believes that it is led by the Spirit of the Lord who fills the whole world. Impelled by that faith, they try to discern the true signs of God's presence and purpose in the events, the needs and the desires which it shares with the rest of humanity today. For faith casts a new light on everything and makes known the full ideal which God has set for humanity, thus guiding the mind towards solutions that are fully human. (11)

The church "travels the same journey as all of humanity and shares the same earthly lot with the world: it is to be a leaven and, as it were, the soul of human society in its renewal by Christ and transformation into the family of God" (40).

That the "earthly and heavenly city penetrate one another" (40) had not been taken into consideration by earlier theology. Exchanges take place between the peoples. "The church believes that through each of its members and its community as a whole it can help make the human family and its history still more human" (40). The church "is not unaware of how much it has profited from the history and development of humankind" (44).

The church "profits from the experience of past ages, from the progress of the sciences, and from the riches hidden in various cultures, through which greater light is thrown on human nature and new avenues to truth are opened up. . . . Nowadays, when things change so rapidly and thought patterns differ so widely, the church needs to step up this exchange by calling upon the help of people who are living in the world, who are expert in its organizations and its forms of training, and who understand its mentality, in the case of believers and nonbelievers alike. . . . It is the task of the whole people of God . . . to listen to and distinguish the many voices of our times and to interpret them . . ." (44).

Without the ecclesiology of the people of God neither *Gaudium et Spes* nor *Ad Gentes* would have been what they are, but once the people of God was seen to be fully human, participation in the movements of humankind began to take on Christian and saving meaning.

PEOPLE OF GOD AND ECUMENISM

A second aim of *Lumen Gentium* in the mind of John XXIII and the bishops was to encourage ecumenism with other Christians and indeed with all religions in the world. The key for Christians would be recognizing the Christian and ecclesial value of other communities or churches that call on Christ. That was where the concept "people of God" allowed the doors to open. If the church comes from the hierarchy there is no hope for other Christians who do not submit to that hierarchy; they do not belong to the church in any fashion.

The concept of people of God opens a door, indicating that there are various ways to belong to a people, and that is what the council recognized. The discussion revolved around the well-known formula "*subsistit in*" ("it subsists in").[16] After long discussions the council deliberately sought to open the door of the people of God to all peoples in the world, when it opted for the word "*subsistit.*" Rather than saying, "This church, constituted and organized in this world as a society, is the Catholic Church governed by the successor of Peter . . .," the council decided to say, "This church . . . subsists in the Catholic Church . . ." (LG 8).

Innocuous as this replacement might appear, it sought to express something fundamental. By saying that the people of God *subsists*, i.e., *is present*, in the Catholic Church, the text does not rule out the possibility that the people of God might subsist elsewhere—in other Christian communities or possibly other religions. The council text says, "this church, constituted and organized as a society in the present world, subsists in the Catholic Church, which is governed by the successor of Peter and by the bishops in communion with him. Nevertheless, many elements of sanctification and of truth are found outside its visible confines" (LG 8). The decree *Unitatis Redintegratio* states that "it is through Christ's Catholic Church alone, which is the universal help toward salvation, that the fullness of the means of salvation can be obtained" (UR 3). Yet that same decree to some extent spells out the elements of truth in other Christian confessions.

These texts place the difference in the means of salvation: Catholics have them in their fullness whereas others have them to varying degrees. The opposition does not lie in faith, charity, or sanctity, in which the Catholic Church does not claim superiority. All do not use the means of salvation equally, and their dispositions can vary. There is no reason why great sanctity cannot be achieved with only a portion of these means. That is the basis for building dialogue.

In the early post-council years, significant work was done on ecumenism, particularly under Cardinal Augustine Bea, but then misgivings began. In official statements, ecumenism is always said to be a priority, but things are different in practice. Ecumenism is often limited to relationships of courtesy and good conduct, perhaps simply due to the style of the Western world where religious relativism and pluralism force everyone to observe the rules of good behavior, based on tolerance. Other churches generally have the impression that ecumenism with the Catholic Church has come to a halt, even though the pope repeatedly says that it is one of the priorities of his papacy. Despite friendly relationships between persons of different religious confessions, there is an indisputable retreat between the churches institutionally, denials by the Catholic Church notwithstanding.

It was predictable that once the theology of the people of God had been abandoned, motivations for fomenting ecumenism would decline. People of God and ecumenism are bound together; they rise or fall together. When the theology of the people of God is abandoned, the Catholic Church folds in on itself, feels obliged to affirm its identity more emphatically, and closes the doors to the contemporary world. Ecumenism looks threatening and suspect because it can surreptitiously open the doors to the contamination of the world. One of Vatican II's greatest concerns cannot be officially rejected, but in practice it is nullified.

What lies at the basis of this retraction? Very likely the return to the precouncil conception of truth has been at work. Signs of this shift, clearly expressing an intention to stand apart from the contemporary world, are found in the encyclicals *Veritatis Splendor* (1993) and *Fides et Ratio* (1998), which reaffirm an intellectualist conception of truth. In the second millennium of the Western church, a conception of truth inspired by Greek philosophy was built up ever more rigidly, with tragic consequences in practice.[17]

First, an intellectualist type of knowing was given primacy in salvation. Knowing means knowing the concepts that truly represent reality. Knowing reality means having the proper concepts in the mind. Second, language is given full confidence, i.e., knowing the words for fully expressing the concepts. Knowing the right words means knowing reality. Third, it is the church's teaching authority that defines the correct words. Of course such a system can lead to the inquisition—which the church practiced and defended in good faith and good conscience for centuries. Convinced that truth was evident to any sincere spirit, the hierarchy could not understand that someone might not recognize this "evident" truth. To do so was to sin against the truth—the gravest of sins, because if it continued, it was a sin of obstinacy meriting death.

Vatican II started out from another conception of truth, one more open to the entire evolution of thinking, from the break with the inflexibility of Greek intellectualism. Truth is not everything—love has primacy. Truth is not exhausted in concepts, which are not so universal, univocal, or evident to everyone. Given the diversity of cultures, the concepts of one culture are different from parallel concepts in another. No translation is perfect because concepts are not exactly aligned. Moreover, language is not the immediate expression of concepts. Language has its autonomy, rules, and evolution that thought cannot control. It is relatively independent of thought and forces one to think in a particular way. A person cannot think as he or she wishes, but is constrained and limited by language.

Finally, the magisterium does not have a full intuition of the correct concepts, nor the revelation of the most suitable words. It does not own the meaning of words, nor is it above culture. Everything it says is a reflection of its own cultural world. Everything is culture: the pope or bishops cannot say a single word that is not directed by a culture and is not the expression of a culture.[18]

With the idea of the *signs of the times*, John XXIII recognized that there is a source of knowledge of the truth in the world which is achieved inductively and not simply deductively. Vatican II recognized that it could learn from others. This conception of truth allowed for dialogue with other Christian confessions. Returning to the previous conception is not acceptable to people of goodwill.

The situation is no better with regard to the broader ecumenism, i.e., with other religions. Although Vatican II was rather evasive about it, the theology of the people of God has allowed for a positive opening. This theology makes it possible to recognize and proclaim what all human beings share in terms of what they are and where they are heading. "All are called to this catholic unity of the people of God which prefigures and promotes universal peace. And to it belong, or are related in different ways: the Catholic faithful, others who believe in Christ, and finally all of humankind, called by God's grace to salvation" (LG 13). The words ". . . all who belong in any way . . . to the people of God" (UR 3) lie at the foundation of the ecumenism with all religions. Otherwise, no dialogue is possible. Even so, the council document on the other religions did not go very far, apparently for lack of sufficient preparation.

Although what Vatican II says about other religions is still very timid and seems to fear venturing into unknown territory, its intention is clear. The church "reflects . . . on what people have in common and what tends to bring them together. . . . Humanity forms but one community" (*Nostra Aetate* 1). The bishops urge Catholics in "discussion and collaboration" with others to "acknowledge, preserve and encourage the spiritual and moral truths found among non-Christians, together with their social life and culture" (NA 2).

What legitimizes dialogue is community between peoples. If Christians are defined as a people, they can enter into dialogue; if they are defined as a perfect society, they have no reason to dialogue, and can only demand that other human beings be converted—by entering the church. One often has the impression that the Catholic hierarchy has no other aim but having all human beings, all religions, enter the Catholic Church as it is now, without waiting for it to open out to other cultures. That is tantamount to seeking the impossible.

The 1986 gathering at Assisi, when the pope met with the world's main religious leaders, aroused hope, but there was no follow up. Everyone prayed together, but they all prayed in their own culture and affirmed their own identity, with no rapprochement. Hence, little advance could be made.

Recently, in *Dominus Iesus*, signed by Cardinal Ratzinger, the message was that there is no solution to ecumenism and that it makes no sense. The document returned to the formulas prior to *Lumen Gentium* (*"subsistit in"*) to state that people of God and Catholic Church are equivalent. The document makes an exception for the Eastern churches because they preserve the episcopacy in its ancient form. The other Christian confessions cannot constitute local churches because they do not have episcopal succession. This document was very discouraging to the separated churches and to all Catholics who believe in ecumenism. The conclusion is that no ecumenism can take place until there is a change in Rome. Only a change in ecclesiology will allow for a return to ecumenism—in tandem with the theology of the people of God.

PROMOTION OF LAY PEOPLE IN THE PEOPLE OF GOD

By choosing the "people of God" theme the council assembly sought to enhance the role of the laity and overcome clericalism. Many thought the theology of the people of God would be the starting point and theoretical justification for promoting lay people. For two centuries lay people have taken initiatives and acted in the name of the church in the midst of the struggles of the world, thereby giving rise to social, cultural, and intellectual movements. The council sought in some fashion to recognize that lay people had reached adulthood, and it wanted lay people to feel that their importance in the church was finally acknowledged.

Whether the council fathers succeeded and remained faithful to their theology of the people of God is more questionable. We believe that the hesitation and relative intellectual confusion over the laity—and the essence of the laity—could reflect hesitation and confusion over the role of priests (and even bishops). In their theology of the laity, they were not consistent with the theology of the people of God.

Lay people are people of God and everything having to do with them comes from being part of the people of God; being lay adds nothing. Everything that lay people are is collective and social and belongs to the people of God. There is no priesthood of the laity alongside the priesthood of the ministers. There is a priesthood of the people, collectively—there is nothing priestly about a lay person in isolation. There is nothing priestly about a priest by himself, because he is at the service of the common priesthood, providing specific functions. The same is true of other attributes.

Lumen Gentium did not have to add a special chapter on the laity, because everything ought to be included in the chapter on the people of God. Individually, lay people are no different from ministers; they are all equal. Chapter 4 on the laity does not help promote lay people. That was done in chapter 2, and chapter 4 only weakens what was said previously in chapter 2. The insertion of a special chapter later had consequences; it justified a synod on lay people; the document *Christifideles Laici*, far from advancing lay people, left them in confusion.

The council fathers were well aware of what they did not want, but they were not so clear about what they wanted. They were trapped by fragments of the very theology from which they wished to break free. They did not succeed in going all the way and freeing themselves from the old theology of the two categories of Christians in which they had been schooled in their seminary training or theology departments. Not even the most advanced, including Congar, were able to break free of the traditional schemes. Congar was censured in Rome for his theology of the laity, but even that theology was quite conservative—as he himself acknowledged after the council.

What they did not want can be represented by a famous text from Gratian, the canon lawyer and founder of the discipline of canon law, who collected Christian texts that might have legal validity in order to lay the groundwork for Christian society. Gratian's words have been repeated millions of times over eight hundred years: "*Duo sunt genera christianorum.*" Even more interesting is the description of these two classes of Christians in the church, which make up two well-separated "orders." First, according to Gratian,

> there is the class of clerics, who being devoted to divine service and given over to contemplation and prayer, is dispensed from the turbulence of temporal things. They must be content with their food and clothing and may not have any property, for everything among them is held in common. . . . There is another class of Christians, the lay people. For *laos* means people. They are permitted to own property, albeit only for use. They are allowed to marry, till the earth, be judges, place offerings on the altar, pay tithes, and thus be saved, provided they avoid vices.[19]

There are many such texts in the Middle Ages. For example, Stephen of Tournai (d. 1203) teaches that "in the church there are two peoples, two orders, clergy and laity; two lives, spiritual and carnal."[20]

This theme has remained in theology and the minds of Catholics to this day. In 1888 Leo XIII wrote in a letter to the archbishop of Tours: "It is, in reality, constant and evident that there are in the Church two naturally distinct orders: the shepherds and the flock, which means to say the leaders and the people. The first order has the function of teaching, governing, directing men in their lives, imposing rules; the second has the duty of being subject to the first, of obeying them, of carrying out their orders and rendering them honor."[21] More recently (1955) Pius XII wrote: "By the will of Christ, Christians are distributed into two orders, clerics and lay people. By that same will, a twofold sacred power has been set up: that of order and that of jurisdiction. In addition, likewise by divine disposition, access to the power of orders—that which creates the hierarchy of bishops, priests, and ministers—comes by receiving the sacrament of holy orders; the power of jurisdiction, for its part is directly conferred by divine right on the supreme Pontiff, on the bishops and by virtue of that same right, but only by the successor of Peter."[22]

In these texts, which could be confirmed with many thousands more, the clear distinction between two types of Christians comes from the distinction between the sacred and the profane. The clergy do not become involved in the profane things of this world but are reserved for sacred activities, and thus belong to the sacred world. Lay people act in, and belong to, the world.

But what does "sacred" mean in Christianity? In paganism, and even in the Old Testament (the prophets notwithstanding), the sacred means temples, sacrifices, and priests. All this is set apart for God. Thus the distinction between sacred and profane was very clear in the Old Testament and in the ancient religions. In Christianity, however, there is no more temple, and God is everywhere: in people, in the disciples, and especially in the poor. There is only one sacrifice, that of Christ, and there are no more priests because there is only one priest: Christ, and with him the entire people of God is priestly. That is the New Testament teaching. Christians are lifelong priests. The sacrifice that they offer God is their life, and the temple is the world. Sacred and profane are no longer distinct. Everything that is from Jesus is sacred, that is, the profane is sacred and the sacred is profane.[23] What makes the sacred is the presence of the Holy Spirit in any human reality.

So how could there be two classes, one devoted to the profane and the other to the sacred? The sources of this arrangement are pre-Christian and hence the word "sacred" used in the texts could create confusion. This distinction is still in the council texts, because they retain something of the earlier period in which the sacred-profane distinction prevailed in the church.

One reason why this distinction between the sacred and profane, clergy and laity, lasted for so many centuries was that it—and only it—could justify the privileged position of the clergy in Christendom starting with Constantine. Indeed, the clergy had received many privileges, including not having to work for a living. This situation, which has no basis in the New Testament, had to be justified in religious terms.

Another reason is the legacy of the ancient religions—which were still present in people's minds. To all pagans it was obvious that there had to be priests devoted to temples. Constantine had churches built and they then needed activities and persons devoted to these activities—the clergy.

This theology of the two classes also made its way into *Lumen Gentium* and lies at the base of the strange chapter 4 on the laity—strange because it repeats a great deal. Actually lay people are people of God, and whatever is said of them comes from being people of God. Participation in the priesthood is not theirs from being laity but from belonging to the people of God. The same is true of their participation in Christ's prophetic and royal role. All this fits in the chapter on the people of God with no need for a separate chapter on lay people.

By including this chapter, the bishops fell into a trap. In seeking to define laity in contradistinction from clergy, the council returned to the old distinction between the two orders, one devoted to sacred things and the other the world. Here is the clearest, and most questionable, text: "To be secular is the special characteristic of the laity. Although people in holy Orders may sometimes be engaged in secular activities, or even practice a secular profession, yet by reason of their particular vocation they are principally and expressly ordained to the sacred ministry, while religious bear outstanding and striking witness that the world cannot be transfigured and offered to God without the spirit of the beatitudes. It is the special vocation of the laity to seek the kingdom of God by engaging in temporal affairs and directing them according to God's will. They live in the world, in each and every one of the world's occupations and callings and in the ordinary circumstances of social and family life, which, as it were, form the context of their existence" (LG 31).

This theology is completely based on the distinction between sacred and profane as expressed in the texts of Gratian and his followers, though this distinction was the very thing that they were trying to overcome. Indeed, the text has very strange statements, showing that it is not in accord with Christian reality. First, it says that the clergy is expressly devoted to the sacred ministry, but it recognizes that "they may sometimes be engaged in secular activities." Actually, until the current vocation crisis, a large portion of priests, both diocesan and religious, were devoted to teaching in Catholic schools. It did not happen "sometimes": tens of thousands of priests did so. Almost all Jesuits were involved in teaching, and the same was true of many other religious order priests. They were teaching secular subjects, not religion, and they were not exceptional cases at all. So why exclude the profane from the life of priests? It says that the mission of religious is to practice the beatitudes, but Jesus did not reserve the practice of the beatitudes to religious. They are the rule for the entire people of God—including lay people.

Lay people are said to "live in the ordinary circumstances of social and family life." In the East priests live in family conditions, as do married deacons in the West. Hence, this characteristic is not proper to lay people alone. As for social life, everyone is involved in it—even the desert fathers were, at some points in their lives. No one escapes social life—except in the illusions of an isolated convent life. (Carmelites, for example, are always well-informed about what is happening in the city.) So this distinction simply does not stand; it is invented to somehow justify the distinction between sacred and profane, and the existing relationship between clergy and laity. The bishops wanted to change but did not put forward directions for change.

What enabled a teaching so contrary to the doctrine of the people of God to enter the council was the theology of Catholic Action.[24] The popes, particularly Pius XI, received Catholic Action as providential, a kind of life preserver for the church. Catholic Action would make it possible to get into environments where the clergy no longer had access, and could be a presence of the church in a secularized world. The idea returns in *Lumen Gentium*: "The laity . . . are given this special vocation: to make the church present and fruitful in those places and circumstances where it is only through them that it can become the salt of the earth" (33).

This idea is very questionable. Today there is no place where a priest cannot enter, and there is a strong sense that the priest's presence is stronger than that of a lay person, and hence it is more meaningful and necessary everywhere, especially in those places most distant from the church. But at that time, Pius XII wanted to maintain priestly status: as a sacred person, the priest had to remain in the sacred world and not be soiled in the midst of the world and humanity. To preserve that status, the hierarchy believed that the lay apostolate would be a kind of substitute for the apostolate of priests, and thus would be a kind of participation in the apostolate of the hierarchy in those places closed off to priests. Pius XII avoided using the term "participation"—which to him looked like giving too much importance to lay people—and preferred to speak of "collaboration." Speaking of the lay movements of previous decades, the council says: "Deservedly praised and promoted by the popes and numerous bishops, they have received from them the name of Catholic Action, and have most often been described by them as a collaboration of the laity in the hierarchical apostolate" (*Apostolicam Actuositatem* 20).

Yet in speaking of the theology of the people of God, the council speaks of lay people participating directly in the priesthood of Christ, and in his prophecy and rule (34-36), all in harmonious collaboration between lay people and hierarchy (37). Lay people are not said to be participating in the mission of the hierarchy but assuming the responsibilities of the people of God, aided by the services of the various ministries. Hence, the council provides the basis for the promotion of lay people in the church, even though the presence of some remnants of the previous theology creates some confusion about the relationship between clergy and laity.

The problem lies in the application to the life of the church. *Lumen Gentium* says, "The sacred pastors . . . should recognize and promote the dignity and responsibility of the laity in the church. They should willingly use their prudent advice and confidently assign offices to them in the service of the church, leaving them freedom and scope for activity" (37). This is very edifying but what happens if the "sacred pastors" do not follow these fine recommendations? There is no way to force the "sacred pastor" to do his duty. The council could hope for a Code of Canon Law that would be inspired by their guidelines, but the one issued was in line with the 1917 code, which in turn comes from Roman law (Justinian). It was not written to proclaim the rights of citizens and defend them from rulers, but to announce the duties of subjects and rights of rulers. Whereas in Western society law has increasingly moved toward defending the weak against the strong (Lacordaire), canon law is set up to defend the strong against the weak. In practice, relations between hierarchy and laity have changed little, except in style, and that reflects not the gospel but good manners as observed in contemporary Western civilization.

If, however, as Hans Küng says, the power of the laity comes not from the hierarchy but from Christ, why must all decisions be made solely by the "sacred pastors," with lay people reduced an advisory role in parish and diocesan councils, and even the Roman curia? The only answer is "because it has always been that way." But it has not always been so—and even if it were, it cannot be proven that it was explicitly willed by Jesus.

"It is very much the wish of the church that all of the faithful should be led to take that full, conscious, and active part in liturgical celebrations which is demanded by the very nature of the liturgy, and to which the Christian people . . . have a right and to which they are bound by reason of their Baptism" (Liturgy, 14). But the liturgical reforms went only halfway. They were heavily inspired by the advice of "experts"—liturgists, archaeologists, historians, pastoral specialists—who wanted to return to the simplicity of the ancient liturgy, but that is far from what our contemporaries feel.

There are vast numbers of people expert in all the arts, particularly oral and symbolic communication. Why not consult them? The liturgical reforms have responded more to the concerns of monks or clerics than lay people, and hence the liturgy has no drawing power. Charismatic movements draw thousands of people to their praise, while the official liturgy remains cold, formal, and restricted to the elderly and to those who like to depend on priests. The reforms have halted halfway. For example, even though the liturgy is now celebrated in the language of the people, the language of the translation remains archaic and does not respond to contemporary modes of expression. Only lay people can make a liturgy adapted to lay people. Unfortunately, the Roman authority declared experimentation over when it had scarcely begun.

Recognition of the universality of charisms provides the basis for the reinstatement of lay people: "it is not only through the sacraments and the ministries that the Holy Spirit makes the people holy, leads them and enriches them with his virtues. Allotting his gifts 'at will to each individual' (I Cor 12:11), he also distributes special graces among the faithful of every rank" (LG 12). "The apostolate of the laity is a sharing in the church's saving mission" (LG 33)—Pius XII would have written "in the hierarchy's saving mission." Chapter 4, with some deference, nevertheless states, "To the extent of their knowledge, competence, or authority the laity are entitled, and indeed sometimes duty-bound, to express their opinion on matters which concern the good of the church" (LG 37). Vatican II thereby ends 150 years in which the distinction between *ecclesia discens* and *ecclesia docens* held sway.

In practice the participation of lay people is still not clearly manifested in the structures. The bishop in the diocese and the priest in the parish retain their monopoly on power. Although diocesan and parish councils exist, their members are chosen by the bishop or pastor. Even so, the council has put in place principles that over the long run question those structures, and will ultimately have their effects.

To conclude, the doctrine of the people of God has still not made its way deeply into the various areas of the church's practice. What remains of the distinction between sacred and profane, clergy dedicated to the sacred and lay people to the profane, must be overcome. The theology of the people of God, the great new contribution of Vatican II, has still not been applied consistently—not even in all the council documents. But this situation only means that this doctrine, far from being abandoned, must be further developed. The theology of the people of God must enter all chapters of ecclesiology, because it is the key to connecting the divine and the human in the church.

Chapter 2

HISTORY OF THE IDEA OF PEOPLE OF GOD

Understanding the scope of Vatican II's teaching on the people of God entails situating it in the history of theology and of the church institution. The idea did not drop down from heaven. Even though it is the teaching of the New Testament and the entire patristic age, it fell into disuse and was marginalized by the dominant theology for centuries. When it reappeared in the nineteenth century in the works of theologians influenced by the Bible and the church fathers, it was still ignored by most theologians almost until Vatican II. Yet little by little it spread in northern European countries in the twentieth century. Although it emerged triumphant in the council, the minority resisted and influenced the texts, leaving some dualism and ambiguity.

THE PRE-VATICAN II HIERARCHICAL MODEL

Catholic theology arose as a separate discipline in the fourteenth century in the context of the struggle between pope and empire (the king of France or England), i.e., the struggle between two powers wishing to be supreme. It drew inspiration from the canonical texts governing the church after the eleventh century. Ecclesiology thus came into being as a juridical conception of the church, defined as a complete and perfect society that does not recognize any human power above it. The formal constitutive element that generates and rules this society is the hierarchy with its powers of order and jurisdiction. On that juridical foundation, the theologians built a system in which juridical aspects are always paramount.

Early Christianity had no such notion—because it had no basis in the Bible nor in the early communities, in which the concept of people always prevailed and no one imagined that *people* could derive from a higher human power. The people had direct contact with God. Mediation between Christians and Christ was through the people, the church as people.

How then did it happen that a theological construction was established as strongly as though it were by divine institution? Where did *hierarchology* (Congar) come from? We will simply make some general observations on which there is some consensus among theologians.

First, we should consider the influence of (Platonic and especially Neoplatonist) Greek philosophy, which entered theology through a number of routes, but especially through the work of Pseudo-Dionysius the Areopagite, who was highly regarded in the Middle Ages and even later, because he was believed to be a disciple converted by St. Paul in Athens.[1]

From Neo-Platonism comes fascination with unity, with the One. Intellectual life consists of reducing reality to the One. The One is outside this multiple world in which we live, but everything comes from it. The One unifies everything existing, and everything derives from the One. Multiplicity derives from unity, but it is flaw and decline. Human beings are in an intense decline because they are bound to matter, which is sheer multiplicity. Through the spirit humans have something of higher unity, but it is in a degraded form. It does not come from the One God directly but through a series of ever more multiple mediators. Creation is fall and decline, because it entails separation from the primordial unity. The aim of life is therefore to return to unity. By drawing apart from matter, humans may rise through contemplation of spiritual ideas and approach God, that is, the primordial One. Unity thus lies at the beginning and at the end. Life is departure from unity and return to unity. Almost all of medieval philosophy and theology was inspired by this framework (e.g., the *Summa Theologica* of Aquinas).

When this framework is transferred to the church, the higher element in the church, that which comes directly from God, is regarded as the One. In the East the emperor can claim the role of unity and be the head of the church. In the West the pope was able to unseat the emperor and impose himself as the principle of unity: everything derives from the pope—bishops, priests, laity. From pope to bishop, bishop to priest, and priest to laity there is decline and degradation. In any case, the principle of unity and salvation lies in the unity constituted by the pope. This framework of unity had to provide support for the pope's total conquest of power. He did not succeed with Christendom in its entirety, but he was successful in the church. As the people lost power in society, his power grew in the church—all in the name of unity.[2]

This conception of unity does not fare well in the Bible, where unity comes from a covenant among several. The people of Israel comes from the covenant of twelve tribes and the church of Christ is founded on the group of twelve disciples. In the Bible unity comes from covenant, which is a human intention of unity rather than a necessary metaphysical process independent of human beings. In the Bible and in ancient Christian tradition the fundamental theme of the church is the covenant, not the One. Therein lies the contradiction that will emerge between the interpretation of the pope's role in unity and the biblical message. It is not about the role of Peter, but the role of the One. However, the ideology of the One comes to encompass all Catholic theology—or at least the dominant theology, which guides those who wield power in the church.

In addition to neo-Platonist philosophy, the role of the ideology of empire must also be emphasized. Its roots lie in the ancient empires of the East, but it also made its way into the Roman empire, and by the time of Constantine it had fully taken hold. A key to the system is "One God—One world—One empire—One emperor." All power derives from the one God, who created a single world and placed it under a single unity—at least that would be the perfection of the world. The world has been entrusted to the empire, and the empire to the emperor, who owes his power to God whom he represents.

The Roman emperors chose Christianity as the imperial religion because in their eyes it was the most perfect representation of the ideology of imperial unity, thanks to its strict monotheism. In this ideology the emperor receives everything from the one God and owes nothing to his subjects. On the contrary, they owe everything to him.

This ideology was accepted, recognized, and transmitted by the Christian church starting with Constantine, as recorded in the works of Eusebius of Caesarea. In the East it persisted until the fall of the empire in Constantinople, and was then transferred to Russia and served as the basis for the Russian empire until 1917. Certain elements remain to this day, as shown by the attempt by some members of the Russian church to seek the canonization of the last czar, Nicholas II.

In the West, after the fall of the Roman empire, the imperial ideology was restored, and the empire was bestowed by the pope himself on the king of the Franks, Charlemagne, on whom the pope conferred the title of emperor. This empire lasted until 1806 when it was abolished by Napoleon. Meanwhile, the pope, who had launched the new empire, came into conflict with it. For two hundred years the empire dominated the pope's religious power and often placed the persons it chose on the throne of Peter. Starting in the eleventh century, the popes reacted, and the empire and the "altar" (the pope) battled for centuries, each claiming supreme authority in Christendom and Christian society.[3]

Pope Gregory VII, the most representative figure of this movement, claimed the attributes and symbols of empire for himself, and demanded that he be treated as an emperor. His successors waged that same battle until the time of Boniface VIII (d. 1303). After him the papacy went into crisis, but it never surrendered the predominant role in Christendom, as temporal as well as spiritual head.[4] The formula "one emperor" became "one pope" and the pope became ever more exalted as head of the universe through a mandate received from Christ himself, king of the universe: "One God—One Christ—One Christendom—one pope."[5] This was the ideology that enabled Pope

Alexander VI (d. 1503), acting as master of the world in the name of Christ,[6] to divide the world between the kings of Spain and Portugal.

Within this perspective the bishops were delegates of the pope's imperial power over the whole world, priests were powers at a lower level, and the people were the object entrusted by Christ to the pope to be dominated and led to salvation. The only savior on earth was the pope; he was *"vicarius"* of Christ, replacement of Christ on the earth, he alone. This was how a hierarchical vision of the universe, humankind, and of the church was constructed. It was persuasive during the Middle Ages, especially the twelfth and thirteenth centuries, declined in the fourteenth and fifteenth centuries, but was taken up again and adapted to the church under the impulse of the Council of Trent, and it constituted the core of ecclesiology until Vatican II.

When the pope lost temporal power, he transferred the imperial ideology to the church. This took place in two stages, the French Revolution, which humbled the pope's power, and then the loss of the papal states in 1870. Pius IX and his successors were able to utilize this loss of temporal power to exalt their spiritual power. The pope became the sole head of the church, garbed in Christ's own authority, a true spiritual emperor. A cult of the person of the pope was created and it has grown to this day. Everything in the church comes from the pope and the levels of clergy constitute the degrees on which his power is built. *Hierarchology* continued in the church. Indeed, recent popes have sought to recover throughout the world a kind of worldwide moral leadership that would be at least a partial restoration of the ancient imperial authority. However, it seems that this claim will encounter major obstacles.

None of this is rooted in what was established by Christ.[7] This structure derives from Greek philosophy and Roman political ideology. This formidable power has been established by the Roman curia, which has worked with remarkable continuity since the eighth century. However, for the people of God this power is very problematic. What is left for the people of God within the arrangement of papal power? What can the people of God be— an army at the service of papal power?

THE "OTHER" CHURCH

"Official" Catholic writings—documents of the magisterium, theology, canon law, church history—seek to give the impression that vertical ecclesiology (*hierarchology*) has always enjoyed the support of the Catholic people and been triumphant. It was the only possible orthodox ecclesiology; anything else was heresy. In fact, however, *hierarchology* has not always been unanimously accepted. Since the eleventh century, i.e., from the moment when the dominant official doctrine (hierarchology) was articulated in the church, a diametrically opposite conception, in which the Christian people is manifested as direct heir of Christ, began to find expression.

For ten centuries, up to the twentieth century, a conception of a hierarchical, vertical, juridical, authoritarian, uniform church, in which obedience is the highest virtue and the source of all the others (obedience to the hierarchy being identified with obedience to God) ran parallel with the horizontal conception, based on the people of God, one that is evangelical, pluralistic, community-oriented, participatory, and in which the highest virtue is obedience to God as distinguished from obedience to human authorities (even in the church).

This last current has given rise to numerous movements that were condemned as heretical. Their heresy always consisted in a rejection of the hierarchical system as it existed in the church of their time. But these heresies were simply some extreme phenomena that expressed in a way that could be condemned, an underlying movement which was a huge protest against the *hierarchological* system. These movements never managed to convince or convert the hierarchy and they remained in the shadows, or completely underground. Some of their members appeared publicly and were harshly put down. The dominant system thus had the impression that it was defending the sole truth against many challengers.

The victory of orthodoxy, thanks to the political and military support of kings and princes, seemed to be the triumph of the truth over error with God's help. Victory was the confirmation granted by God to the single, which was the obligatory ecclesiological system. For ten centuries, therefore, we have had a clerical church supported by the dominant forces of Christendom, the empire, the monarchies, and feudalism, over against a more popular grassroots church, with no support. It was not necessarily anticlerical, but it gradually became anticlerical as a result of the inertia of the system.

This antagonism reached its apogee in the nineteenth century. If it has lessened in the twentieth century, it is not because there is more peace, but because the church is weakened and on the defensive, trying to salvage what can still be saved. The history of Christianity in the West is made up of this antagonism, which was the most fundamental in society, and even today marks the imagination and sometimes the action of our contemporaries.

Where was the people of God? The *hierarchological* system has always called on the testimony of the people, and always claimed to speak on their behalf and claimed to have their support. Indeed, the great masses, especially in the countryside, have always fully supported the established church. It must be kept in mind that these masses were illiterate, completely ignorant of the Bible, and understood nothing of the ecclesiastical system, which spoke in Latin. They also had no ability to become organized and were completely passive vis-à-vis the clergy. These masses have always supported the church—and still do so where they exist (the "alliance between the church and the ignorant"). But was this mass people of God? Did it merit the name "people"?

Those social groups and peoples that became more educated, freer, more capable of acting, kept strengthening movements of opposition to the system. This has been the overall thrust of things from the Middle Ages to this day. As people become more educated, many break away from the Catholic Church and seek other churches or counter-churches. In these new places they believe they encounter greater respect for their personhood, because it offers them a better future and greater opportunities.

Having access to education, such persons come to see themselves as a people, no longer belonging to the ignorant masses (e.g., members of the medieval communes).[8] Their consciousness as a people was initially still the consciousness of the Christian people or people of God. Starting in the seventeenth, and especially in the eighteenth century, the consciousness of people split off from church consciousness, and the concept of a people without reference to a religion emerged. In practice, however, the emancipatory movements of peoples still bore many Christian elements, albeit unconsciously.

There is no proof that this distancing from the church is due to Christianity in itself—quite the contrary. The inchoate peoples wanted to be Christian and wanted to be people for Christian reasons. The reason for the separation must lie in the top-down, authoritarian system that the ignorant masses accept because for them it constitutes a refuge and support, but that is rejected by people seeking freedom to this day. Teaching people to read means preparing them to leave the church and join Pentecostal churches and social movements independent of the church. When young people go to high school, they lose their faith in the Catholic Church.

* * *

At first the hierarchical church had no difficulty imposing its authority on rebellious movements. Nevertheless, as time went on, the world emancipated from feudalism grew, and the power of the clergy declined. Opposition became ever harsher. Let us note that this is not opposition to religion or to Christ, but an opposition to the hierarchical system (not to the church), an opposition in the name of the Christian people to the power abusively assumed by the hierarchy and by the clergy as a privileged class in society and as a class in the church with a monopoly on power and all decisions.

In the sixteenth century the church could no longer suppress the opposition. A century before, four crusades reduced the resistance of the Czech people which arose in response to the call of Jan Hus. With the advent of Protestantism, a century of religious war was unable to reduce the schism. Finally, the Peace of Westphalia (1648), which the pope did not recognize, defined a situation of mutual tolerance in Europe. The pope had to bow to the facts.

Protestantism presented itself as the "other," true church, the one that had been founded by Jesus and was faithful to the Bible. For the first time the "other" church became embodied in history. With the Council of Trent—and particularly with the integralist interpretation imposed by Pius VI and the Jesuits[9]—the Catholic Church was unable (and unwilling) to interpret the signs of the times. It did not recognize the voice of the people of God, and stifled that voice as though it were heresy, apostasy, and rejection of Christianity.

In the eighteenth century, the church lost the intellectual leaders even in Catholic countries, and could no longer control the movement of ideas and social movements. Liberal ideas, which were not against religion or Christianity, but were increasingly opposed to the power of the hierarchy and the clergy, came to the fore. Anticlericalism exploded in the French Revolution and from there it spread to the entire Western world. In Latin America anticlericalism entered all countries with greater or lesser intensity. In Mexico, Guatemala, Ecuador, Colombia, and Chile it led to battles. Liberal parties arose almost everywhere and slowly managed to overcome the resistance of conservative parties maintained by the church. In Brazil as well, during the monarchy of Dom Pedro II, liberalism succeeded in curtailing the church's power, with the closing of the novitiates and measures to bring the hierarchy under the control of the system. Over time each party became more entrenched as intransigence and refusal of any dialogue increased. Only with John XXIII did there begin a process of rapprochement, reexamination of the past, and an effort at reconciliation and understanding.

The hierarchy interpreted this entire evolution as a struggle between truth and error, Christ and anti-Christ, God and atheism, God and the devil. It could not see that it was something else, a struggle within the church between two parties, one of which affirmed the hierarchy as power over the church, and the other the rights of the people of God. Over time the idea of the people of God became the banner of the party of the people, the laity, and it became a sign of heresy, schism, and opposition to the church for the clergy. Hence it aroused mistrust: one who affirmed the rights of the people of God was suspect of anticlericalism. It was eliminated from official theology (that of the hierarchy) which dominated church institutions.

The opposition invoked the people and wanted to represent the people. It was the people against the clergy, and this was really a Christian people, imbued with Christian values, generally seeking to follow Jesus. In the end it was a battle with no escape. The upshot was the weakening of the church and the secularization of society. To this day the reasons for secularization and secularism are not recognized. It is still being blamed on diabolical intervention as an expression of the power opposed to Christ. The hierarchy has issued denunciations, condemnations, and prophecies of disasters—as though it had no responsibility itself. It was the time of the "prophets of doom" (in the phrase of John XXIII). They failed to see that two ecclesiologies were in contention; without dialogue, which the hierarchy always refused, the end result could only be hopeless struggle. Over these ten centuries of struggle there were voices—popes, bishops, priests, and lay people—who sought rapprochement, but they did not prevail.

The two churches elaborated two ecclesiologies, which were not arbitrary theoretical creations. The two ecclesiologies represented two models of church: one always the winner and the other always defeated—but now "raising its head" since Vatican II. The official church ignored the other theology, assuming that anything that did not agree with it was heretical or quasi-heretical. Today, however, it is increasingly evident that there have always been two parallel ecclesiologies, as there were two parallel churches within orthodoxy—and outside it when there was no more room inside.

It is crucial, especially for ecumenism, to recognize that the schisms and so-called heresies in the West are always linked to that "other" church—the church that did not accept the imperial, vertical, authoritarian arrangement. At particular times members of this "other" church were expelled from the body of the church for disobedience. Others remained, always in an uncomfortable situation, because they were always suspected of favoring heretics or falling into heresy themselves.

There is no need to present this whole history of conflict between these two theologies over the second millennium.[10] We will simply recall some of the major lines to express more concretely what we have just stated.

In the eleventh century there appeared some social movements that appealed to the people and affirmed the existence of a people over against the predominance of the clergy.[11] In the twelfth century these movements grew, and went in two directions.[12] On the one hand, social movements sought to obtain a space of autonomy within the feudal system where the clergy and the nobility owned everything. The communes and other urban movements, but also movements of independent farmers seeking land,[13] expressed an affirmation of "people." These movements often clashed with the hierarchy which owned a great deal and could lose privilege, power, and wealth. On the other hand, there were spiritual movements, struggling for a church free of corruption, an evangelical church, a poor church of poor people. Such movements sometimes came into conflict with the clergy for condemning the vices and corruption of the clergy and bishops. The tendency was to make the church the "congregation of the elect" or of the predestined, of those who practiced the gospel in real life.[14] Of course these two thrusts often crisscrossed. The peoples who wanted a more evangelical Christianity were also involved in popular movements for political and economic emancipation.

A good part of the history of the Middle Ages consisted of the struggles between the dominant system and the first movements to challenge it. They were all suppressed, but from that time on there emerged the concerns and the historical forces that after four or five centuries would bring about the reformation with its schisms and the progressive secularization of modernity.

Gradually the church was proposed to be *congregatio, fraternitas*, a *corpus* of believers. As conflict with the hierarchy increased, the popular movements, the movements of the poor, and the spiritual movements advocated a church with no hierarchy or clergy, an *Ecclesia spiritualis*.[15] After all, for many people "cleric" meant "bad Christian."

The movement against the hierarchy had no significant theological expression until the late twelfth century when Abbot Joachim of Fiori proposed a theology of history that overturned the entire tradition and upset all of medieval society. His theory envisions three ages of church history. First came reign of the Father (Old Testament) when the flesh rules, under the law; it was the age of slavery and fear. Then came the reign of the Son, which began with the New Testament and extends to the thirteenth century. In this reign, the time of the flesh and the time of the Spirit coexist under grace: it is the age of filial obedience and faith. Then comes the time of the Holy Spirit, when people live in the Spirit under a more abundant grace: it will be the time of freedom and charity. According to Joachim of Fiori the time of the Holy Spirit has not yet arrived but it is imminent. Each age is marked by a class of people: in the first age married people, in the second, clerics, and in the third, monks. Thus, Joachim was accused of "denigrating the clerical order."[16]

Joachim's theology of history was condemned after his death, but even so it had a great deal of impact, first in the Franciscan movement and subsequently throughout the history of the West. It would not have attracted attention had not St. Francis and his masses of followers appeared a few years after the death of the holy abbot. Many saw the coming of St. Francis as the sign of a new world, one inspired by the Spirit, of absolute poverty, of the emergence of a people of the poor, independent of the clergy. The Franciscan movement seemed to be a miracle. In a few years it spread astonishingly throughout all of Europe and drew in thousands, tens of thousands of members and sympathy from millions of Christians.

St. Francis was unaware of Abbot Joachim's prophecies, but when the direction of the order began to be debated, some spiritual Franciscans resurrected his prophecies to show that the time announced by him, the time of the Holy Spirit, had arrived with St. Francis. They believed that everything had to change and that henceforth they had to live in a reign of the Spirit. Francis embodied the aspirations of the popular movements and ushered in a new era in Christendom.[17]

The Franciscan movement did not remain united. That was impossible, for the life of St. Francis and his first companions was a miracle, but one that could not last. His disciples could not live the same way. Moreover, St. Francis's life was a radical challenge to virtually the whole church—but especially to the hierarchical model of the church, despite the immense respect that St. Francis always showed toward the representatives of the hierarchy. Francis was able to win over Pope Innocent III and his immediate successors. With the pope's support, Francis was able to free himself from the clergy, the bishops, and the priests. The pope apparently thought that both Francis and Dominic could help him reform the church, without having to go through the clergy, which was unwilling to be reformed. Let us not forget that until the mid-thirteenth century the popes led church reform.

But even then it could be foreseen that the popes would not allow Francis's way of life or his thinking or way of understanding the gospel to become widespread in the church. This gospel of Francis was not the same as that of the popes, who had to manage a church made up of sinners but also of power. The popes wanted to bring the mendicants into their own politics. The split came with the rebelliousness of the spiritual Franciscans, who were seeking Abbot Joachim's reign of the Holy Spirit,[18] and the popes of course could not adopt that position.[19]

Some less radical movements, like confraternities and third orders, were recognized by the hierarchy. They tried to promote lay people, that is, the people of God, in a way that the clergy and hierarchy could tolerate. They accepted the established system, but with the help of the mendicants they sought to win rights and privileges that would bring them close to the privileged situation of the clergy.[20] This awakening from passive submission to the clergy was a step forward for the people of God.

With the Avignon popes (1309-1378) the separation between the radicals of the reign of the Spirit and the hierarchical church became so great that reconciliation seemed impossible—even though people at the time had not become aware of the gravity of the situation. These popes provoked increasingly strong opposition from lay people, especially because of their financial policy and the many taxes they imposed on all Christendom. They constituted a scandalous rejection of the spirit of poverty of the tradition of St. Francis and of Joachim's spiritual movement. Rebellion against the pope's policies took various forms. By the end of the century, the powers of the hierarchy were first challenged by a lay church in the theology of John Wycliffe,[21] who was condemned by Gregory XI in 1377.

With the Great Western Schism (1378-1415) and the coexistence of two and even three rival popes, the pope's power entered into crisis. It was Emperor Sigismund who, together with the bishops and the universities, convoked the Council of Constance (1414-1418) to reestablish the unity of the church. Several alternative theologies to the prevailing ecclesiology emerged and were given the general name "conciliarism," because they all held that the council was higher than the pope by himself. These alternatives were led by bishops and universities, and they entrusted power in the church to bishops and university scholars, but they did not essentially change the structure, despite the emperor's initiative (Constance was the first council convoked by an emperor in the West).

In the first half of the fifteenth century the popes managed to restore their authority and eliminate the conciliarist alternatives. Even though conciliarism did not bring about solid efforts at restoring the people of God, it played an important role historically because it served as a defense and legitimation against the efforts of the popes to increase their power in the church. Whenever there was any resistance to further steps of concentrating power in the hands of the popes, they invoked the specter of conciliarism. That memory served to erect strong barriers against the aspirations of the people of God.[22]

The Council of Constance itself condemned the Czech reformer Jan Hus, the national hero of the Czech people and nation. Hus and Jerome of Prague were condemned, and Hus was burned at the stake in 1415. The popes had to send four crusades against the resistance in Bohemia in order to destroy the popular resistance seeking to save his legacy. The Hussite movement was both a revolution of the poor and reform of the church,[23] and it foreshadowed the whole left wing of modernity. Out of it come the Anabaptists, Methodism, and (implicit and explicit) Christian socialism.

All efforts to restore an institutionally recognized active role of the Christian people were in vain, and efforts at a Christian humanism were systematically opposed by Rome. The most famous of those preaching reconciliation was Nicolas of Cusa (d. 1464), who proposed a theology that allowed for coexistence between the power of the hierarchy and the Christian people conceived as people, *communio, fraternitas*,[24] but it did not gain acceptance. Flemish mysticism and the *devotio moderna* can be regarded as a way of conciliation. Lay people were schooled in mysticism and thus became a well-trained, cultured Christian people sincerely devoted to the faith, recognizing the powers of clergy and hierarchy but drawing its spirituality from other sources. In the course of the fifteenth century a group of highly developed lay adults emerged, but most joined the Protestant reformation, attracted by its message.

On the eve of the Protestant crisis, there were many outstanding Christian humanists, like the emblematic Erasmus and Thomas More, who advocated peaceful reform of the church; they did not challenge its structure but only how its powers were used. Unfortunately, in the war between Luther and the Jesuits, Erasmus and the humanists were condemned by both sides. The Catholic Counter-Reformation wanted condemnation, and those advocating reconciliation were stamped out. The Catholic Church apparently still believed in the possibility of political and military reconquest. Unlike the humanists, church authorities did not grasp the tenor of their times.[25] There was no longer any third party—the church was irrevocably divided. No pope after Hadrian IV wanted to reach any agreement. The people could not come together; clerical power was too strong.

Into this situation came the explosion of the Reformation, which was a huge disaster. The vision of Christendom split into two poles: one invoking the hierarchy and the other the Christian people, one the power of the hierarchy and the other the power of the Bible. The centuries-long aspiration for church reform *"in capite et in membris"* finally broke out in the great schism which cut Christendom in two: North and South. In reaction to the Protestant Reformation, the Catholic Church resolved to undertake its own reform: the Council of Trent. However, rather than facing the problems that had arisen in the people of God, Trent shored up the past and its structures, and closed all doors.

The council itself remained close to the patristic and medieval tradition; its theology is less polemical than the interpretation made of it starting in the late sixteenth century.[26] Here the Jesuits played a key role, starting with their privileged position at Trent, when Diego Laynez became a kind of vice-pope, as sole interpreter of the pope among the bishops. Later the Jesuits assumed leadership, and over the centuries of modernity imprinted their combative spirit and rigid structure on the church. Although the Jesuits were suppressed by the popes in 1773 under pressure from the Catholic monarchs, when the suppression was lifted in 1814 they became an even more fearful army at the disposal of the popes, combating modernity, liberalism, and all the errors of the modern world.

The Jesuits legitimized and helped shape Roman centralization. They took as the aim of their own activity and that of the church the Catholic reconquest—first against Protestantism and then against modernity. Great apologists and debaters, they had no sense of any initiative or participation by the Christian people,[27] but sought support from kings and elites. The humanist aspiration for the participation of the people, as in the early church, was stifled and practically disappeared from view. No one could conceive of challenging the "Tridentine" system, which was destined to last four hundred years.[28]

Tridentine Christianity revolved around obedience, a virtue at the heart of Jesuit spirituality, which was inculcated into the entire people of God. Any slight wish for change was ruled out: wanting to change something was an act of disobedience. Sanctity was synonymous with obedience and the purpose of the church was to inculcate obedience in everyone. Obedience to whom? To God, it was said, but in practice obedience to God meant radical submission to the mind and will of the hierarchy. Because the hierarchy became ever more subordinate to the pope, the route to salvation became quite simple: salvation meant obeying the pope.

The other (Protestant) Reformation failed to remain true to its origins. Two principles lay at the root of Protestantism: the aspiration to freedom on the part of the Christian peoples (the more educated but also among the ordinary people in town and countryside, everyone who did not accept clerical authoritarianism), and the aspirations of the scholars who, drawing on humanism, wanted to return to the Bible and the simplicity of early Christianity, free of spurious later additions. Although they agreed in their rejection of the clerical system, the people were on one side and the scholars on the other.

Initially the scholars prevailed. Protected by princes, their reformation shaped a new clergy, that of the scholars, which maintained most of the medieval ecclesiastical system—everything in tradition compatible with the principle of *scriptura sola*, understood more or less flexibly. The people were not very strong in the Lutheran, Anglican, or Calvinist Presbyterian churches.

Thomas Münzer and the Anabaptists seized the other principle, that of the people. The radical conflict between Luther and Münzer expresses well the incompatibility between the two projects, that of the people and that of the new hierarchy. Luther remained faithful to the model of alliance between the political power and the new clergy, while Münzer became the sounding board of the people in the countryside and the city.[29] The Reformation aroused in the people a great hope of liberation. Luther opted for the support and security offered by the princes, while Calvin and Zwingli sought support from the emerging bourgeoisie. The people were left with the bitterness of defeat and disappointment.

What was salvaged from the disaster of the popular reformation were the Anabaptist movements, which found refuge in Holland and then in England. The English Anabaptists, the Puritans, actually took power in England in the Revolution of the Saints (1640-1660), which was the first great manifestation of the idea of the people in the history of Europe. For twenty years the Puritans governed England in the name of the people, rejecting the divine right monarchy and the hierarchical Anglican church connected to the king.

This is not the place to rehearse the history of Puritanism or of the English revolution. Our concern is how the people of God enters history along a winding path. Rejected by the Catholic Church and by the reformation churches, the people of God appears in a parallel sect. However, this route had a great deal of influence in the subsequent movement of the life of the West. Rejected by the great churches, the people of God will later be secularized and clash with the dominant churches.

The Puritans emigrated to the English colonies in the Americas where they formed the United States of America. The U.S. Constitution (1787) begins, *"We, the people of the United States."* The people had arrived: the Declaration of Independence of the United States gave rise to contemporary democracy. In the United States, religion and politics are intimately connected and the people identify their democracy with their own Christianity. However, this is essentially the Christianity of the free, non-hierarchical churches, independent of both the Catholic Church (which was absent in the beginning) and the historic churches, particularly the Anglican and Lutheran. The concept of people of God grew in this context, whereas it was completely absent from the Catholic Church.[30]

Europe moved toward increasing separation between the church and the people, as the people became increasingly secularized. The signs were ignored: no one in the church seemed to notice that a concept essential to Christianity was being taken up by social movements outside the established church.

Initially, it was the bourgeoisie who claimed to be the people. They were not part of the privileged orders of society (clergy and nobility), but they saw themselves as a class spurned even though it was they who produced the nation's wealth. They were the people, the polar opposite of clergy and nobility. Until the seventeenth century, no distinction was made between the bourgeoisie and manual workers. By the eighteenth century, as it grew rich and powerful, the bourgeoisie no longer wanted to be confused with the poor. Since then the word "people" has meant essentially workers, manual workers, who are in fact the poor.[31]

In their struggles against the clergy and nobility the bourgeoisie called on the poor for help. That is what happened in the French Revolution and in the other bourgeois revolutions of the nineteenth century. The same thing happened in the Latin American wars of independence. The Indigenous people were called to sacrifice, and spilled their blood, but after victory, the local elites took all the power for themselves. The French Revolution was a victory of the bourgeoisie, and the people were shunted aside.

In the nineteenth century, the bourgeoisie fought primarily against the remnants of monarchy and aristocracy and against the power of the clergy. The bourgeoisie wanted a rational religion, i.e., deism, as exemplified in Freemasonry.[32] In religious terms, the bourgeoisie sought to distance itself from the people, who remained faithful to the rural religious traditions of the Middle Ages, and which the post-Tridentine clergy carefully cultivated as the main source of their social power.

From the eighteenth until the end of the nineteenth century, the main struggle took place between the clergy and the deist bourgeoisie, now emancipated from the clergy. The bourgeoisie won all the battles and gradually transformed society into its image and likeness. The Tridentine church was not prepared to deal with the forces enhancing the power of the bourgeoisie. It was armed to struggle against Protestantism, but it did not understand what was happening with the advance of the bourgeoisie—science, technical progress, the freeing of the critical spirit from popular religion, and the antiquated way Christian revelation was presented.[33] The clergy drew support from the declining aristocracy and the rural masses and elaborated a purely defensive strategy for dealing with the bourgeois assault.

The solution adopted by the popes and the ever more submissive clergy was to settle into the castle, separated from bourgeois, urban, industrial society under the "Enlightenment." The popes simply issued condemnations. For example, almost all French literature was put on the Index of Forbidden Books, and so French Catholic youth were unaware of what was being thought and said in their country, and had to be content with series of apologetics by Catholic writers who were well intentioned but completely out of touch with their own times.[34] The hierarchy's response to liberalism was to seal off the borders, seeking to isolate Catholics from any contact with modernity, and to close their eyes to the fate of humankind in order to defend the remnants of their privileges. The Protestant churches did practically the same thing.

To bolster the church taking refuge in their castle, the popes increased centralization. They thought that with the support of the people (which, in fact, was not a people but a mass identified with medieval popular religion) they could defeat the liberal movement—they need only wait for the liberal world to destroy itself. They were absolutely certain that a society in revolt against the church and God could not stand. But it is still standing to this day. Facing the persistence of the unbelieving liberal bourgeoisie, the popes thought that even more centralization was needed. The process has continued to this day, when centralization is without precedent.

During the nineteenth century, the popes gradually reserved the appointment of bishops for themselves, thereby destroying the ancient traditions that allowed local churches some involvement in the choice of bishops. On the eve of Vatican II, only two dioceses in the world still had structures of participation inherited from the past, Basel and Sankt Gallen in Switzerland.

This centralization gave rise to a submissive episcopate, completely out of contact with the outside world, impervious to being contaminated by the errors dominating society, tirelessly defending orthodoxy, bureaucratic, concerned over the application of laws, and faithfully carrying out instructions from Rome—separated from the people. The bishops no longer felt that they were representatives of a portion of the people of God—they were representatives of papal power to that portion. Their role was to impose the pope's policy on their people, but not in any way to direct or guide the action of their people. Strong personalities capable of questioning instructions from the Roman Curia were gradually excluded.

This was the response to the rise of the bourgeoisie and the civilization it created. Blinded by the struggle against liberalism, the clergy failed to recognize what was happening with the people. The church lost the people— when it is supposed to be a people. Earthly people and people of God go together. Leo XIII (1878-1903) recognized the extreme poverty of the workers and the great injustice suffered by the working class at the hands of an ambitious, greedy, arrogant bourgeoisie haughty with its new power. But he failed to see the most important thing: that this people was changing and becoming conscious of itself. Workers learned to read, to think for themselves, and became aware of their social power. They wanted to be actors in history, but the clergy still wanted an ignorant and submissive people. While the hierarchy thought it could still count on the support of the ignorant masses, they disappeared.

After 1870, the church could have been out in front of this people seeking freedom, dignity, and a share in the vast wealth being produced by its labor, but the hierarchy was afraid, and under Pius X (1903-1914) it forged an alliance with its worst enemy, the bourgeoisie.[35] The church had unconsciously assimilated the bourgeois mindset, and to this day it is unaware of the extent to which it has absorbed the values and structures of the bourgeoisie.[36] That is why it lost the people.

This situation helps us appreciate the revolutionary scope of Vatican II, which sought in some manner to correct everything that had been done— and especially what should have been done—for a thousand years, to respond to unanswered questions, and to repair so many sins of omission over the years. Asking forgiveness for the sins of Christians is fine, but there must also be repentance for errors in governing the church. What did the popes do with the total power they accumulated in the church? What was it good for? What guidance was given to the church? At decisive moments, they failed.

This power in one person is illusory, for the Holy Spirit's real power comes from his presence in millions of disciples of Jesus. Why such a lack of vision? Perhaps the clergy was at least dimly aware that its strategy was empty, but there was no courage to change such an ancient system with so much inertia. What was missing was faith and trust in the power of the Holy Spirit in the people. The church could have been at the forefront of the worker's liberation movement, but it used its power in purely symbolic things—words, rituals, gestures—rather than entering the world.

In the twentieth century, a discreet movement began to grow and, despite threats, it continued to grow, against all hope. It achieved the miracle of Vatican II, thanks to the miracle of John XXIII, but it is clear that Vatican II is still too frail for confronting a thousand years of building up a useless, illusory power. The people of God has been absent for centuries. What was most visible was the conflict between the clergy and the civil power—which monopolized the role of lay people, who included the emperor, kings, princes, and the bourgeoisie, i.e., those who hold social power. When the people raised their heads they encountered repression.

Socialism started out Christian, and socialists were Christians until the late nineteenth century (although its intellectuals were liberals). Abandoned by the church, socialism sought a churchless Christianity, and at the end of the century was taken over by atheist ideologues. Socialism was contaminated by the spirit of the bourgeoisie, adopted the ideas of development, and turned bourgeois. That was when Catholics were allowed to make alliances with socialist parties, but by this time the people were gone from the church.

The church had not completely ignored the people, but it treated them paternalistically. The poor were treated as an object of charity, not recognized as "people." They were not the church, but the object of its paternalism. Then, little by little, Catholics opened their eyes, discovered the world, and unwittingly prepared Vatican II.

BACK TO THE SOURCES

The previous pages have shown how the Catholic Church came to see itself increasingly as a supernatural and purely spiritual entity, above the world and outside history. In the early twentieth century a new Christian avant-garde sought to discover the historic reality of the church. Two movements came together: an *intellectual* movement that accepted modern historical and critical methods for thinking about Christianity; and a *social* movement that recognized the world of the poor, the people, and accepted its challenge. Both recognized the truth in liberalism and socialism and sought dialogue with Western society and its ideologies. Whereas the previous theology had used history to find arguments in support of the official theology, the use of historical methods now led to a realization that the church's past was quite different, and hence to a questioning of the official theology.

The biblical movement, best represented by Fr. Joseph-Marie Lagrange OP (1855-1938) and the École Biblique he founded in Jerusalem, had to endure many condemnations and many decrees from the Pontifical Biblical Commission, which was set up to restrain it. For a time, the biblical movement operated more or less underground, but then came out in the open, and Rome was forced to tolerate it. Likewise the patristic movement showed that the origins of Christianity were quite different from the official version, and in figures like Goerres and Duchesne, Rome had to accept the beginnings of a new church history which attempted to find out (in von Ranke's expression) "what really happened." The liturgical movement (Dom Odo Casel, abbey of Bueron) sought to restore a liturgy closer to Christian origins. All these movements inspired movements of Catholic youth after 1918 (notably Romano Guardini in Germany). The ecumenical movement led Catholics to take up relations with separated Christians in dialogue rather than combat. Some eventually discovered that the heretics were not so heretical, there were many values in the separated churches, and not all practices in the Catholic Church were as above question as the apologists said.

Alongside this intellectual movement was a social movement. The history of Social Catholicism and Christian democracy will not be repeated here. In Germany Catholics formed powerful social associations and a political party with social concerns (the Center) and similar movements arose in France, Belgium, and Switzerland.[37] The hierarchy, and especially Pius X and Pius XII, resisted, as it has to this day. The social action of Catholics continued until Vatican II opened things up; it was too late for Europe but Latin America responded with Medellín and Puebla.

There were two reasons for the conflict between "social Catholics" and the hierarchy.[38] First, with the "church's social teaching" the popes sought to offer a single ideal doctrine to be followed by everyone, a body of doctrine that would take the place of ideologies. The result was a continual gap between the doctrine and real problems. Catholics seemed to float in the realm of ideas, rather than action. All political parties could claim to be following Catholic social doctrine. Social Catholics exerted pressure for the church to become involved, but the hierarchy refused and even issued condemnations (Luigi Sturzo in Italy, worker priests in France).

Second, the hierarchy rejected any expression of class struggle, a Marxist idea and a banner of socialism. The reason given was the gospel's message of peace, but the real reason might be more political: accepting class struggle meant breaking with the bourgeoisie.

What united these movements was a desire to situate the church in human history, and in its own origins. Out of these movements, especially after 1918, there emerged a new ecclesiology, which was summed up and symbolized in the concept of the "people of God." Social Catholicism, Christian democracy, the youth movements, Catholic Action, the new missionary movement of young clergy, and the liturgical movement all gave a sense of the people of God. What was lacking was a theory, and that came through the biblical movement. Between 1937 and 1942 biblical scholars—Protestant and Catholic—rediscovered the concept of the people of God in the Bible.[39] One influential pre-Vatican II work was Lucien Cerfaux, *La Théologie de l'Église suivant Saint Paul* (1942), which shows that Paul's theology is built on the concept of the people of God. Patristic studies had already shown that the notion of people of God was more prominent in the church fathers than had been thought. Historical study of theology and the church made it possible to retrieve forgotten ideas.[40]

In 1943 Pius XII responded with *Mystici Corporis,* in which he sought to derive ecclesiology wholly from the notion of the Body of Christ. He did not succeed in imposing that theology. The Body of Christ is an important and necessary concept in Catholic ecclesiology, but it is not a summary of all ecclesiology. An ecclesiology totally based on the Body of Christ would remain unhistorical, disembodied, unconnected to human realities. It would not help lay movements or change deep-seated clericalism. Thanks to the council theologians and experts, who had suffered and struggled to change the face of the church, Pius XII's theology did not prevail.

By enshrining the concept of people of God, the council fathers wanted to approve, legitimize, and stimulate the intellectual movements and those pastoral movements that promoted the laity as Christian people.

What happened at the council was almost miraculous. No one imagined that theologians condemned just ten years before could be the intellectual authors of the conciliar theology. Yet something was still missing, something that both Cardinal Lercaro and John XXIII regarded as central, the centrality of the poor. It was only in Latin America that the theology of the people of God reached its broadest expression.[41]

Chapter 3

PEOPLE OF GOD IN LATIN AMERICA

Nothing indicates that Latin American bishops were interested in the ecclesiology of the people of God before the council. They had generally studied theology in Rome or Spain, and were quite faithful to the doctrine of the *societas perfecta* and alert to new heresies and the danger of communism.

And yet there are many signs that the rejection of the idea of the people of God at the 1985 synod and in subsequent official ecclesiology was in response to Latin American liberation theology as understood in Rome. In order to see how this could happen in so few years, we will look at how the theology of the people of God emerged in Latin American awareness and writings, and what the condemnation from Rome meant.

THEOLOGY OF THE PEOPLE OF GOD IN LATIN AMERICA

How to explain that what was impossible before Vatican II could happen in Latin America, i.e., the identification of the people of God with the poor? There may have been social reasons, but the primary reason had to do with specific people. The social reason was the awakening of the people of God, who had been silenced for four hundred years. Social movements began to appear in the early twentieth century, often led by a new tiny but conscious intellectual class which sought to awaken the consciousness of the people and make them agents of their own liberation. These movements were sporadic and quite limited until 1950, but then they began to expand—to the point where they even drew attention in the church.

At that point a new generation of priests and religious appeared, including a generation of prophetic bishops, few in number but endowed with unusual spiritual strength. They first sought to become familiar with the human reality of their parishes and dioceses. They discovered that the reality was poverty—shocking poverty. Many of the poor were Catholics, and their oppressors, those responsible for their poverty, were also Catholics quite close to the church.

Even before Vatican II some bishops drew closer to the poor, and having discovered the real people, the people of the poor, committed themselves to the liberation of this people. They had no theology to guide and strengthen that commitment, but they received one at Vatican II. Although they were a minority among the bishops they were the soul of Medellín, and they took their stand before most of the great inert mass of bishops knew what was happening.

They were prophetic bishops, but they had the advantage of being unaware of how the hierarchical machinery worked; they did not realize what they were up against. They were innocent, or as Jesus said, as simple as children. They thought it was safe for a bishop to live the gospel. They took on risks without knowing what lay in wait. But the Vatican, aided by the Latin American elites with their loyal bishops, waged unceasing battle to undo what had been done at Medellín, and these bishops were spied upon, discredited, rebuked, and blocked, and their work was dismantled after they retired. Archbishop Oscar Romero, for example, was converted by the reality of the people of El Salvador—in whom he discovered the people of God. He thought it was his duty as a bishop to speak, but he was increasingly isolated, and condemned by most of the Salvadoran bishops conference and by the Roman Curia.[1] He only lasted three years.

Today most of these bishops are dead or retired. Their replacements do not have the same prophetic vigor, but their work remains. They gave another face to the church in Latin America—the image of what a Vatican II church would be.

THE PEOPLE OF GOD AND THE CHURCH OF THE POOR

Since Vatican II the people of God and the poor have been linked (as they were apparently for John XXIII). In Europe, where the long labor struggle and a Marxist terminology of class struggle had left their mark, the term "people" no longer evoked the poor. "People of God" invoked instead the ancient theology of the Bible and tradition. In Latin America "people" meant the vast majority of the poor population in the countryside or on the outskirts of cities, made up of Indigenous people, Black descendants of slaves, or people of mixed ancestry.

Latin America offered the new prophets a favorable setting. Religion was still present in all areas of individual and social life. It was not unusual for the church to be present in public life, although its public presence generally bolstered existing structures. Unlike Europe with its long history of secularization, the church could be brought around to defending the people.

Another reason for the emergence of this theology of the people of the poor is that in Latin America the state is weak and the church is strong—institutionally, socially, and culturally—whereas in Europe the state is strong and the church is weak. Liberal and socialist movements were much stronger in Europe, and they eventually succeeded in involving most of the population, thereby strengthening the state. In addition, a strong middle class was able to provide the state with efficient administration, something that has not yet happened in Latin America, at least not sufficiently. Thus the church could play a much more important role than in Europe—if it wished.

In Latin America there was a rural people primarily living under conditions of shocking exploitation (in 1968), and an incipient proletariat, but especially a huge urban population without jobs, with no defined social status, living precariously. The gap between the wealthy ruling class and the vast masses of the population was startling, and it has only continued to grow. It is Latin America's "distinction" to have the greatest social inequality in the world. More than elsewhere in the world, there was and still is a huge population that looks just like those sheep without a shepherd who moved Jesus to compassion. Indignation and compassion for this huge abandoned mass was what aroused the cry of the prophets.

Yet this was a deeply religious people, still unfamiliar with modernity. Religion meant worldview, philosophy, culture, morality, meaning of life, code of behavior—all at once. The religious celebrations that broke up normal everyday work were a high point in life. This situation has changed a great deal since then, especially since the arrival of television, which has flattened out cultures and has largely taken over the place of religion. But that is how things were then.

The conditions were in place: a vast people of the poor and some prophets in their midst. The only thing lacking was a jolt to cause a revolution—which had not happened in Europe. The jolt was Vatican II and its theology of the people.[2] Most Latin American bishops went into the council not knowing what they wanted, but by the time they left they did.

Paul VI explicitly asked Bishop Manuel Larrain, the president of CELAM (the Bishops Conference of Latin America), to apply Vatican II to Latin America. That was just what the group of prophets wanted. The Latin Americans understood that they could now be more independent and take initiatives. Prior to the council it was assumed that the church had to reflect the European church, and changing anything in the structures from colonial times seemed inconceivable. To apply the council the prophets had to get together. There already was a group of bishops who had learned how to communicate—thanks to the creation of CELAM (1955), and they had recognized leaders like Larrain and Bishop Hélder Câmara of Brazil.

There was also a group of young priests studying theology and social sciences in Europe and in contact with new developments in theology and in social movements. Impressed by the worldwide movement of decolonization, they envisioned a decolonization of Latin America. The upshot was a new prophetic kind of pastoral work committed to the liberation of the poor, and a new theology that sought to provide a theoretical foundation for this liberation movement. They stayed in contact and exchanged ideas through seminars, training sessions, and reflection groups.

These theologians played a role different from that in Europe, where theologians had to remain in the academic world and had no role in leading the church. To be a theologian was to be suspected of possible deviations. From the outset in Latin America bishops and theologians were linked, and hence theory and practice were likewise linked. Bishops and priests committed to changing society, along with theologians, immediately embraced the idea of the people of God. It was very relevant to the needs and challenges of the time.

In Latin America the term "people" made it possible to say many things, to symbolize the entirety of the aspirations of the population, with the exception of the ruling oligarchies. People of God was what was sought, a people with its rights and dignity restored.

* * *

The concept "people of God" offered the gateway to a church of the poor. During Vatican II, some bishops who were meeting at the Belgian College wanted the council to declare its identification with the poor, and support a church of the poor, as desired by John XXIII. Bishop Charles-Marie Himmer of Tournai said on the council floor (October 1963): *"primus locus in ecclesia pauperibus reservandus est."*[3]

"People" meant the multitude oppressed by an exploiting ruling class. "People" also meant the world of poverty. "People" meant the true church because the poor masses were the most attached to the church. "People" meant solidarity and unity in winning a better world. "People" meant this latent energy, now awakening. "People" meant emancipation from colonization, independence from the colony or colonial situation. "People" meant the new agent of history, humankind liberated. It meant all these things together.

The word "people" (Spanish *pueblo*, Portuguese *povo*) took on a special resonance with the awakening of populist nationalism in the early twentieth century in intellectual and university movements in almost all countries. "People" was the key word in almost all populist movements. Socialist movements adopted the populist vocabulary, and the people themselves had a populist understanding of socialism: it meant the liberation of the people from the traditional yoke of the oligarchy. Class struggle was experienced as the struggle of the people against their traditional masters. Among the people both populism and socialism were religious. Even if the leaders professed no religion, they had to be present for the religious acts of the people, because religion was part of the people.

The concept of "people of God" facilitated linkages between theologians, Catholic activists, and the religious masses in populist or socialist social movements. Neither the bishops nor the theologians wanted to be isolated in either the church or the popular movements. In their mind it could all go together. They were seeking to renew the church, and the church was a huge potential force. By "church" they meant that institution or organization which has played and continues to play an important social role in Latin America.[4] Their aspiration was that this huge potential force should be placed at the service of the people's liberation. They thought that the church ought to be of the people; the aim was to restore to the people what was theirs. The people should become church and the church should become people. Was that an illusion? Time will tell; for now we are in a dark night, and only the future will reveal whether someday the dawn will come.

In the mind of the group of bishops and theologians who were the driving force at Medellín and Puebla, the church in Latin America is a moral and cultural power indispensable for liberation. In any case, Medellín and Puebla allowed the hope of the poor and the church to come together.

Surprisingly, the term "people of God" does not appear much in the Medellín texts, although the idea is at its core. The reason is that the concept of "people" was in process: everyone was aware that the church ought to be, but is not yet, people of God. Being people of God is the goal, the project, the endpoint of the change sought. That is why the texts speak more of the transformation process. In the terminology of that time, this process is often envisioned as a conflict between three models of the church in Latin America: Christendom, neo-Christendom, or liberation. This three-part scheme can be seen throughout the Medellín documents and became a widely used framework for talking about the church.[5] That is why the church is always spoken of within a historic context. These three models are in conflict in the church, which is called to reach the third model, which means becoming people of God.

On the last page of his book *A Theology of Liberation*, Gustavo Gutiérrez says, "but in the last instance we will have an authentic theology of liberation only when the oppressed themselves can freely raise their voice and express themselves directly and creatively in society and in the heart of the People of God." Leonardo Boff states the implications of the theology of the people of God: "Having the courage to allow a popular church, a church of the people to grow, with the people's values, in terms of language, liturgical expression, popular religiosity, etc. Until recently the church was not of the people, but of the priests, and for the people."[6]

Everyone is aware that without Vatican II's theology of the people of God, there would have been no liberation theology. If the church were to be identified with its power, i.e., with the clergy, no change would be conceivable. They were also convinced that the people of God could only be the people of the poor and that "people" meant the poor.[7]

At Vatican II only a minority could see this clearly because in Europe the central issue was the relationship between hierarchy and laity. The movement was prompting lay people to seek greater recognition of their value in the church with the support of biblical and patristic theology. The return to the authentic documents of revelation and the aspirations of lay people went together. In Latin America the central problem was the antagonism between the people's church and the elite church, church of liberation and church of domination. "Lay" consciousness was weak. The issue was confronting poverty: the prophets tried to force the rich to face it.

The church was (and still is) divided at all levels: bishops, clergy, religious and lay people, all split, as a result of the history of the church in the Americas. From the outset, the church, i.e., most of the clergy and official church institutions, have always been on the side of the ruling classes and the system of oppression, in colonial times and in the states that appeared after independence. Yet there have always been prophetic voices speaking on behalf of the forgotten people. Vatican II led to critical study of the historic role of the church. One portion of the church was led to criticize what was done during the long period of collaboration between those on top and the clergy, and the latter have felt unjustly attacked, because they were unaware of the role they were playing in society.

Hence, the struggle against the domination of one portion of the clergy (and bishops) against the other is part of the struggle of the people against the dominant elite. One portion of the church, which is still the larger, is part and parcel of domination; the other portion is convinced that the church must be freed of the bonds tying it to the dominant classes and stand with the people in their struggle for liberation. The struggles against social domination and clerical domination are not the same thing, but they are inseparable.

This context helps explain the rediscovery of a fundamental biblical teaching that had long been hidden, at least since the fourteenth century: the church is the people of the poor. The people of God is the poor. Nothing is more basic and obvious in the Bible. How to understand that this truth was hidden for so many centuries, except in the minds of some prophets who went almost unheeded in their own time? Understanding this is the great challenge in Latin America.

At Vatican II Cardinal Lercaro made a heartfelt plea to the council to proclaim the priority of the poor as a central truth of Christianity. Everyone knew that Lercaro was committed to the poor.[8] The assembly was deeply moved but not ready intellectually. The problem was clericalism not poverty; by affirming the church as people of God, the bishops wanted to highlight the fundamental equality of all the baptized. In Latin America the problem was not the situation of lay people but the situation of oppression of entire peoples with the complicity of the church—five centuries of oppression sacralized and legitimized by the church as an institution.

John XXIII's expression "church of the poor" was not taken up by the council, but in Latin America it has been made central to ecclesiology. The "church of the poor" indicates what is in the people of God, but it adds something fundamental: this people is a people of the poor. The true people of God is the people of the poor.

In the 1970s the term "popular church" was sometimes used ("popular" is synonymous with "poor"). The people is comprised of everyone oppressed by the ruling elites (whether called "oligarchy," "aristocracy," "upper class"). The term "people" is used to express opposition to those on top. The term "popular church" was open to misinterpretation by someone who was not aware of how people speak in Latin America. It served as the basis for the great campaign before and after Puebla against base communities and against Medellín pastoral work in general and the option for the poor. The popular church was condemned as a "parallel" church, in opposition to another, i.e., the "institutional" church. As a church "born from the people" it was said to be denying the divine origin of the church.

At his inaugural speech in Puebla, the pope took up the attack and severely warned the popular church (1.8). The assembly took up the pope's criticisms and rejected the expression "popular church" (Puebla 263). The advocates of base communities and the preferential option for the poor tried to make known the true, utterly correct, and orthodox meaning of the expression. But they were unable to convince their foes who had found it to be a dangerous weapon, and they thought it better to abandon the term to save the reality. From that point on the expression "church of the poor" gained currency.

The "church of the poor" includes everything that was in the conciliar expression "people of God," but it adds something fundamental to it, because it sets forth where this people of God can be found, the feature that makes it possible to identify it in human history. It removes the abstract and purely theoretical character from "people of God" and makes it concrete. The "church of the poor" is located within humankind, whereas "people of God" can leave things fuzzy, or allows for identifying the people through symbolic characters: a person would be regarded as belonging to the people of God if wrapped in Christian symbols: words from dogma, sacramental acts, expressions of obedience to the hierarchy; what he or she does in the world or life does not matter. That is not what it means in Latin America.

To illustrate a few major aspects of this concept we turn to Jon Sobrino's *The True Church and the Poor*, which is the clearest and most complete exposition of the idea of the church of the poor.[9] Sobrino notes the difference between the conciliar idea of the people of God and that of the "church of the poor," while recognizing three advances in the council's teaching on the people of God: 1) it counterbalanced the excessive weight of the idea of the Body of Christ; 2) it limited the "hierarchological" idea of the church, and restored the importance of the laity; 3) it helped end the monopoly over the faith by discovering it "throughout the people." The perspective of the people of God helped bring a new appreciation for the historic character of the church's earthly pilgrimage, the fundamental equality of all Christians, the recognition of the value of every human creature, the revaluing of local churches—with some hints of a priority of the poor. Vatican II was very important for beginning to broach the notion and reality of the church of the poor, but it did not define the link between the church and the poor.

Sobrino likewise indicates some weaknesses of the conciliar theology: 1) the church as people of God remains very abstract (all lay people are equal, as if they were not situated in a human history of domination and exploitation); 2) the issue of the church "for the poor" remains an ethical problem, whereas the problem posed by the poor is ecclesiological (being "church of the poor"); 3) the church of the poor cannot simply be a part of the church as though there were a church of the rich or anyone else, each on its own; the church as a whole must make the centrality of the poor a starting point.[10]

Recognizing the church of the poor must lead to a change in power relationships. The aim is not to transfer the power of the hierarchy to the poor, but to change what power means in the church. There is a poor way and a rich way to exercise power. The change does not mean moving from a historically structured church to a purely spiritual church. Obviously, the church must be structured to be able to exist in history or in the world of human beings. The change entails moving from a church drawing support from the political, economic, and cultural powers of this world—even being imprisoned by those powers—to a church that follows Jesus Christ, and that draws support from the faith of the people.

A church connected to the powerful inevitably becomes rich and powerful. It ends up sacralizing, legitimizing, and imitating the power system in human societies with their injustice, becoming complicit in injustice, even when it is justified by a pseudonecessity: "There's no other way, no other answer." Sobrino shows that the four notes of the church are present in the church of the poor and that hence it is the true church. This is not a new church emerging from the old, but a resurrection of the old church starting from the poor. This is the project launched in Latin America and is still going on today, despite contradictions and opposition.[11]

The Puebla conference (1979) did not produce the theological synthesis sought by the Medellín theologians; in fact, they were excluded from the conference. "People of God" and "poverty" were assigned to two separate commissions, thereby affecting the conclusions. A third commission dealt with the church by commenting on the council teaching, without adding anything fundamental. Commission eight, which had the preferential option for the poor, drew up the most significant portion of the final document, but it was disconnected from the question of the essence of the church. The upshot was that no ecclesiology in which the poor are the people of God was launched. Even so, in the reception of Puebla, it was clear that the chapters on the church and the option for the poor shed light on one another.

It is important to be aware that Puebla intended to say something new about the people of God: "CELAM prepared the groundwork for the Catholic people to open up somewhat more easily to a Church that would also describe itself as a People. This universal People permeates other peoples to help them grow toward the greater communion and brotherhood that Latin America itself was beginning to envisage. The Medellín Conference spread the new vision, which is as old as biblical history itself." [12]

One aspect of the idea of the people of God that Puebla wanted to highlight is the following: "the view of the Church as the People of God seems necessary if we are to complete the transition, initiated at the Medellín conference, from an individualistic way of living the faith to the great communitarian awareness opened up to us by Vatican II" (35). The word "transition" stresses the newness, i.e., the community aspect of the church.

The idea of people of God relates the church to the peoples of the earth, which it "permeates" to help them grow toward communion. "Our peoples have been living through important moments. . . . Amid this process they are discovering the presence of this other People that accompanies our natural peoples through their history." (234). "The church is a universal people," and hence it "is not in conflict with any other people. It can take on flesh and blood in all peoples to introduce the Kingdom of God into their histories" (237).

Likewise the people of God is something real in history, immersed in the history of peoples; it is "journeying through history" (220). The church is "the Family of God, pictured as the People of God on pilgrimage though history and journeying toward the Lord" (232); "universal people; the Family of God on earth; a holy People; a people on pilgrimage through history; a people that is sent out" (236). "The citizens who make up this People must journey by way of this earth" (251). "In viewing itself as a People, the Church defines itself as a reality in the midst of history that is journeying toward a goal not yet reached" (254). This theme of pilgrimage was developed extensively from paragraphs 254 to 266.

If the church is on pilgrimage in the history of peoples and of humankind, it cannot but be influenced by changes taking place in peoples; it too must change. Puebla emphasizes this topic of change, bearing in mind the pope's warning that the changes cannot affect the core which stands throughout the ages. "Another critical problem in Latin America, which is bound up with the historical condition of the People of God, is the whole matter of changes in the church. As it moves through history, the church must necessarily change, but only in external and accidental ways" (264).

Puebla highlights the social aspect of the people of God: it is a "historical, socially structured people," a "historical, institutional People" (261). It must be "visible as a socially structured entity. . . . Emphasis on the historical aspect brings out the necessity of giving institutional expression to this real-ity" (255). Puebla does not indicate the changes needed in the institution, except very abstractly: "A great change can be noted in Latin America in the way that authority is exercised within the Church" (260). The Puebla docu-ment also states the biblical attributes of the people of God: "People of God . . . invested with a universal priesthood . . ." (260), "a People made up of servants . . . sent out as prophetic People . . ." (267) "being inhabited by the Spirit, the People of God is also a holy people . . . a messianic People" (250). (Who could have imagined that just six years later the teaching on the people of God would be rejected by the hierarchy—at the 1985 extraordinary synod charged with further developing Vatican II?)

The option for the poor (chapter 1 of Part Four, "Preferential Option for the Poor") is the charter of Latin American theology. It is so well known that there is no need to summarize it, but the two chapters on the church and the poor must be brought together because they are complementary.

Being poor in Latin America, being "people," means being nothing, be-ing marginalized and exploited—it means being regarded as an object to be used when needed and thrown away when no longer needed. It is precisely in the midst of these poor that Jesus gathers the people of God—he gathers the people that the Father has chosen in the midst of this people. God has chosen "this people" to make "his people."[13]

The church is the people of the oppressed which finds in Jesus Christ its hope of full liberation—liberation as true human beings, worthy and free—and it receives from the Holy Spirit the strength and courage to struggle for this liberation. This is the figure of the church that is closest to the biblical teaching and to the manner of the early church.

CHURCH OF THE POOR ON TRIAL

The harmonious development of the Latin American church from Medellín to Puebla was broken by interference from Rome. After the ecclesial coup in Sucre, Bolivia, in 1972, when Rome imposed Alfonso López Trujillo as sec-retary general of CELAM,[14] the Curia was able to use CELAM itself to undo what had been achieved over the previous decade. It could launch a major campaign against the new Latin American ecclesiology, and from there against the council theology on which it was based. This was part of a systematic struggle seeking to discredit and ruin popular movements, Christian base communities, and anything related to the church of the poor. CELAM waged its campaign against liberation theology in the name of defending the church against Marxism.

The 1978 Consultative Document given to the bishops conferences in preparation for Puebla met widespread rejection because it was clear that the aim was to stamp out the influence of Medellín.[15] The critique of liberation ecclesiology was aimed first of all at the "popular church," an expression in which its adversaries sought to find the surreptitious presence of Marxism. In opening the meeting, the pope gave voice to these criticisms, and they then became part of the Puebla document. At Puebla the bishops made a distinction between acceptable and unacceptable meanings of the expression "popular church" (Puebla 262-263). The primary objection was that the term suggested the existence of another "official" or "institutional" church, thereby entailing division in the church and a denial of the function of the hierarchy.

In view of that opposition from the hierarchy, the expression "popular church" was abandoned, as we have said. The expression, which had become ambiguous, was dropped but the teaching about the people of God remained. However, it was clear that the criticism against the "popular church" was a pretext for discrediting all movements drawing inspiration from the theology of Medellín.

The Puebla document was received with relief, because the expected general condemnation of anything having to do with the people, community, or liberation did not occur. Despite its ambiguity, the advocates of Medellín adopted a tactic of highlighting what was positive and not criticizing what was negative, and thus the general opinion was that Puebla had confirmed Medellín and legitimized pastoral work for social change. Neither liberation theology nor base communities had been condemned.

The accusation of an attempt to oppose a "popular" church to an "official" or "institutional" church is completely gratuitous, because in liberation theology the opposition is between the church of the poor and the church of the oppressors. No one is opposed to the hierarchy as structure; quite the opposite, a good portion of the hierarchy was, and still is, at the forefront of the struggle for liberation. The aim was not to eliminate but to convert the hierarchy, which for centuries had almost always been on the side of domination, after an initial generation of prophetic bishops in the early sixteenth century. The aim was for the bishops to stand with the oppressed, and they have often done so.

Even without the term "popular church," opposition to the theology of the people of the poor became harsher after Puebla. This criticism came largely from certain sectors of the Latin American church, particularly CELAM, now headed by Alfonso López Trujillo and his advisors, including Roger Vekemans in Bogota.[16] Vekemans organized a three-way alliance between Rome, Germany (Koenigstein), and Bogota. He worked hard and persistently to prepare condemnations from Rome, convincing the Roman prelates that the Marxist danger had made its way deeply into the Latin American church, and that the poison had to be removed before it was too late. The Roman Curia welcomed this criticism, and the pope's crusade against communism in Poland provided a favorable context. The pope could be convinced that the struggle in Europe had to be extended to Latin America.

Communism was the same in both places but the danger was greater in Latin America because the enemy had succeeded in penetrating the church itself.

On August 6, 1984, the "Instruction on Certain Aspects of the 'Theology of Liberation'" was published under Cardinal Ratzinger's signature.[17] Its thesis was very clear: liberation theology was nothing but a Christian or theological garb for revolutionary Marxist ideas. Latin American theology was being condemned for the same reasons as French "progressivism" (*Jeunesse de l'Eglise* in the mid-twentieth century).

The condemnation of ecclesiology was especially harsh:

> The "theologies of liberation" . . . go on to a disastrous confusion between the poor of Scripture and the *proletariat* of Marx. In this way they pervert the Christian meaning of the poor, and they transform the fight for the rights of the poor into a class fight within the ideological perspective of the class struggle. For them the *"church of the poor"* signifies the church of the class which has become aware of the requirements of the revolutionary struggle as a step toward liberation, and which celebrates this liberation in its liturgy (IX, 10).
>
> The "theologies of liberation" of which we are speaking mean by the *church of the people* a church . . . of organized struggle for freedom. For some, the people, thus understood, even become the object of faith.
>
> Building on such a conception of the church of the people, a critique of the very structures of the church is developed. It is not simply the case of fraternal correction of pastors of the church whose behavior does not reflect the evangelical spirit of service and is linked to old fashioned signs of authority which scandalize the poor. It has to do with the challenge to the *sacramental and hierarchal structure* of the church, which was willed by the Lord himself. There is a denunciation of members of the hierarchy and the magisterium as objective representatives of the ruling class which has to be opposed (IX, 13).
>
> As far as the church is concerned, this system would see it only as a reality interior to history, itself subject to those laws which are supposed to govern the development of history in its immanence (IX, 8).

Many bishops thought the letter was aimed especially at them. The Vatican was annoyed at the support the Brazilian episcopacy was giving to popular movements and liberation theology—two cardinals went to Rome to support Leonardo Boff. The Instruction was no doubt an indirect reproach against the bishops, but the pope recognized that it was too harsh and sent a letter to Brazil (April 1986) almost apologizing for what had been said earlier—but without taking back any of the content of the Instruction. In March 1986 Cardinal Ratzinger issued a more positive document ("Instruction on Christian Freedom and Liberation"), but the real message was in the first statement. The other documents took nothing back, but merely sought to soothe feelings.

The presence of prominent Catholics and priests in the Sandinista government in Nicaragua was another reason for the Instruction. The serious incidents that took place when the pope visited Nicaragua in 1983 and the Vatican's inability to force the priests to resign from their positions as ministers in the government convinced the Curia of the need to end collaboration between Catholics and Sandinistas. The fact that Sandinista Catholics appealed to liberation theology was clear proof to the Curia of the dangers of liberation theology.

The Instruction's interpretation of Latin American ecclesiology was baseless and arbitrary. Certainly dictatorial governments and traditional elites must have sent thousands of condemnations of the "Communist church." Some people invoked liberation theology at their own whim, and some people may have advocated Marxism in the name of liberation theology. Some members of Catholic communities could have said things that were disturbing, especially to the traditional elites, who know nothing of Christianity, and for whom any reference to social matters is communism. The problem is that Rome, rather than consulting with the bishops conferences, which are normally well informed about the situation in their country, preferred to believe criticism from irresponsible people.

One need only read the writings of the theologians to realize that the notion of "people" does not come from Marxism or any Marxist sociology. It is the traditional Latin American notion of "people," which was embodied in many popular movements in the 1970s, and which was an expression of the people of God. Indeed, there are elements in Marxism that could be valuable for Christian theology[18] but Latin American theologians did not use them. Religion is always part of popular movements in Latin America. People understand themselves as people of God and see their faith in God, the God of Jesus, as the source of their struggle and of the energy that allows them to survive. It has nothing in common with social class in the Marxist sense. If the members of the Curia really wished to understand Latin America, they could have compared the Latin American people to the people in the European revolutions of 1848. They made no effort to learn because they thought they already understood.

Why did they do this? One suspects that after John Paul II had chosen his aides, it became clear that the Curia was made up of people who did not accept Vatican II and were resolved to undo it. They obviously could not deny it, but had to combat the council by invoking it, and empty the council documents of their content by citing them.

Rome's central concern was not Latin America but Vatican II. Latin America was of interest insofar as it provided arguments for changing the content of Vatican II. It required no particular genius to discover that the key to the council's ecclesiology was the people of God, which provided a basis for lay initiative, different pastoral options, and temporal commitment, varying by country and continent. The notion of the people of God was the most serious threat to Roman centralization, because it was a justification for the decentralization of power in the church: everyone else would gain but the Curia would lose. No bureaucracy passively allows its power to be reduced; it seeks more power and centralization, which it calls unity.

In Rome the extraordinary synod, convoked for the twentieth anniversary of the end of Vatican II, was being prepared. To the Curia, Latin America seemed to offer good examples of the dangers of a "false interpretation" of *Lumen Gentium*. The Curia needed Latin America's deviations to provide arguments for its proposal to revise the council's concepts. The 1985 Instruction may be explained as a preparation for the synod (next chapter). All indications are that Latin America was chosen to provide proof of the dangers of the doctrine of the people of God. Most bishops had little direct experience of this continent and believed all the documentation collected by Father Vekemans over fifteen years and sent to them by the Curia.

Chapter 4

REVERSAL AT THE 1985 SYNOD

On January 25, 1985, Pope John Paul II surprised the Catholic world by convoking an extraordinary synod to celebrate the twentieth anniversary of the end of Vatican II. The announcement aroused misgivings and fear in Latin America. It was hard not to make the connection to Cardinal Ratzinger's condemnation of liberation theology a few months earlier. In a climate of artificial euphoria, the synod's stated intention was to deepen the council—when in fact it was to revise it. The publicity campaign was intended to soften resistance from those bishops who had taken part in the council.

The suspicions were not without foundation.

CARDINAL RATZINGER'S THEOLOGY

Cardinal Ratzinger had already set forth the synod's conclusions in his famous "report on the faith" which appeared as an interview with the Italian journalist Vittorio Messori. His overall vision of the church was quite pessimistic. Certainly the cardinal could not avoid the theme of the people of God, which was to be at the center of the major reversal made by the synod. In a word, he managed to discredit and utterly reject the concept of people of God, as though it were not at the heart of the council's ecclesiology.[1]

Cardinal Ratzinger's "report on the faith" first attacks the theme "people of God," censuring those who want to limit the entire ecclesiology of the New Testament to this expression, or who want to consider the church as only people of God. He gives the impression that speaking of "people of God" means falling into the danger of reducing everything to this theme. (As though by speaking of God the Father one would automatically be suspect of denying God the Son and God the Holy Spirit, so that it would therefore be better to suppress the Father.) The cardinal does not rule it out, but he discredits it by making it suspect of being reductionist.

Next, the cardinal announces two dangers linked to the "people of God" theme. The first is the danger of going back to the Old Testament, because "people of God" is an Old Testament theme, and hence less representative of Christianity than the Body of Christ—a theme not found in the Old Testament. By that logic, it would be better to suppress the themes of God and the Ten Commandments, because they are Old Testament.

In the "Body of Christ" theme, the church is said to be given a name more representative of the New Testament, and hence ecclesiology should be focused around the Body of Christ. To bolster this very weak argument, the cardinal says that one enters the church not by belonging sociologically, but through baptism and the eucharist—which bring one into the Body of Christ. Baptism and the eucharist are said to show that entry into the church is primarily entry into the Body of Christ, and thus that there is no need for the notion of people of God.

Certainly incorporation into the Body of Christ is signified by the eucharist, but it is not clear that entry into the Body of Christ is signified by baptism. Nothing in baptism represents or signifies entry into the Body of Christ. Indeed, from the outset baptism signifies incorporation into the new people of God gathered by Christ. Baptism is the entryway and it comes before the Eucharist. The person enters the church by baptism. Thanks to infant baptism, millions of human beings belong to the church before they receive the eucharist. The eucharist does not mean entry into the church but fullness of participation. Reducing everything to the Body of Christ means changing the meaning of baptism.

At no point in the "report on the faith" interview did the cardinal allude to the fact that Vatican II explicitly sought to change the ecclesiology of Pius XII, who in *Mystici Corporis* made the Body of Christ the center from which all ecclesiology ought to flow. Vatican II explicitly tried to place the people of God before the theme of the Body of Christ as more all-embracing and more fundamental. Nowhere, however, did either the council or Vatican II's followers indicate any wish to suppress, diminish, or devalue the title "Body of Christ."

The cardinal poses a false alternative: entry into the church either takes place through the sacraments (and entry into the church is signified as entry into the Body of Christ, thereby enhancing this theme) or one enters sociologically. Does "people of God" mean "sociological belonging"? With this line of argument, the cardinal hints that people of God must be a sociological concept, and hence of lesser value. He does not say so clearly—because he knows that it is not true—but he leaves the suspicion.

The second argument spells out what has already been hinted, namely that those who support the idea of "people of God" do so because of "political, partisan, collectivist suggestions."[2] Without saying so explicitly, he hints that "people of God" is a Marxist-inspired idea which exposes the church to Marxist infiltration, and he points to Latin America, where many are said to have fallen into Marxism led by the idea of the people of God.

From now on, it would be more prudent to avoid the theme so as not to be exposed to Marxist distortions. While not spelled out fully, his reasoning is clear enough.

The Ratzinger interview established the context for the 1985 extraordinary synod, which was intended to "rectify" Vatican II.[3]

THE THEOLOGY OF THE SYNOD

The synod (November 24 to December 8, 1985) signaled a radical change of direction for the church, which decisively abandoned what most of the participants themselves had understood of the council. The synod was intended to legitimize the radical changes then under way. Anyone who did not understand it at the time did so later when the results of the new direction became apparent.

The clearest signal of the reversal was the replacement of "people of God" with "communion" as the center of ecclesiology. More than just a sign, it was a change that influenced the entire council message.[4] In a written contribution to the synod, Cardinal Aloisio Lorscheider had said, "The church as people of God is the key idea of *Lumen Gentium*." And yet in the synod's final report Cardinal Godfried Daneels said, "The ecclesiology of communion is the central and fundamental idea of the Council's documents."[5] Who was right? Certainly for the council participants at that time, *people of God* was the central idea. But twenty years later, after a rereading, *communion* is found to be the central idea. Was this not a reading of the text on the basis of a new concern? Might not Cardinal Daneels's reading be wishful thinking: "We would have liked the council's central idea to have been 'communion' and so we are stating that it was its central idea"?

In the final report, the sole mention of the "people of God" is made in a way that makes the notion itself insignificant.

> The whole importance of the Church derives from her connection with Christ. The Council has described the Church in diverse ways: as the people of God, the body of Christ, the bride of Christ, the temple of the Holy Spirit, the family of God. These descriptions of the Church complete one another and must be understood in the light of the Mystery of Christ or of the Church in Christ. We cannot replace a false one-sided vision of the Church as purely hierarchical with a new sociological conception which is also one-sided.

This paragraph clearly shows how far removed the synod was from the council perspective. It had completely forgotten what the council was about (or deliberately intended to reject the conciliar perspective).

The council had made a clear distinction between the visible and the invisible in the church, that is, the divine and the human, the relationship with God and the human reality (*Lumen Gentium* 8). Chapter 1 deals with the mystery of the church, namely its relationship to God. It lists various biblical metaphors, but not the "people of God," which appears only in chapter 2, which deals with the human reality of the church.

The synod's report presents "people of God" among the metaphors that express the relationship with God, forgetting that this title has to do with the church's human reality. Indeed, the report completely leaves out the visible or human aspect of the church. The upshot of its failure to understand the placement of the title "people of God" is that any consideration of the church's human reality vanishes: the church is sheer divine mystery. Later, however, it will be necessary to speak about the hierarchy without saying explicitly that it is a visible and human element in the church. In practice, the synod returns to the pre-council theology: the only visible reality in the church worthy of being singled out is the hierarchy. There is also ambiguity about its divine or human reality. In any case, no distinction whatsoever is made between the divine and human in the church.

To treat the idea of the "people of God" as a "new sociological concept" reflects ignorance of both the Bible and sociology. The final sentence about a unilateral sociological conception is astonishing. The sociological concept which is being condemned is plainly the theology of the people of God, which is accused of being sociological. An attack on the theology of the people of God at this point is astonishing, but it is very significant because it shows what underlies all the synod's reasoning and concerns. The sentence fits the theology developed throughout the whole paragraph, and it makes plain the theology running through the entire document. The implication is that "people of God" is not a theological concept, but a one-sided sociological concept brought into theology and with it a threat of secularization, or worse, a connection to condemned teachings (Marxism of course).

However, Vatican II never understood "people of God" as a sociological concept—its analysis is essentially biblical and theological, referring to something revealed by God and founded by Jesus. It expresses the visible aspect of the church, but it is no less a theological concept than the concepts of the sacraments or church ministries. These are all visible things, and could all be studied by religious sociology, but what the council addressed has nothing to do with sociology. The church is God's work, in both its visible and invisible aspects.

The synod sought to remove any theological consideration of the church's human reality. The council's adversaries knew this could be accomplished by removing any consideration of the "people of God." The hierarchy would not be threatened because it would be regarded as part of the mystery of the church rather than a human reality in the church. The hierarchy wanted to return to the pre-conciliar theology based on the documents of the sixteenth-century Council of Trent. The synod's solution (although most participants probably did not realize this) was to suppress Vatican II's chapter on the people of God.

This is a return to Tridentine ecclesiology: everything in the church is divine. Yet this church which is viewed so one-sidedly in its divinity has very real human activity, even if that activity is not a theological reality and does not draw on gospel principles. The church's human action is purely contingent and has nothing to do with the reality of the church: in its human action it can get away with following the criteria of any human institution (e.g., the criteria of power). The church acts with pragmatism and opportunism; that is certainly how the Roman Curia acts, though this has no basis in the council. Everything human in the church was disqualified as nontheological—taken away from theologians and handed over to canonists and church politicians.

However, by emphasizing the people of God theme, the council intended to subject ecclesiastical politics to gospel criteria by affirming that the entire human reality of the church ought to obey gospel criteria—because the church is within the full human reality, for it is God's creation, even though it is incarnated in human history. The being and acting of the people of God is subject to gospel criteria, which it must obey in its behavior in the world.

During Christendom, that behavior often followed purely human criteria for conquering or defending power in society. The council bishops wanted a church with a gospel presence in the world. That is what they intended in making people of God the subject of chapter 2, thereby laying the groundwork for a theology of the human reality in the church. The hierarchy would also have to submit itself to the criteria guiding the entire people of God.

What the Curia wanted, however—and what the synod consciously or unconsciously ratified—was quite different. It wanted to free ecclesiastical politics from those criteria and to keep engaging in politics as it had in the past, i.e., following the criteria of human power. It wanted a church free to act like other powers in the world. Such submission to the criteria of power would not affect its divine reality at all; there would be total separation between the mystery of the church and the everyday behavior of the institution among the powers of this world. The church would continue to be equally divine, no matter how the institution acted in the world. It could be guided by the same criteria that guide other human institutions.

This was the very thing that the council wanted to change. It wanted a church led by the gospel—in all its temporal activity. Its way of being in the world would be the manifestation of its divine mystery. This was all in the theology of the people of God, and it all had to be brought down with the synod. The entire sector opposed to the council, the sector that has become so strong during John Paul II's pontificate, wanted to return to a church that struggles for power using the weapons at hand, such as support from the political and economic powers of this world. That is why it sought to eliminate the theme of the people of God, and it was successful in doing this, at least temporarily.

It is worth noting that the Latin American churches were well aware of what was at stake. The issue was not so much the danger of contamination by Marxism, but the question of how the human reality of the church is to be understood; whether the behavior of the church, hierarchy, and people in the midst of human history is to be guided by the gospel or by opportunism. Latin American theologians and all the prophetic bishops were convinced that poverty and the option for the poor are not purely ethical issues; they belong to the essence of the church because they are qualities of the people of God, i.e., the human reality of the church. When the notion of the "people of God" is removed, the option for the poor ceases to be an important issue, and the poverty proclaimed by the church is reduced to a pious spiritual exhortation addressed to each individual Catholic, without committing the institution as a whole.

In his initial report, which ought to have provided a summary of the presynod work and suggestions from bishops conferences, Cardinal Daneels was even harsher: "The core of the crisis lies in the area of ecclesiology. Many speak of an overly one-sided and superficial reception of the council doctrine on the church. In particular, the concept of Church–People of God is defined ideologically and separated from other complementary concepts considered in the council texts: body of Christ, temple of the Spirit."[6]

This clearly means that the issue at the synod was the people of God theme. From the outset "people of God" was viewed negatively. Various bishops conferences were said to have criticized the superficial understandings of the "people of God," but the synod did not say that other bishops conferences insisted on the importance of the idea. Moreover, the existence of superficial interpretations does not justify suppressing a whole chapter of *Lumen Gentium*.

Even supposing that there were many superficial interpretations of the idea of the people of God, the normal response would be to pursue more deeply the meaning of this council concept. The response proposed by the synod, however, was to eliminate the concept, or at least to reduce its importance to the point of insignificance. In regarding the people of God as one of the images represented in the mystery of the church, the author fails to see the scope of *Lumen Gentium* 2, and does not recognize the difference between the concept people of God and the images of the mystery. He fails to see that "people of God" seeks to express the human reality of the church, and that ignoring that human reality entails a return to the pre-conciliar theology.

The issue of the concept of the people of God is far from being a problem of terminology. It is the most important thing that the council said about the church; what is at stake is nothing less than the church's presence in the world. What the church is in its mystery must be manifested in how it is human, in its action, its relationship with the world, peoples, and cultures, and the hopes and sufferings of the world. That is why we cannot passively allow a synod to simply cancel out what an ecumenical council has taught.

The synod did more than simply interpret or explain the council, it changed its content on essential points; it corrected the council, replacing a major part of its content with something else. That is why the synod must be reexamined, and the importance of its decisions put into perspective. The concept of the people of God must be restored—even with all necessary explanation. Otherwise the council's ecclesiology would be largely eviscerated.

THE AMBIGUITIES OF "COMMUNION"

Since the Roman synod, a theology of communion has been put forth to replace the theology of the people of God, which is suspected of falling prey to sociology, secularism, or reductionism. Increasingly, "communion" has been presented as a definition of the church. All official speeches since that time lack any reference to the people of God, while presenting communion as the theme that best sums up the church.

The Final Report of the 1985 synod said, "The ecclesiology of communion is the central and fundamental idea of the Council's documents." The apostolic exhortation *Christifideles Laici*, which quotes this sentence, is the most complete exposition of the theology of communion seen from the Roman viewpoint (chapter 2, 18-31).[7]

The substitution of "communion" for "people of God" is all the more significant in that as a foundation of the post-synodal theology, it adopts a line from St. Cyprian, which actually says something else: "The Church shines forth as a people made one with the unity of the Father, Son and Holy Spirit." For St. Cyprian, the fundamental concept was clearly that of people, but the document draws the very opposite from it. Of course this is a lapse, but it is significant. The theology of the people of God is not seen even in the most explicit texts.

No one doubts that communion, which has been the subject of many useful works,[8] is basic to ecclesiology. Communion was an important theme at the council, e.g., regarding collegiality in the church. But communion does not exclude the people of God nor should it take its place. Communion is a more restricted theme than "people." People means a kind of communion but it includes other elements.

Indeed, when posed as the central theme of ecclesiology, communion merits some observations or cautions. First, "communion" refers to the invisible, divine aspect of the church. The church is communion through bonds with the Father, Son, and Spirit. There is communion between human beings who are children of God, members of Christ, enlivened by the Holy Spirit. This unity is invisible, although it has visible signs (sacraments, word of God, ministries, entire life of the people of God). Communion expresses the divine nature of the church, not its human nature; it belongs in chapter 1 of *Lumen Gentium*, but not in chapter 2. Chapter 2 is thus emptied and there is nothing left to represent the human nature of the church, which is absorbed into the divine.

"Communion" does not express the church's human nature, unless the human in the church is reduced to the means of salvation. But the church's human nature is made up of full human beings, men and women, not just doctrines, liturgies, or juridical organization. Human beings are not reduced to these signs of unity or communion. Doctrine, sacraments, and government are signs of communion, but not communion itself, which is lived in the daily lives of followers of Jesus as divine mystery.

If the aim is to make communion the most all-embracing concept of the church, connecting the divine and the human, it must be said that this is a new kind of ecclesiological Monophysitism: human nature is absorbed into the divine element in the church. This choice of "communion" leads to a return to the spiritualization of an increasingly disincarnate church. The change of ideas expresses or causes a change in the church's practical behavior. In the past twenty years, the church has drawn ever more apart from the world and its joys, anguishes, struggles, and triumphs, and has taken refuge in its suprahuman and suprahistoric nature. The new theory of the church justifies the new practice.

A church that is sheer communion has no body, no matter, and does not evoke anything concrete. It is purely immaterial, a communion of souls somehow touched from time to time by material signs—the same for everyone. This church is a soul without body, matterless spirit. It soars over history rather than entering into it.[9]

This church, like any communion, has no history. A people has history: it is made up of the succession of many generations, each bringing something new, journeying, groping, trying to find its way amid a huge diversity and multiplicity of works and efforts by millions of people and human groups. A communion has no history, knows nothing of time, and is changeless over time. It has no historic character and is thus not human.[10]

Obviously, a church of pure communion cannot explain conflicts and struggles, the diversity caused by these conflicts, clashes of mindsets, projects, sensitivities, and cultures.[11] A communion has no conflicts. However, a glance at the church's history shows that it is full of conflicts. The greatest saints were surrounded by conflicts and took sides.[12]

Edifying hagiography has always tried to conceal this history by creating a conventional vision of the saints, projecting over them a vision of communion in which they are all equal, and any particularity in their life disappears. This distortion begins even before the death of people who are considered to be marked for canonization. The reality is different: each of them lived within a defined reality and became holy precisely by confronting this historic reality. They are the result of God's grace and also their time and their bodily situation in the world.

The hierarchy tends to spiritualize the church and silence its human reality, or it exalts it as communion, peace, truth, happiness—which amounts to the same thing. By concealing the human reality, it seeks to escape all criticism. The Catholic hierarchy does not willingly submit to sociological or anthropological analysis, as if being a divine communion put it beyond the reach of such disciplines. If the church is also a human reality, that reality can clearly be the object of critical or analytical study, performed with the disciplines existing in a given period. As a divine reality, the church cannot be studied by the social sciences, while as a human reality it can. This is what a good portion of the hierarchy does not like to acknowledge, and it is scandalized when social scientists examine its behavior. While such analyses do not explain everything, they explain a good portion of the reality, and the church can only gain thereby.

Indeed, the church gains nothing by seeking to conceal its human character, which inevitably sneaks back in. If the people of God disappears, what reappears as the church's human reality is the clerical bureaucracy, the bureaucratic centralization of the Roman Curia and its practice of very human (in the pejorative sense) and scarcely Christian politics. When the people of God is denied, what is left is the post-Tridentine church, centered on its own juridical, clerical, bureaucratic structure, stuck in a defensive, polemic stance; a church at war with Protestantism and modernity. Rejecting the idea of people of God means going back to the church of Pius IX and Pius XII.

Second, it should be borne in mind that in Catholic theology "communion" is always ambiguous. One suspects that this ambiguity is intentional and it may have been the reason why the theme of "communion" was chosen as the broadest and most representative of Catholic ecclesiology. Yet communion can be both vertical and horizontal. Vertical communion is created by the hierarchy and is the result of common acceptance of the dogmas and the trusts assimilated into dogmas, the reception of the sacraments, and submission to the hierarchy, especially the pope. "Communion" means common submission to the pope. So communion means being in submission to the pope—and the pope decides everything, including who is or is not in communion with him.[13]

With this notion we lose contact with the mystery of the church. "Communion" also applies to a sociological reality: belonging to a visible, social institution, which may also be observed from outside. Thus "communion" takes on another meaning, and may lead to confusion or overlapping meanings. One can easily come to the conclusion that canonical communion with ecclesiastical government and participation in the communion of the divine persons merge together as do canonical communion and communion-as-mystery. This confusion is in the minds of many Catholics of good faith precisely because of confusion in official terminology. The canonical meaning does not show up so often in theological documents, but one still has the suspicion that the aim of this theology of communion that identifies the institution and the divine mystery so radically is to return to the Tridentine theology of Bellarmine which became common teaching until the twentieth century and Vatican II.

In his apostolic letter *Novo Millennio Ineunte*, Pope John Paul II appeals for a spirituality of communion. At the end, he writes, "Consequently, the new century will have to see us more than ever intent on valuing and developing the forums and structures which, in accordance with the Second Vatican Council's major directives, serve to ensure and safeguard communion. How can we forget in the first place those *specific services to communion* which are the *Petrine ministry* and, closely related to it, *episcopal collegiality?*" Communion is first of all obedience to the pope. All the talk of spirituality leads into this statement.

However, if "communion" is also intended to express the horizontal relationship between the members of the church—i.e., the sociological reality of the church, and not only its divine mystery—it should be remembered that there is another meaning to communion (we discount the purely emotional or psychological meaning, sometimes dressed up as spiritual communion, which, if it exists, is purely superficial). Communion between human beings arises through agreements between persons. There are countless kinds of agreements, such as those in the family, between siblings, colleagues, co-workers, participants in the same cultural activity. There may be communion between players on the same team, advocates of the same cause, people committed to human rights or democracy, and so forth. Agreement may be spontaneous or deliberate, thought about, and rationally defined.

It should be recalled that the people of Israel was founded on an agreement—the covenant between the tribes. To some extent a people is always founded on an agreement, a covenant made by history or through a public and legal act such as the constitution of a nation. All shared life is to some extent a communion, insofar as it assumes at least an implicit agreement. The agreement, pact, covenant, or "social contract" is the foundation of a democracy or republic.

Thus it can also be said that the church is also called to be a communion, because it was founded in an agreement between the disciples of Jesus. There is shared life, mutual aid, mutual acknowledgment, and so forth (next chapter). Yet this communion is not recognized in the Tridentine system, and it has no expression in canon law. Hence the suspicion: when official church documents speak about communion, it would seem to come from the unity that comes from common obedience to the pope, combined with an emotional unity of feeling among all his subjects.

Horizontal communion is not top-down; it emerges among equals through reciprocity. There is room for governance, but with the knowledge that ultimately what matters is agreement between persons. Without such agreement, any imposition remains superficial and does not create true human communion.

The conclusion to this chapter is clear: the aim in putting the "people of God" aside was to return to pre-Vatican II ecclesiology. That aim was not stated, giving the impression of fidelity to Vatican II. But in reality, the theme of the "people of God" has been missing from official church documents for twenty years, and the practice of the hierarchy has gone back to being just as it was in the time of Pius XII. After twenty years of gradual, persistent endeavor to return to the previous period, the job is almost completed. Will a new papacy be able to resurrect Vatican II?

Chapter 5

THE CHURCH AS PEOPLE

After four chapters summarizing the history of the idea of the people of God at Vatican II (preparation, definition, and reception) we now turn to consider it systematically. We will attempt to understand the content this theme of the "people of God" brings to the church.

SCOPE OF THE CHOICE OF THE THEME OF THE PEOPLE OF GOD

The Christian concept of people arose in the Bible, but in the course of Christian history it has been very much enriched over the course of Christian history with elements from various civilizations, especially the Greco-Roman world, i.e., the Greek city and the Roman republic. Through many episodes, distortions, and deviations, it has always reappeared, finally prevailing at Vatican II (subsequent efforts to correct it notwithstanding).

As a starting point, we must recognize that the concept of "people" applied to the church is similar to the concept of people applied to all peoples on earth. The idea of "people" has arisen and grown as a secularization of the Christian concept, and constitutes an extension of the reality of the people of God. The church did not receive the notion of people from humankind; humankind received it from the church.

That the church is people of God means that its mystery of communion with the Father, Son, and Holy Spirit is lived and realized under the condition of people. People, as we will see, includes the entire human reality in its concrete diversity. The mystery of the church is not lived out in a world parallel to the world of earthly peoples, in a spiritualized, supraterrestrial world, a purely religious world of souls. Religion is part of a people, not the people itself. The fact that the church is people means that it is not limited to the religious dimension of life, but permeates the full range of the human being.

The 1985 synod seems to have been drawn to a pseudotraditional figure of the church corresponding to what Hans Küng denounced as a "hypostasized church":

63

If the church is really the people of God, it cannot be seen as a quasi-divine hypostasis between God and human beings. . . . The church would then be separated from the concrete human beings comprising it, and would be idealized: an *Ecclesia quoad substantiam*, a suprapersonal institutional mediation between God and humankind. The church as community is certainly more than the sum of the individuals. But even so it is and always remains the community of believers brought together by God to form his people. Without this people of believers, the church is nothing.[1]

Several speakers at the synod expressed a fear that the idea of "people of God" could lead to the thought that the church is the work of human beings rather than of God.[2] That bishops or theologians should raise this objection is astonishing. After centuries of debate between Molinists and Banezianists it is time to realize that God's causality and that of human beings are not exclusive: God acts and so does the human being; God is free and so is the human being. God makes the church through the freedom of human beings. God and human beings always act together, each at their own level. Exalting human power means exalting God's power. God makes the church through free human creatures—as Jesus founds the church through his humanity and not simply by decree of his divinity. It is founded by a series of fully human acts, and there is no conflict between Jesus' divinity and his humanity. Similarly, the church must be said to be the work of God and of human persons.

Christians are members of the people of God in all their human activities and within the culture of a particular people. Being a member of the people does not mean being separated from others in order to practice religious acts apart. Such acts are useful as preparation and formation, but they are not the reality of the church, for Christians are priests offering their lives to God in the midst of their people, as St. Paul says.

If the church is a people, it cannot live in a ghetto apart from the real world. Even at the beginning of the Christian era, when there were many persecutions and Christians were officially outlawed by Roman law, they saw themselves as citizens of the empire, responsible for that empire where they were, and in their action they always situated themselves at the center of this world. The church was a people in the midst of peoples and not a ghetto apart, as sects are.

However, since the time of Jesus the people of God has never constituted yet another people set apart in separate territory in a separate history. It is not a people alongside other peoples, but like them in everything; it is a people within other peoples. In this regard, the history of Christendom from Constantine to the present has been mistaken: Christendom was a people alongside others, a society alongside others, a particular people. It thought of itself as universal because it knew little of other existing peoples—except for the Muslim people, which was regarded as the kingdom of the anti-Christ. But it was a particular people with universal pretensions.

Christendom had the illusion of being both the universal people and the people of God, a complete earthly, fully Christian people in which a natural people would be completely identified with the people of God. This project was never fully realized, but as an illusion it gravely distorted the meaning of Christianity, because there was a temptation to confuse things (thus the crusades, the inquisition, the privileges of the clergy, the claims of the pope in the temporal world, the use of the secular arm, the superiority of spiritual power, etc.). Voices of protest in the name of the gospel have always been raised, but they did not prevail in the institution which attempted to hold onto Christendom to the end.

Christendom is gone, leaving only monuments, memories, relics, and—for many—nostalgia. From now on we know that the people of God lives in other peoples. Or rather, that it lives from others, for its members are also members of a particular people. Christians in some sense belong to two different but convergent peoples. Being a Brazilian does not mean being a member of the people of God, although Brazilians may be Christians only as Brazilians with all their peculiar features. There are no generic Christians, only particular Christians, each within his or her own people.

What is now called eschatology had to be rediscovered. The church is an eschatological reality, i.e., it will receive its perfect and complete expression only in the new world after the resurrection in the new Jerusalem. Until then, it exists and lives struggling to reach its complete form—as though it were a new species seeking to come alive in the midst of other species (with the difference that in the end the people of God will unite all the peoples of the earth).

In the present the people of God lives in the midst of the people, as a leaven seeking to transform the entire people into people of God, knowing that this task will never be complete in this world. Hence, the church exists within the peoples of the earth, although distinct, because it is the project that lies at the end of each people. It initiates a journey that is to lead all peoples to their final destiny. Until then, like an active leaven, it seeks to transform the mass (all the peoples where its members are found). Vatican II devoted an entire chapter (*Lumen Gentium* 7) to the eschatological nature of the church. Although it is an eschatological or messianic people, the church is a true people, and we must examine this concept in all its richness.

When we consider the human element in the church, we do not intend to deny or minimize the importance of the divine element, the mystery—quite the contrary. The aim is to place the mystery in its real, concrete, human place where it becomes present on earth. Divine mystery and human reality coexist in their fullness. There is no need to take something away from the humanity to exalt the divinity or to take something away from the divinity to appreciate the humanity. According to the formula of the Council of

Chalcedon, humanity and divinity each subsist in their fullness, although they are united concretely in existence. We will not know the mystery well if we do not know how it is lived out in human life.

Chapter 1 of *Lumen Gentium* deals with the church as mystery, i.e., the divine aspect of the church. The following chapters consider its human aspect. Pope John Paul II forcefully highlighted the church's human character when he asked forgiveness for a large number of sins committed by it. It was a courageous act because it broke with a long tradition of hiding everything negative in the history of the church.

Traditional apologetics has so often sought to hide or minimize the facts, and regarded those who brought them up as enemies of the church. It has thus concealed the humanity of the church and defended an interpretation of the church that deserves to be called Monophysite (everything in the church regarded as divine or of divine inspiration). Such a sacralization of the church may convince masses of people still sunk in the mindset of the ancient Neolithic religions, but it is not convincing to a more educated and critical population.

However, the humanity of the church is not limited to highlighting the negative aspects of its history. Negative aspects are inevitable in any human institution, but they cannot hide everything positive in the action of Christianity in the history of the last two thousand years.

Everything that is positive and human in the church comes from humankind and is permeated by cultures and by human history; there is nothing that is not marked by human history. Just as Jesus' humanity does not undermine or block his divinity, likewise the church's humanity does not prevent it from also being the Body of Christ and the dwelling place of the Holy Spirit. These divine realities are lived humanly within a human context despite human limitations.

The Bible chose the theme "people" to speak of the church's humanity, no doubt for many good reasons. Indeed, "people" describes a practice as well as a theory. The church was born and has grown as people. The church is called "people" because it is people and exists as people. God chose this way of being for humankind.

Naturally, the people that is the church draws inspiration and support from the Old Testament people of Israel. The church grew out of a change within the people of Israel, as an authentic continuation of the people of Israel, although the continuation takes place in a paradoxical manner because in some fashion it constitutes a complete reversal. However, not only has the church never lost contact with the people of Israel and the Old Testament, it has often sought to recover and adapt Old Testament ways of living and ideas. Even after the New Testament, the Old Testament has continued to exercise influence in the New—sometimes excessively and without much discretion.

The people of Israel drew inspiration from the surrounding peoples.

Throughout its entire history it has struggled against the tendency to be assimilated into other peoples, while imitating them in everything—as if finding it hard to break away from a rigid structure that it shared with the neighboring peoples. The prophets reminded Israel that it had a specific unique vocation, obliging it to live differently. Israel was a different people, but it was still a people tied to a land, a culture, and a language.

The church is likewise a different people—different from the peoples of the earth and from Israel. But it is still a people, and retains the fundamental structures of a people. Far from being an out-of-date category, "people" is more necessary than ever for understanding the church. Today more than ever we must insist on the reality of people, of the collective life of the disciples of Jesus, because we are in a period of extreme individualism. Individualism seemed to have reached its high point in modernity, but the last few decades have made it clear that the individualism of modernity still bore many elements from the community life inherited from traditional peoples.

Individualism has now become much more acute, and the remnants of community life are being destroyed faster and faster. The total market society makes each human being nothing but a consumer, and consumption is conceived for the individual. The entire ideological apparatus, which comes from the United States and Europe, exalts individualism, and anyone who still believes in community solidarity is regarded as backward or intellectually weak and incapable of comprehending the direction of history.

Individualism also affects religion—perhaps especially religion. The triumph of the neo-Pentecostals and Charismatic movements is a visible sign of the movement toward religious individualism that is increasingly winning over leaders of religious movements, including the heads of the Christian churches.[3] The crowds mobilized and seduced by the universal church or by some priest known for his use of the media do not form church. These crowds are made up of isolated individuals who with a great deal of emotion are seeking relief from their sufferings, escape from loneliness, and palpable contact with the divine.

The churches are imitating the way so many religious groups burgeoning around the world act: they become agencies for distributing religious services, religious therapies providing health and happiness, prosperity, and inner peace. Perhaps twenty or thirty years ago the church was in danger of leaning too far toward a purely secularized liberation—although such a diagnosis should be treated with great reservation and is not accepted in Latin America by the advocates of Medellín and Puebla. However, this is not the place to discuss a past which is well behind us.

In any case, today everything is different and the challenge to the church is the religious individualism invading the world along with other phenomena of so-called globalization. Someone who seeks religious services (healing, happiness, wealth, solution to emotional problems) from the church is not assuming a commitment to any religious institution. He or she comes to

church seeking the benefit promised and goes back home to enjoy the satisfaction received, with no need even to pay back the promise to the "saint,"
as used to be the case. Today Jesus gives everything and does not need to be
paid—though you do have to pay the religious organization proclaiming
him.

Some try to imitate the methods of the neo-Pentecostals, adopt their
themes, and turn the Catholic Church into a copy of the universal church:
taking the battle to the foe's terrain, which means allowing oneself to be
transformed by the foe. The Catholic Church might thereby manage to defeat the universal church, but the price will ultimately be that it turns into
the universal church.

In opposition to the invasion of religious individualism, it must be forcefully asserted that the church is not an agency for distributing religious services—providing health, psychological tranquility, wealth, or the solution
to economic problems. The church is shared community life, it is people; it
saves human individuals by integrating them into a people. Personal freedom is never ignored, but it grows in a life of mutual service, in a people
established by God.

The only way to understand this people is by starting with a consideration of the peoples of the earth. Obviously there are many differences between the peoples that were contemporaneous with Israel and Jesus and the
peoples of the twenty-first century, but even today the similarity is greater
than the difference. Peoples today are very similar to ancient peoples.

We have just seen that the concept of "people" can only be understood
on the basis of our current questions, fears, and hopes. We understand the
Bible on the basis of a pre-understanding that comes from our contemporary issues. That does not mean that we necessarily project our current realities onto the past, but that we raise questions on the basis of these realities,
thereby enabling us to measure the distance between the ideas of that time
and our own. We need not insist on this point, which can be found in intro-
ductions to the Bible. However, we certainly cannot live now as people of
God in the categories and behaviors of biblical times. The people of God is,
and must be, different today, even if it remains faithful to biblical inspiration.

PEOPLE: BONDS OF SHARED LIFE

"People" is constituted primarily by shared life: life suffered and assumed
in common. To say "people" rules out the idea of a group of individuals
each seeking to take care of themselves. In pointing to the church as a people,
the council closed all the doors to individualism—at the very moment when
individualism was beginning to triumph in Western society. It was a challenge,
a banner raised in opposition to the current direction of Western society.

If the church is people, its unity does not consist simply in communion in faith, sacraments, and government. These functions generate a spiritual communion, but that communion must take flesh in a human community. Otherwise it remains ethereal, an empty illusion of communion. What unifies the followers of Jesus is rooted materially and concretely—it is embodied in a people. The people of Jesus are the multitudes who follow him, or the disciples who accompany him, and collect his teachings and put them into practice in the life of their people.

Sheer unity of faith, sacraments, and submission to governance is a disembodied unity with no human content or value, an illusory union. Is that not the impression left by so many parish or diocesan communities when they remain at a formal unity outside real life—a unity of feeling but not human unity, which is lived out in the struggles for earthly existence? The unity of the church is constituted by shared endeavors, community struggles, confrontations, tasks, movements working together in an effort to change the world.

All peoples have a memory of symbolic events when they felt united because they were acting together (e.g., the 1985 campaign for "Direct Elections Now" in Brazil). In such events one could feel the community of life, acting jointly, feeling united as a people. Many peoples experience their peoplehood in struggles for independence, in wars, in victory and defeat.

Today many peoples become aware of themselves in sports events, the Olympics or soccer championships—the symbol takes the place of reality. What is being expressed is not a people but a symbol of a people. Individualism prevents new shared achievements, while there is an oversupply of athletic events that are sheer spectacle.

In a natural people, community of life comes not by free choice but by de facto situations. They are people living in the same region brought together by history; they work the same way, speak the same language, intermarry— all of which reinforce differences from other peoples. They live the in same climate, eat the same food, build similar houses using similar materials, share the same landscapes. Rivers, mountains, beaches, cities, fields, and forests shape peoples. Someone born in another country or even another state can communicate immediately with people from the same place. They cherish fond memories of the land, landscapes, food, music when they are far away. Affinities with one's birthplace are never extinguished, for those who choose to leave. You can be angry with or ashamed of your people, or you can despair over it, but it is always your people.

The shared life of a people is corporeal. Bodies are used to one another and recognize one another as similar. That is the source of the problems encountered by peoples of different colors or races, and migration problems. The difference does not have to be large, e.g., in Rwanda and Burundi where two groups of Black Africans cannot live together in peace, or problems in Europe with Jews or Gypsies.

The church is also a people because it is shared corporeal and cultural life—primarily corporeal. They are people who live together during at least one important part of their life. They are used to one another, their bodies are mutually adapted to one another, they learn to relate, and hence can have a shared human life. They understand the many thousands of signs that make life together bearable or even pleasant. The church is also exchange and communication between persons who—by exchanging goods, services, and signs—become like one another. They constitute a specific way of living together, sharing thousands of small details that create mutual recognition and sympathy.

Shared life is realized in small communities, because a people is woven together of small communities, not isolated individuals. Today these communities are defined not by physical proximity alone, but also by cultural proximity. A people is made up of thousands or millions of particular associations, which form complex networks with multiple relationships. No people is made up only of people in isolation. That is why in today's world the reality that sustains peoplehood is at risk, because the consciousness of belonging to a people and solidarity with the people is declining. Individualism destroys peoples,[4] and it destroys the church as well, insofar as the church is people.

Given human reality, a community of faith entails bodily community, a shared life of bodies making the same movements, and recognizing one another by their signs. What is specific to the Christian people is community of faith: following Jesus in community as did the apostles. In a spiritualistic conception of the church, Christian community could be based on people who were physically far apart, by the mere fact of participating in the same faith or practicing specifically Christian signs such as the sacraments, without any perceptible material or emotional communication, and with no shared feelings. Today many communities use internet communication, but that does not build a people because there is no experience of shared life between people who gather physically. Without bodily presence there is no real solidarity. The example of hermits could be invoked,[5] but they represent an extreme exceptional case, and even they had shared human contacts, albeit less than other Christians.

In practice, human contacts, shared life, acting in community are always part of the church. Even if the community of faith disregards material realities, it needs human support, sympathy, and communication. Community always entails shared food and drink, celebrations, a calendar, ongoing relationships between those involved. A community of pure faith would be without feeling and emotion, and would not work. Faith has to be lived in community, and a shared life of faith is embodied in a community. That is what is done, but it is not analyzed and evaluated in the light of Christianity.

Not all kinds of community life are participation in the life of a people; some even turn the group in on itself. Hence the question for the church's community life today: does this community life of the church belong to a people or not? Is it the shared life of a people or of a particular association? In the ages of rural civilization, parish and municipality were coterminous. The parish was the center of cultural life, and it had a great deal of political and economic influence. By acting in the parish, Christians acted in the world. Parish life was an expression of the life of the people of God.

With the advent of urbanization, the old rural communities are disappearing even in Latin American countries. Most parishes are now urban, but they are not coterminous with the life of the city. The parish often becomes self-enclosed in a ghetto, a world apart, a kind of sect. The parishioners may be content because the parish offers them a refuge that enables them to remain far from the problems of today's world. Their action is focused around the parish itself. Around the parish is shaped a circle of works that include a portion of society, generally very small.[6] In few cities does the parish manage to reach 10% of the population. Only in a few states in Brazil can that happen, and even there parish communities are unlikely to create the city environment.

Consequently, the church lives like a sect isolated from society as a whole (though it still cherishes the illusion that it speaks on behalf of the entire people). A parish acts collectively, but that action does not constitute a people. The activities of different parishes in the city or region are not integrated for the sake of a common goal. Each parish is an island with its own set of works. This does not foster peoplehood. The church does not take on the reality of the city nor does it project itself into the city. The church's material and temporal reality is not coterminous with that of the world. It does not take on the reality of the world. The church's human element is no longer a part of the world, and hence it thinks ever less as people. The material part is spiritualized because it is isolated from its human whole.

In Latin America this problem goes unnoticed because the mindset of the hierarchy and clergy is still that of Christendom. Some do not recognize the fact that Christendom no longer exists; others think it can be rebuilt. Of course, some fragments of Christendom remain, particularly on the outside façade, but the really dynamic elements of society are no longer in Christendom. The church can retain the illusion that it is giving direction to the world, but it is not. Such an illusion is dangerous because, thus deluded, the church continues to trust in structures that remain in place formally—even when they are devoid of content.

The reality of the vast majority of parishes serves to encourage the illusion of Christendom. For example, the slogan of the 2001 Brotherhood Campaign, organized by the Brazilian bishops, was "Life yes, drugs no." To have been effective, that campaign would have had to be organized on the citywide level, seeking to affect the city on an institutional level: drug distribution, how drugs get into schools, where drugs are concentrated, the media. The campaign would have had to be coordinated with other institutions dedicated to issues of health, human rights, education, and so forth. But what happens when the Brotherhood Campaign reaches the parish? What does the parish do? A lot of talk to the small circle of parishioners who are already convinced. In practice nothing happens; the parish is not in the world. But the illusion of Christendom creates the impression that the parish reaches society. As long as this illusion remains, new responses to the challenges of evangelization in the contemporary world will not be sought.

In Christendom, Christians are aware that they are a people with all the characteristics of a people: they are people of God, but a people like the other peoples of the earth. There is no difference between the structure of this people and other peoples. Christianity—as seen from Christendom—is no longer a people among peoples, a leaven inspiring peoples eschatologically. Christianity then becomes a particular people, the culture of one people, and things operate within it as happens in other peoples. Today with Christendom gone, "people of God" is a symbol. Parishioners try to be convinced that they are people of God, but they are a symbol rather than a reality.

Under Christendom everyone is people, albeit ambiguously, because the people of God is confused with a political entity. From the beginning of Christendom with Constantine, all the empire's inhabitants were born Christian. Baptism simply ratified the Christian character of the person, who was such from birth, and it enabled people to be officially registered. All were subject to the traditional customs inherited from the past. They learned Christianity by way of custom, absorbing it from their family and neighbors. Being a Christian simply meant doing what everyone else did. Little by little, no more difference could be seen between the Christian people and the Muslim or Hindu people. The customs were different, but the way of living was the same. The gods had different names, but worship had the same meaning, namely the legitimation of the established society.

Under such conditions, the people calling itself "Christian" was no more the Body of Christ or dwelling place of the Spirit than any other people. The name "Christian" was simply a symbol of identity, without necessarily having any impact on how people acted. The mystery of the church became an ideological garb. In reality, the religion lived by the vast majority was simply custom; it was a religion similar to the other religions in the world. Evangelizing meant conquering, bringing other peoples into the Christian people— changing symbols without changing reality. Fortunately, the church and the true people of God remained in the minorities, who were willing to disregard superficial customs and follow the gospel of Jesus Christ.

Christendom is well represented in a letter of Pope Gregory I to missionaries sent to England. He says that the missionaries should tear down the images of the idols in the sacred places of the pagans and replace them with images of Christian saints. That way peoples would keep practicing their worship thinking that they were addressing their gods, but would actually be addressing Christian saints. They would become Christians without even noticing anything new. They would be called Christians but nothing would really change, because their religion would remain pagan in terms of human awareness—with a Christian surface. Under such conditions anything that was done was Christian activity and part of the Christian people. Such Christianity obviously did not take into account the central message of Jesus.

Under Christendom, prophets arose and raised their voice for 1500 years with little effect, except for maintaining the continuity of the prophetic current itself. Had outside forces not come into play, Christendom would still exist. In many places in Latin America the hierarchy with the aid of well-off Catholics spares no efforts to recreate it (e.g., Mexico, Chile, Peru, Venezuela, not to mention Argentina, where the hierarchy has never departed from that model).

Many people still have a Christendom mindset and do not recognize what is going on in their country. They are little involved in collective life and so they think that nothing has happened and that everything is still the same as it was in their grandparents' time. Even though Christendom no longer exists there is an illusion that parishes are a continuation of Christendom. Indeed, people in a parish find there all the cultural elements that could be found in Christendom: worship, charitable works, catechism. They think that nothing has changed because all of this survives, and do not realize that the meaning of it all has changed. It used to reach everyone, but today reaches a minority, and often superficially, because the larger society is no longer Christian. But parishioners are unaware of that. They are isolated from the world outside and still think that the parish is everything. Many think that everyone is still involved in the parish, and have still not discovered that it is a minority. From the parish angle, Christendom does not seem to be finished. The institutions continue in the parish, but the fact that they no longer have the same effect goes unnoticed. They are no longer the culture of a people—the Christian people—but a subculture within the larger society. In any case, consciousness of peoplehood is gradually extinguished because parish consciousness becomes stronger. We are no longer a people, we are a parish.

This cannot be the church. The church is people of God, not a particular people but an eschatological people present in all peoples as leaven, a force transforming all peoples until one day all may achieve peoplehood. Shared life takes place in the midst of the world, the shared life of all those who are working together to transform this world into people of God. This community of life is also participation in the world with all its activities. Even so, not everyone in the world shares in this common life, but only those who transform the world, the people whose goal is the people of God, or Reign of God.

The Reign of God cannot be sought in isolation, on one's own. This Reign is not sought in the remnants of Christendom, or in those things retained by the parish. The Reign of God is sought in active communities, in a network of communities of many different kinds, but where there is solidarity among all—where all are inspired by the same mystery of the church, and all take part in the same material reality in which they are struggling, helping to form the people of God in the current phase of its journey in the midst of the world.

THE PEOPLE: COMMUNITY OF DESTINY

Peoplehood is created by a community of destiny, and hence a community of hope. The church is also called to be a community of destiny. All human beings have a personal destiny, manifested by the situation in which they find themselves: their birthplace, social class, moment in history, and the challenges of the society in which they have been born and to which they belong—a destiny set to some extent from birth. There is a whole condition that a person cannot change, within which his or her life must be lived out. If you are born Indian, your destiny is marked—you will have to struggle for the emancipation of the Indigenous. If you are born Black, your destiny is marked—you will have to confront racism throughout your life. If you are born poor, you will always be marked, even if you succeed in becoming rich. Your entire life is conditioned by your country of birth and mother tongue. Destiny does not control everything: within such conditions the individual can seek a range of solutions, but the range is limited, without many options.

Peoples also have a destiny. That of a powerful people is different from that of a weak people. A developed people will have a destiny different from that of an underdeveloped people. The latter will have no escape from the challenge of the backwardness of underdevelopment for entire generations. Over time a people goes through different situations, each generation facing a different challenge. Such is its destiny.

In addition to destiny set at birth, there are events that change destiny or mark a new one (war, disaster, revolution). Since 1959, the Cuban people has been marked by the Castro revolution, and there is no way to be a Cuban outside that destiny. A Brazilian's destiny is marked by the fact that it holds the world championship for social inequality. Facing that extreme inequality will be the inescapable challenge of the Brazilian people for several generations.

The people arises and grows in a country when its inhabitants begin to feel in solidarity and practice solidarity in challenges and in the acceptance of their shared condition. Without solidarity the people cannot yet be said to exist. We can see that complete solidarity is quite unlikely, but it appears to varying degrees. For example: there is no solidarity between the White, mixed-blood, and Indigenous populations. Whites do not take on the needs of the Indigenous, as is obvious throughout the Americas. Hence, the Indigenous say that they make up a different people. They do not feel that solidarity includes them. Nor was there solidarity between the nation and workers in the nineteenth century, or with Black slaves; they were not recognized as members of the people. Where differences of race or culture hinder solidarity, there is no people. Places without segregation are rare, hence it is hard to find a people with real peoplehood.

Latin America is a case in point. The meaning of the word "people" (*povo*, *pueblo*) is marked by the opposition between the "people" and "them," namely the oligarchy, aristocracy, large landowners, politicians, or the powerful in general.[7] The upper classes do not like the word "people" because it reminds them of their privileges and so they prefer to avoid the word. They use pejorative words: *rotos* [broken ones] in Chile, *matutos* or *caipiras* [backwoodsmen, hillbillies] in Brazil. Every country has its own half-ironic, half-insulting words to designate the mass of the poor.

Yet the word "people" is the title of nobility par excellence for the poor. The people are precisely the ones who come together in solidarity as a single force, as in the cry of the Popular Unity government of Salvador Allende in Chile: *El pueblo unido, jamás será vencido* [The people united will never be defeated].[8] So strong is the term that political movements have adopted the people as symbol, theme, and project, e.g., a "people's party." These movements have been called populist precisely because they were for the poor and sought to represent the poor in action: Cardenas (Mexico), Perón (Argentina), Haya de la Torre (Peru), Velasco Ibarra (Ecuador), Getulio Vargas (Brazil).[9] Populism has now almost entirely disappeared from the state in Latin America, pushed aside by neoliberal capitalist globalization, but it is not destroyed and could reappear at any time (e.g., the government of Hugo Chávez in Venezuela can be compared to populism). The military dictatorships suppressed the word "people" from their official vocabulary. To speak of the people challenged the established power—their power.

A people is made up of human beings who feel in solidarity with each other. Those who are not of the people are not in solidarity; they dominate, exploit, and are indifferent to the needs of others, and they govern for their own gain without taking the common good into account. On one side is the people and on the other those who abuse the people. The elites are precisely those who refuse to be in solidarity; they build the nation not for others but for themselves. That is why all Latin American revolutions are uprisings of the "people" against the traditional ruling elites.

Hence the challenges to the church. Traditionally many have felt that the church was not with the people, not interested in it, that it made alliances with the powerful against the people, showing contempt for it. This began in colonial times, when the hierarchy and clergy became linked to the owners and exploiters. In their way of thinking the people see two churches: the one that is suffering with them and defending them, and another church that is not with the people, and is always on the side of the powerful.

We may note that Archbishop Romero described "the people" as composed of the following: 1) the popular majorities made up of the people living in inhuman conditions of poverty, not because they are lazy, weak, or incapable, but because the majorities are exploited and oppressed by unjust structures and institutions by oppressor countries or exploiting classes, which taken together constitute structural and institutionalized violence; 2) the popular organizations which suffer repression in their struggle to give the people a popular project and popular power enabling it to forge its own destiny; 3) all those, organized or unorganized, who identify with just popular causes and struggle for them. Being people entails two elements: poverty and the struggle to escape from poverty. To truly be the people of God, according to Archbishop Romero, the church must be incarnated in the people's history, that is, in the people's struggle for justice and liberation. The characteristic of the people of God is being a Christian leaven in struggles for justice. What makes the people of God is encouraging the people of the poor seeking freedom and justice. What Archbishop Oscar Romero embodied until his martyrdom was simply what the Puebla Conference had taught: "We affirm the need for conversion on the part of the whole Church to a preferential option for the poor, an option aimed at their integral liberation" (Puebla 1134).

A few days before he died, Pope John XXIII dictated to Cardinal Cigognani words that summed up his vision of the future of the church:

> Today more than ever and certainly more than in past centuries, we are called to serve man as such and not only Catholics in connection with the rights of the human person and not only the rights of the Catholic Church. The present circumstances, the demands of the last fifty years, a deeper understanding of doctrine, have led us to new realities—as I said in my inaugural address at the council. It is not the gospel that changed; it is we that understand it better. Someone who has lived a long time, and who early in the century faced new tasks of social activity involving the whole man, one who has lived, like I, twenty years in the East, eight in France, and who has been able to deal with different cultures and traditions, knows that the time has come to recognize the "signs of the times," to take advantage of the right moment and to look far ahead.[10]

Many of our parishes may have the impression that they are with the people, because many people attend these parishes, but that shows that they have not discovered that the people are no longer there. Being in solidarity with just those who are in the parish, ignoring everyone else, amounts to practicing at most a symbolic aid of charity, giving from what is superfluous, but the parish as a whole is not thereby serving the real people.

Thirty years ago there were parishes committed to the causes of the people;

many people involved in these parishes were also victims of the oppression suffered by the people. Through them the whole parish experienced the problem of the people. When these major conflicts disappeared, the people outside were forgotten. They do not express their needs for solidarity any more. Each parish has once more closed in on itself. But a church outside the people is not people of God; it is a sect, a religious movement, but not the church of Jesus Christ. It is not incarnated in the human reality. It is only people if it is within the peoples, engaging in solidarity that forms a people. Certainly many Catholics are committed to the people, but they are not acknowledged as the church committed to the people. The sense of people dissipates, and the church is again spiritualized, disembodied; it soars in the heavens, far from this earth.

Yet there are plenty of challenges. The people are being crushed by a system that devotes all the country's resources to accumulating capital and the resulting rise of the elites, whose power is increasing enormously. The whole country is shaped as a country by an elite of 20% or 30% in more privileged countries like Brazil, or by 10% in Central America, Bolivia, or Paraguay. The masses are abandoned, unemployed, without government services and, especially, without hope.

The worst thing for a people is to lose hope, because hope is what constitutes it as a people. Without hope a people falls apart, falls into a state of anarchy and violence. The masses lack hope and the results are plain: violence keeps rising, drug consumption increases each year, open or hidden unemployment grows, i.e., the number of people surviving in the parallel market from the crumbs dropping from the table of the powerful keeps growing. The situation grows worse for young people who know they have no future, know they will not have a job, they will never be able to enroll in the courses that would bring them into the national economy, and will never have the cultural level necessary to have access to the goods of society. They know that all avenues are blocked; they are stuck in an empty, hopeless wait. Not everyone falls into violence, but all become discouraged and resigned. They accept this situation of anarchy because they have lost hope. They no longer want to build a future, but it is the future that makes peoplehood.

The church seems to be almost passive vis-à-vis this challenge, the greatest in human history, given the number of people involved. It issues documents which almost no one reads, but there are no visible signs of solidarity with the poor who are left out. Some local groups offer signs, but most are at their ease in parishes cultivating their good conscience.

Today experts in Catholic "marketing" talk about increasing the church's visibility. Visibility of what? Visibility of parish signs? Higher towers? A more visible display of the sacraments? Or simply producing Catholic spectacles? Indeed there is a great lack of visible signs—signs of solidarity with the excluded masses, condemning the complicity of the universal silence.

This universal silence could be blamed on the environment. The system has succeeded in demobilizing and dispersing the people, making it feel guilty as though the people were the enemy of the nation's progress and of development and the economy. The breakdown of the people is taking place in absolute silence. If violence rises, the answer is said to be more and better police. The social question is again a matter for police, as in the time of the Old Republic.

But the church ought to be the first in remaining alert and seeking the rebirth of the people. Should not the church itself be people? Isn't solidarity the visible sign of the people? Isn't the gospel good news, and a message of hope? A hope not in word alone, but in action.

THE PEOPLE AND ITS MARTYRS

Every people has heroes—including the people of God. Heroes are a reminder of the deeds of the past, and in a way they embody history because the only history familiar to the mass of the people is the names of heroes or some of their deeds. But remembering heroes gives a sense of dignity, enhances solidarity, creates unity, and is a reminder of collective responsibilities today. It makes the past of a people and propels it toward the future.

A people with no heroes, no mobilizing symbols, is incapable of sacrifices. Unless the leaders of a people can appeal to the example of heroes, they will not accomplish anything. Certainly the pseudodemocratic governments in Latin America today are lacking heroes. They would not even dare to evoke the heroes of the past because they are too far from them. Thus, they fail to achieve anything; citizens look after their own interests and cheat the government whenever they can. The result is corruption which stems from the low regard for authority.

This function of heroes can easily be seen in the history of Israel. What propels the people is the memory of the heroes of the past; the great book of the people is the history of its heroes, Abraham, Isaac, Jacob, and especially Moses, the superhero always invoked, ever the standard. Later come prophets like Samuel, King David, Elijah, and Elisha. In addition there were the writing prophets, Isaiah, Jeremiah, Ezekiel, Daniel, and the minor prophets; at the return from exile, Esdras and Nehemiah, and later the Maccabees. The people of Israel never lacked for heroes, and that is certainly one of the foundations of the great awareness of people that is proper to Israel.

The heroes of the Bible were those who embodied in their lives the values of the people. They are the founders, those who kept the founders as a living memory, who reminded Israel of its values, its destiny, the calling that gave it its dignity. They were challenged, argued with, persecuted, and killed for their fidelity to the calling of their people. Their death was a testimony to the vocation of their people.

Israel's culture and religion can be said to have consisted of reciting the lives of the heroes of the people to draw inspiration from them. Every child could identify with these heroes, including women like Sarah, Rebecca, Miriam, Moses' sister, Esther, Judith, and Anna, the mother of Samuel. Continuity between heroes keeps alive the hope that a new hero will come when the situation seems alarming. In the time of Jesus everyone was hoping for such a hero.

There was a big difference between Israel and the contemporary ancient peoples and their religions. The heroes of the other peoples were gods, or at least superhuman beings with semidivine qualities, as in Greece or Rome. In Brazil, in Candomblé, the heroes are the "Orixás," and each individual has ties to an Orixá, who is not simply a man or woman, but a higher being. In Israel, heroes are human persons like us. Sometimes a cult grows up around them, especially after their death, exalting, venerating, and invoking them as though they were superior to human beings and endowed with supernatural power, but the certainty that they were men and women like us never disappears. Legends attributing miracles to them appear, but they never lose their weak and mortal human character.

Identification with a god is unlikely to be able to produce a people. There were never peoples in traditional Africa, and that is why Western institutions adapt so poorly to the African world. Only human heroes can unite human beings in a people; Orixás do not do that. Shared belief in a creator God is likewise not enough to unite a people.

Modern nations, arising out of the secularization of Christendom, and imbued with the Judeo-Christian tradition, have their heroes. Brazil has its own, whose names can be seen on city streets.

In the second half of the twentieth century attitudes changed a great deal throughout a world permeated with Western culture. A new civilization and culture have spread, and values have been completely changed. Among the most noteworthy phenomena is that the old heroes have been replaced by new human types, whose heroism is more ludic and symbolic than real. The hero used to be the savior of the country; today's hero is a successful athlete, or the actor or actress who has succeeded in getting millions of spectators to buy a theater ticket or follow the soap opera, Miss Universe, or the TV host, and so forth.

Radical capitalism, which has reached the point of totally dominating the Western world, eliminating the remains of the older cultures, has installed the worship of champions. Champions are ultimately those who made the most money. Life is organized competitively, there are all kinds of competitions, and heroes are those who win major competitions. Winners, money champions, have replaced heroes, but they produce a market rather than a people.

Consider the United States: its heroes used to be the founding fathers, Washington, Adams, Jefferson, Franklin, and so forth, followed by Lincoln.

New candidates appeared in the early twentieth century: Rockefeller, Morgan, Ford. Today the heroes are Bill Gates and other billionaires. We can add movie stars and athletes. Heroes of this kind are the embodiment of the people of the United States. But can heroes of this kind incarnate a people? Can they arouse the solidarity of a people? Are they not the heralds of the ruin of a people, crushed by the market and its owners?

The need for heroes is satisfied today by the superchampions who earn millions. Is this not a sign that the idea of the people is falling apart and that no one else is standing with the people in solidarity? After all, a soccer champion does not prompt much social solidarity or dedication to the common good. Within this new system, peoplehood is only skin-deep, pride that the national anthem is echoing in a stadium, because our champion reached the finish line first. Citizens therefore swell with pride, but no great solidarity will come from this pride. We may conclude that this deviation in terms of heroes will inevitably lead to the exaltation of individualism and devaluation of peoplehood.

Historically, we may observe that wars have played a primary role in forming almost all peoples. Wars provide the heroes; they are a great hero factory. They have done so through suffering and death. One who dies in war is commonly declared a hero. A cult has been organized around soldiers slain in war. The greatest suffering comes from war. A large portion of history is occupied with wars, so much so that at one time historians devoted themselves solely to wars. Besides wars, there are epidemics, droughts, floods, earthquakes, volcano eruptions, accidents of nature or caused by humans—but none of them produce heroes like wars.

The people of Israel shows the importance of war in the formation and consciousness of a people. The Old Testament attests to the joys and sufferings of the people of Israel, and shows how the people of Israel was formed by suffering in Egypt and the desert and consolidated by victories in the conquest of the land of Canaan. It suffered from invasions, oppression by foreigners or even the kings of Israel, and exile in Babylon, which remained in the memory of the people as the supreme test. Yet they returned to Jerusalem, the capital was rebuilt, and worship and the law of the people were reestablished. All of this was interpreted as a victory over paganism.

The Christian hero, the one who unites the Christian people and brings about peoplehood, is Jesus. As Son of God, he is mysteriously joined to his people, as head of the body. The divine and the human are joined through incorporation of the people into Christ. This incorporation is invisible, for it is contact between human beings and the invisible God. However, this incorporation also has a human and visible element; it responds to a psychological need, to a mental structure of all human beings—a people's need for heroes. In human terms, Jesus acts as a hero, and at the same time changes the model of hero.

This recognition of Jesus as founding hero of the people has not always been so clear to people or to theologians. Spiritualist and Monophysite theology was satisfied to explain Jesus' death by a decree of the Father. In order to forgive sins the Father needed an expiation, and hence the Father condemned Jesus to death so that he could offer a sufficient expiation and the Father could forgive. These ideas were repeated for centuries, leaving the impression that Jesus' death had nothing to do with his life. It was a one-time isolated event. In a way, Jesus' life was useless, and the course of his life was time wasted: it would have sufficed for him to have been created on the eve of his death so that he could die and offer satisfaction. Or, Jesus' life could be the unavoidable time between birth and death, until the moment of sacrifice—like the life of slaves that certain Indigenous tribes set aside to be sacrificed some day. It would be a life without saving value, a waiting period until the sacrifice could be completed.

Yet the people of God needs the example of the hero, the example of human death, a martyr's death, and hence it needs a clear presentation of the human reality of the Jesus, not simply the saving value attributed to it by the Father. It has been Latin American Christology that has insisted most on fully restoring the humanity of Jesus.[11] There must have been human reasons explaining the death of Jesus. Jesus died because he confronted the powerful in his people and wanted to reform all the structures of that people, and so he was rejected by the authorities, while the poor were not strong enough to prevent the order of the authorities from being carried out. That same story was to take place thousands of times in subsequent history. Jesus' death thus has a human meaning and makes him a hero.

After Jesus, the Christian heroes of the people of God are the martyrs, imitators of Jesus. They do not die in war, but are persecuted and killed for their fidelity to Jesus. The church as mystery is born from the Father, the Son, and the Holy Spirit. As a human reality, as people, it is born out of the heroism of Jesus and is renewed by the heroism of the martyrs. Jesus' martyrdom is a sign that is ever present, ever conscious in the mind of all Christians. The image of the crucified one is by far the most popular one and the one spread most widely; it is the image of the martyr hero, the crucified one. In the early centuries, the martyrs occupied a preeminent place in the church. Without them the church would not have survived or remained united. They were a constant presence in the memory of the Christian people. They were the true Christian people, as the writers of that time celebrated it. Even when the persecutions ceased, the memory of the martyrs of the early centuries was always at the forefront of the Christian imagination. Not only the liturgy, but countless shrines, relics, and devotions transmitted the memory of the martyrs, sustaining the faith of Christians in the most painful circumstances of life. Until a few generations ago, the lives of the martyrs were often read in Christian households. Christians felt that they were in the company of the martyrs.

The death of the martyrs was always held up as a victory. One who kept the faith to death was held to be victorious, and hence the cult of the martyrs was a victory celebration, and thus it was encouraging to Christians in the midst of all the difficulties of life. The memory of the martyrs was a promise of victory. Christians have always been encouraged by the awareness of belonging to a church of martyrs. The consciousness of the people of God was held high, despite so much corruption over the centuries, because the church was still defined as church of martyrs, even when it was making martyrs itself, and was killing heretics or unbelievers. In the midst of so many sad spectacles, the martyrs were celebrated. At least they were the image of the church that was desired.

The First World has practically lost the memory of the older martyrs; they have no commercial value and do not register on the market. The church is no longer seen as the church of martyrs there, and hence it has lost consciousness of people of God. Familiarity with the martyrs has been lost. There are no modern martyrs because capitalist society avoids creating martyrs; there is a surer way to destroy the church than persecutions. For many people the church is an agency for individual services, and has nothing to do with martyrdom. No one can even imagine the possibility of being a martyr: martyr for what? Why? Where?

Even so, there were more martyrs in the twentieth century than in all previous centuries combined—tens of thousands of martyrs in Communist countries, especially in Russia and China, but also elsewhere. There were tens of thousands of martyrs in Germany under the Nazi regime, who died in the concentration camps or by firing squad. In Africa Christians have been, and still are, persecuted and killed, particularly under Muslim dictatorships.

In Latin America awareness of people of God has arisen primarily because of the martyrs.[12] Anyone who does not honor these martyrs has no awareness of people of God, and is living a disembodied, spiritualistic religion. Indeed, the true church is the church of the martyrs, who have been so numerous, especially between 1960 and 1990.

Latin American church history preserves the memory of martyrs from its colonial beginning, such as the recently canonized martyrs of Natal, Brazil. Yet there is the troublesome fact that these martyrs were killed by Indians, and hence the question: what did these Indians intend? For them, weren't the missionaries invaders or friends of the invaders? Didn't they support the invaders? So, objectively speaking, wasn't their behavior aggressive? Did the Indians want to expel invaders or persecute religion? Unfortunately, no Indians killed by the invaders have been canonized. These martyrs killed by the Indians were not martyrs in the full sense, and hence they do not found a people. They are there in history and may nourish popular religiosity but they do not create and nourish peoplehood.

The martyrs of recent times have been different. They have been killed not by Indians, but by established governments, governments linked to the ruling classes, or by the wealthy ruling oligarchies, who generally have bishop and priest friends and who claim to be the great defenders of the faith. They killed in God's name. They did not intend to persecute religion as they understood it. They expected the church to support authority and property, and they thought that the church is supposed to preach unconditional obedience to any de facto authority. They persecuted, arrested, tortured, and killed in the name of their idea of the church. As Jesus had announced, they killed his disciples thinking that they were serving God. The martyrs died to defend the true meaning of Christianity and the church. Hence, their memory fashions the people of God, and separates the people of God from caricatures of it. Celebration of contemporary martyrs is in some fashion the firm foundation on which the people of God is built in Latin America.[13]

The martyrs are very much present in the consciousness of the church, starting with the martyr bishops. As bishops they have stood out more, as leaders of a martyr church. Archbishop Oscar Romero is venerated throughout Latin America, canonized by the people and the churches, even though Rome is stalling.[14] Bishop Enrique Angelelli of La Rioja is venerated in Argentina,[15] as is Bishop Juan Gerardi in Guatemala. Some martyred priests are deeply honored in the memory of the people: Father Rutilio Grande, the Salvadoran Jesuit whose martyrdom opened the eyes of Archbishop Romero, whose confessor he had been; Father Bosco Penido Burnier of São Félix do Araguaia, Brazil; Father Hector Gallego, in Panama; and certainly the six university Jesuits in El Salvador, the most well known of whom was Ignacio Ellacuría, one of the main liberation theologians.

As incomprehensible as it might seem, the Roman Curia radically rejects all the Latin American martyrs and the very idea of their martyrdom. The Roman church has managed to convince a portion of the hierarchy and clergy to silence these martyrs. Thus far the martyrdoms of Romero, Angelelli, and so many priests, men and women religious, and thousands of lay people have not been recognized. Yet martyrs are fundamental to the awareness of the church as people. Why this rejection?

Among the signs that this rejection comes from Rome is the fact that in the 1997 Synod of the Americas the bishops had included among their proposals a recognition of the martyrs of Latin America, but this proposal was not accepted in Rome by those who drafted the text signed by the pope. No clear mention of martyrs could be placed in the final document of the Santo Domingo Conference (1992).[16] The Curia, represented by the iron hand of Bishop (later Cardinal) Jorgé Medina, did not allow it: it thought that the martyrs should be simply ignored or that they were not martyrs, thereby taking away from the Latin American churches what was most precious: the blood of martyrs. It is like denying that they are churches, for a church without martyrs is not church.

Why this denial of the martyrs? Is it to prevent the formation of an awareness of people in the Latin American churches, ever treated as appendages to the metropolitan church? Or because a significant portion of the hierarchy is unwilling to surrender its ties to governments that claim to be Catholic but were responsible for the martyrdoms? For the specific feature of the Latin American martyrs is that they were killed by governments claiming to act in the name of God and with the support of representatives of the church. Recognizing martyrdom would be tantamount to condemning the crimes of certain governments and the cowardice of a portion of the clergy and hierarchy. To stifle the memory of cowardice, an effort is made to impose silence on everyone. Is that the reason?

Yet silence is impossible. The martyrs show that the Latin American churches have reached adulthood, and are Christian on their own and not simply in imitation of other churches. The memory of the recent martyrs cannot be removed from the awareness of the Catholic people.

The denial of the martyrs is part of an overall policy. Many signs indicate that the Roman Curia did not and does not want the Latin American church to have its own history and its own shape. The martyrs are the center of this history and this shape but alongside the martyrs there are the prophets who have also been discredited. Furthermore, the Curia stifles all important events, discredits the people who make history, and tries to suppress the memory of Medellín and Puebla. By keeping the church from having its own history, the formation of awareness of the Christian people as people of God is stifled. Christians remain passive objects intended to receive the services offered by the clergy, inasmuch as all of these services come from Rome.

What is the reason for all of this? For the sake of a worldwide policy of having good relations with all governments with the hope of inspiring evangelizing legislation? Is it a repeat of the time-worn formula: top-down evangelizing based on the power of states and governments, accepting even the most corrupt, oppressive, and inhumane?

In any case, the Latin American church already has its martyrs and no one can make them vanish. They are in history and in memory and hence they create peoplehood.

THE PEOPLE AND ITS CULTURE

Every people has a culture. Each people has its own culture. There is no universal culture, for there are many cultures in humankind and all imperial claims to universal culture prove fruitless. It is impossible to unify all peoples in a single culture. Until a century ago, all cultures saw themselves as unique. In the twentieth century, they discovered their diversity and they still have not gotten used to this fact. Not even today's globalization will succeed in enveloping all peoples in a single culture. All peoples will learn to use the same technical means, but they will do so within a specific culture, as can already be seen in Asian countries (Japan, China, Korea, India) which have assimilated Western technology but have their own way of living, and feeling and being in the world.

In human beings culture is almost everything. Culture comes from the immersion of persons and human communities in the earthly world, not passively but actively. Although animals can transform the world to a limited extent, humans can do so infinitely more, even if they are far from being able to do everything they would like.

In recent years, the theological study of cultures has developed considerably, particularly around the issue of inculturation. Here we want to draw attention only to some aspects. Our issue is not inculturation but the "people of God."

Within the vast scope of what is meant by culture, we intend to take up only one question, namely the relationship between cultures and people of God, an issue that is itself very far-reaching. Out of everything related to this issue, we will take only one question: i.e., why Christianity has not been inculturated in recent centuries either in Western modernity or in the cultures of the rest of the world.[17] Let us first examine what we understand here by culture.

The first important distinction is that between culture understood passively and actively. Passive culture is everything that a human person receives, the entire legacy of previous works of humankind: the taste for certain foods or drinks, ways of speaking and taking shelter, working and enjoying life, social relationships, language and all the products of language, the arts and all works of art or of engineering that make cities and their content, and so forth. All of this is received, and a person who has been able to assimilate a good portion of this legacy is regarded as cultured.

This legacy includes the organization of relationships between people and economic, political, or cultural institutions. All this has been built up over hundreds and thousands of years in order to make human beings freer, more in charge of themselves, better able to express their personality to one another. Each cultural configuration reflects a certain way of conceiving freedom and relationships between human persons.

Nevertheless, over time every culture tends to become dead weight. There comes a time when people find that they are imprisoned in their own culture. A culture fashioned for the journey toward freedom ends up suppressing freedom, because it forces everything to work preserving that culture (e.g., the end of Christendom before the French Revolution; the Chinese empire in the late nineteenth century; the Turkish empire at the beginning of the twentieth century). Under such circumstances either a new culture arises and bursts the chains of the previous culture, or the people goes into decline and disappears as a living force in history. We will return to this observation, which is important for the people of God.

Culture is active as well as passive, and in this sense it means the action of a people to break through obstacles, routines, decadent forms, prejudices, obsolete customs, paralyzing administration, in order to establish other relationships with nature and between human beings in order to gain greater freedom. This culture is also particular because the action of peoples is conditioned by the context in which it takes place, and it also depends on the personality of the one leading the process. Every culture brings to the fore certain very strong personalities who are able to imprint new values or new ways of living on their peoples. The word "culture" does not express this constructive activity very well but there is no other word in modern European languages to designate this aspect of things, and hence we are forced to make use of the word "culture," even while insisting on the difference from its meaning in ordinary speech in which culture is passive.

A people is always creating a culture or changing a culture. A living people continually changes or creates new kinds of culture. The purpose of life is not culture but human freedom, and freedom can only exist in a concrete, limited, conditioned way, i.e., in a culture. This culture is constraining, but it is also a condition of existence.

Any culture is social; it is the collective work of many successive generations, because each creative action extends and renews previous actions by other persons. A single person in isolation cannot create a culture, despite the myth of Robinson Crusoe, which is capitalism's founding myth. Capitalism tends to highlight strength of personality and glorify the "self-made man." Capitalism arouses and excites the ambition of each individual, encouraging permanent competition: today the supreme quality is competitiveness. But such people do not create a culture. Only through collective endeavors is a culture fashioned. Hence, an individual alone cannot gain any freedom, but a multitude of active persons can do so.

Hence "people" and "culture" are correlative; there is no people without culture, and no culture without people. Culture may be said to unite this people. When a people stops producing culture, anarchy will ensue. When peoplehood no longer exists, culture becomes an empty form.

When a people has two or more cultures, that people is very weak. Many writers describe Latin American society in general as a society in which there are two peoples, one on top of the other. Since there are two peoples, there are two cultures. Taken literally that is certainly an exaggeration. The Brazilian upper and lower classes share many things, e.g., language, religion, soccer, beans (although the latter is tending to disappear from the table of the well-off except in the form of *feijoada*). Even so in many aspects there really are two ways of living, two ways of dealing with life and the world, two ways of organizing shared life.[18]

There is a culture of the elites, which is increasingly an imitation of the dominant culture in the bourgeois classes in the North Atlantic, particularly of the United States. While they used to copy French culture, now they copy the United States. The upper class regularly visits New York or Miami and finds new items to import into their country. Certain Central American and

Caribbean countries, as well as Venezuela, Colombia, and Ecuador, are fiercely imitative in this manner, because they are closer to the metropole and are
relatively small and defenseless. Even in more developed countries like Brazil, Argentina, and Chile, imitation is on the rise. They hold onto some signs
of their own, but the way of thinking, feeling, and living seeks to imitate
North American fashion as faithfully as possible. Of course they cannot
suppress their distinctive features, but they try to hide them.

Latin American elites continually experience ambiguity toward their own
country. On the one hand, they are boosters and exalt their country and
claim to be fiercely patriotic, and want to be independent. But at the same
time they feel the shame of their country's inferiority vis-à-vis major figures
in the First World, whom they wish to imitate as thoroughly as possible.
Such is the case, for example, of the economists who lead these countries,
whose training and mindset is more American than that of the Americans,
more neoliberal than the Americans, and completely submissive to American principles, out of fear of not seeming as civilized or cultured as the
Americans. There is a huge feeling of inferiority that can sometimes be manifested in a forced expression of superiority.

Their greatest ambition is to attain the status of First World countries.
The elites speculate about when they will enter into the circle of the "blessed."
Their active culture consists not in creating something of their own but in
imitating what others have done. Thus they are always following someone
else's footsteps and they will always arrive late. People who want to propose
a path that will be the country's own are carefully eliminated, with either
soft or violent methods (e.g., by bringing in the armed forces).

The armed forces in Latin American countries are a clear sign of that
schizophrenia. Their role is not to defend the country militarily from outside invaders, which do not exist, but to serve as a violent force in readiness
for circumstances in which the elites can no longer maintain their control.
They are there as a visible sign that a united people is not going to be formed.
They are the ultimate police force to quell insurrections by the people down
below. Their role is to repress the poor, should the elites consider it necessary.

The elite culture is more visible and seeks to ignore other culture, i.e., the
culture or subculture of the subordinate masses, which is dependent on that
of the elites and is not such a well-articulated system as that of the elites. It
is fashioned by combining fragments from the culture of the rich to shape a
way of life. The disparity keeps increasing. In food, the rich eat natural
foods, and the poor genetically modified food. The rich are dressed in brand-
name clothing, and the poor in clothes imported from China. The homes of
the poor are made out of used materials or castoffs from the homes of the
rich, with very little furniture. Teaching in their schools is made up of fragments of culture that do not serve as a preparation for anything. Care in
their hospitals, when they even exist, is reduced to a minimum.

Even with these scanty resources, the poor create a way of life. Sometimes they are happier than the rich, who are caught in a competition that creates an anxiety that brings on nervous diseases and depression. There is a true culture of the poor, an art of getting along with little, and an organization of social relations in which solidarity can be even greater than that practiced by the elites converted to globalization. There is the art of using the few resources available to make life possible. This a culture that does not appear publicly and is ignored by the elites.[19]

This subculture is passed on and tends to create a way of life of the people; it is submissive, and limited, but it exists. The life of the poor is not anarchy and breakdown—at least not usually. Some may fall into that situation, but as a rule, the poor are able to organize a decent and dignified life, albeit separated from the elites of the nation. Such is the case of the culture of the maid which is unknown to the mistress of the house, just as the maid does not understand the workings of the culture of the family for which she works.

Such cultural duality weakens a people or prevents peoplehood from really occurring. Unless culture becomes homogeneous no people can be integrated.

We now apply these considerations, drawn from observations on the relationships between people and culture, to the people of God.

Until Latin American countries achieved political independence, the culture of the church was that of the whole society. In the colonies of Portugal and Spain all culture came from the church. Of course the Indigenous people and Black slaves secretly held onto many elements of their defeated culture, but in public life there was only one culture, that of the church, a clerical culture.

Within the colonial system in the Americas, the church unquestionably created a vast imposing culture whose monuments still stand, and are now the main tourist attractions in the cities. Latin America has a huge cultural legacy in continuity with the culture of the metropolitan centers and with the culture of medieval Christendom, albeit even more clerical. The centers of the old colonial cities in Latin America are museums of the former Christian culture: Mexico City, Oaxaca, Puebla, Guanajuato, Taxco, Antigua (Guatemala), Lima, Arequipa, Quito, Cuenca, Santiago, Ouro Preto, Salvador, Rio de Janeiro, Olinda e Recife, Mariana, Congonhas, Bogota, Cartagena, to name only the main ones.

Merely listing these cities makes it clear that this legacy constitutes a past that was not renewed. The creativity of the people of God was extinguished in the early nineteenth century, or at least declined a great deal. This was true not only in the Americas but throughout what used to be Christendom. The production of the people of God declined in all aspects: literature, music, plastic arts, architecture, ways of life, social organization, joint activities, feasts. There is much repetition but little creation. This is not surprising because the church was banished from public life and sought to save itself in a ghetto.

Today the ancient Christian legacy of culture is one of the great tourist attractions in the world. Christian culture has become a museum, which remains important, because it still witnesses, albeit only nostalgically, to Christianity in a society that ignores it in practice. People need to become familiar with the Bible, if only in order to understand museums, even if they are not interested in its message.

Moreover, the contrast between the marvels of the culture of the past, that is, of the culture that has now become a museum, and what has been produced in the last two centuries shows the impoverishment of active culture today. To illustrate the decline, one need only compare the number of Christian writers in the first half of the twentieth century with those of the second half. Today it is hard to find among contemporary writers a great Christian writer who produces work inspired by Christianity. Latin America has wonderful writers, but it is hard to find a Christian among them. The same can be said of other arts, philosophy, and human thought in general. The Christian presence in culture has declined, Christians produce very little culture. They manage the museum, but they are no longer creators of culture.

If they do not create culture, are they still a people? Obviously, culture is not what is essential to the people of God, but the life of faith, hope, and charity in the mystery of the Blessed Trinity. However, that mystery has to be lived on earth in human works, and they do not exist outside of culture— they are culture. In principle, Christians could ignore culture entirely and live by faith and charity, like the ancient desert monks or the companions of St. Francis. However, those were exceptional vocations which most people would not be able to endure. Even they carried within themselves the culture that they had received since infancy, and without intending to, they created culture, indeed a very strong culture.

So why does the culture of the people of God not appear as activity, creation, transformation of the world? Certainly many Christians are acting, but there is no community of action. They act in a scattered way, and that is the most serious sign that the people does not exist. Otherwise, if the people of God really existed, it would have resisted the many efforts to deny it over the last twenty years that have almost succeeded in extinguishing it from the memory of Christians.

What has happened?

Since the French Revolution, especially starting with the papacy of Pius IX, the Roman church has sought to absorb all local churches and achieve complete centralization in which everything is to come from Rome, and the churches would be mere receivers of guidelines from Rome. For two hundred years this has been done with persistence and tenacity. After a brief interval encouraged by Vatican II, it has been reassumed by John Paul II; even before that, Paul VI lost control of the Curia and was forced to watch as the previous strategy that began in the nineteenth century was restored.

Within this Romanization project, which also made its way into Latin

America somewhat belatedly, there arose a Roman subculture.[20] Rome sought to impose its Romanized culture on all the churches. It suppressed local customs, rites, theologies, and ways of expression. It insisted on appointing bishops to prevent diversification; each bishop was to be the local agent of the Roman subculture. In creating a culture, Rome imposed on all the churches a theology, scholastic philosophy, a catechism, a ritual for the sacraments, a canon law, and a centralized administration that took away any initiative from the bishops. Through its social doctrine, it even imposed a single type of politics, an economic option, a type of social action. It stifled all local initiatives that strayed even slightly from the Roman cultural model. The idea was that every Catholic should be born in a Catholic maternity ward; be raised in a Catholic day-care center; attend Catholic grade school, high school, and university; be a member of a Catholic political party, labor union, or club; be treated at a Catholic hospital, and ultimately in a Catholic retirement home. This ideal was fully achieved in some countries and partially in others. The Roman culture was cultivated in all these institutions.

This Roman subculture was built artificially using fragments from the past. It was a time of "neos": neoscholasticism, neo-Thomism, neo-Gothic, neo-Roman, neo-Byzantine. The upshot was the creation of a philosophy whose main feature was that no one but Catholics knew anything about it. It became a barrier between the culture of contemporary peoples and that of Catholics. Neo-Gothic was a Catholic or churchy style because no one else was building in that style from the Middle Ages when all buildings, including churches, were Gothic. A neo-Gothic church seemed strange in a city that was completely different. A social doctrine for the church was built out of neoscholasticism, a doctrine whose categories were inaccessible to anyone but Catholics.

This was a culture artificially resuscitated from dead elements from a remote past. All Catholics were forced to enter into this model. They wasted huge amounts of energy and were increasingly isolated from their own people and their culture. The Catholic subculture seemed increasingly alien to urban culture, and Catholics created no new culture. No one would claim, for example, that the cathedral in São Paulo could communicate a message. The huge intellectual effort of neo-Thomism produced nothing in the contemporary cultures of the Western world, let alone other cultures.

Rome artificially created a culture that radically cut Catholics off from the outside world, handed them over to the central administration with their hands tied, and forced them to act without inspiration. It was very difficult to escape from this prison, because those who took risks were condemned, and thus isolated from other Catholics.

The results of this effort can be seen today. To begin with, only the clergy and a small portion of lay people assimilated this culture, and they did so passively, with little or no creativity. The clergy did absorb it but lost credibility and social and intellectual impact. How many priests are known, heard, or sought beyond parishes or religious houses? This inability is not due to their priestly character, but to the Roman culture in which they have been educated.

Roman centralization is justified on the grounds that all Catholics around the world are united in a single culture. The Roman subculture is the product of a great anxiety: the fear that the Catholic Church will be absorbed and dissolved in the various cultures of the world. There is nothing evangelical about this: it is nothing but a psychological distortion, a group neurosis. Many have internalized and rationalized this anxiety, and impose Roman culture with a zeal and enthusiasm worthy of noble causes.

It must be acknowledged that creating a universal culture is impossible, harmful, and un-Christian. Christianity calls to human beings who are in their own culture and does not impose another culture on them. Throughout the world, all try to live the gospel within their own particular culture. Indeed, the task of the people of God is to be a leaven within peoples so that each may develop its own culture.

It is a peculiar feature of the people of God that its unity comes not from cultural unity, but from agreement, covenant, friendship between all disciples in all cultures. Unity means agreement, connection, and dialogue between all cultures, with mutual enrichment. Two centuries of attempted centralization have caused great damage to the church, and it will take centuries to repair it.

The second result of Romanized culture is that almost all lay people have been deprived of culture and are "uncultured." They could not assimilate the Romanized culture, which required a long initiation, they have not received a theology or philosophy within their own culture, and they have not been encouraged or tolerated when they sought to create their own culture. Repression has taught them that it is better to do nothing. One need only compare the passivity of the vast majority of Catholics to the dynamism of Pentecostal believers. Why the difference? As people they come from the same conditions. Why does a Catholic who has always been passive become active and dynamic after conversion into a Pentecostal denomination? The answer is simple: Rome sought to impose a Romanized culture on everything and it did not work. The obstacle to evangelization in the world today is centralization around a subculture that has not become part of any people.[21]

Why is there no inculturation? Because the hierarchy has sought to impose a subculture that no one wants. And why is there no evangelization? For the very same reason.

THE PEOPLE OVER TIME

A people is formed over time, through successive generations; it cannot be formed artificially. Bringing millions of human beings into a market is not enough to make a people, as can be observed in the former colonial empires. New nations emerged out of the administrative boundaries of the empires, with the aim of forming peoples out of their inhabitants. In the Americas the nations inherited from the Spanish empire are almost two centuries old and yet they are still not true peoples. The same is true in Africa. In the Middle East, the countries left in the wake of the Turkish empire have still not formed true peoples.

There has not been enough time. Forming a people takes many generations. What can be done by a single generation is limited. A people is built up over a long succession of generations, each bringing new elements, changes, improvements, adding greater complexity to the building.

A people is radically different from a market, although today the aim is to substitute markets for peoples in complete globalization. The market is unaware of generations; its time is uniform continuity. The time of a people is diversified because each generation leaves its own mark, as human beings get old and die, and a new generation comes along seeking to start fresh, even though it is unable to undo 90% of what has been done or transmitted by the previous generation. The market is built artificially, homogenizing consumers. By contrast a people matures by going through many cycles of human life.

The people is made up of young and old people, people being born and people dying. Older people transmit the result of their labors to young people, who choose what they want to receive or not. A people is characterized by the ongoing transmission flowing between generations. Many people spend fifty years or more working hard, and then pass it all on to the next generation which almost never continues the same work. Human works are always unfinished and hence a people is ever unfinished, ever in need of reform, never able to halt.

Moreover, transmission takes place not through equal subjects but is influenced by gender. Men and women are endlessly involved in life and the world they produce is marked by women as well as men. Because of the sex-influenced mode of reproduction, each individual is unique and unforeseeable, thereby giving rise to infinite variety among the generations.

If there were no succession of generations, the world would be forever the same. There would be no people, only a museum. The world changes because of young people not attached to the past. Young people want to change, bring new things, change society and nature. Adults want to hold onto and increase what they have done. The old are afraid of losing their world and defend it against assaults of young people, and delay the changes needed. Peoplehood comes from this ongoing interaction between young and old, some pressuring, others resisting. Hence, a people is always in a state of formation. The old educate the young, passing on their experience. A people is transmitted and shaped going from the old to the young. A people consists precisely of this passage of one generation to another; it is what remains through the succession of generations.

Education may be more or less free and flexible, or constricted and forced. Ancient peoples were generally very rigid in transmission because it took place almost solely in the family. In recent centuries, a good portion of education is outside the family. Young people are formed in homogeneous environments that move forward and are then differentiated from the parents and enter into conflict. Open conflict between generations used to be unthinkable, but since 1968 we know that conflicts will be a constant in the future, unless older people hand everything over to the young, which is not a good solution. Conflicts are necessary because they lead to dialogue, even if by force.

Young people more easily succumb to the market which manipulates them. Young people are consumers who follow fashions and thus depend on advertising. Thus they do not create continuity. If all were to let themselves be manipulated by the market, there would be no peoples left, only consumers. Education would cede to advertising. Today a certain education still resists the attraction of the market, albeit with considerable struggle and protest. Peoples are resisting the suppression of time sought by the market. They still think that they must transmit something more than how to buy and consume.

In the Bible, the people of Israel shows very clearly how a people lives in time and depends on time. The wisdom books transmit the advice of the old to the young. What is most crucial, however, is the recitation of the history that young people will have to assume it and take it forward. This history consists of genealogies, for the people of Israel is transmitted from fleshly fathers and mothers to fleshly sons and daughters, as in all peoples, because it values the transmission of its heritage even more highly than other peoples.

The people of God is a people like others and lives in time, but Christian time is quite different. It is more flexible: it is the place of freedom and hence of availability, not known by any other people (at least that is how it ought to be). The big difference from other peoples is that transmission is not made essentially from parents to children but from disciple to disciple. Yet in practice we know that it is often not that way. Theoretically, faith comes from evangelization, rather than generation—a young person can evangelize an older person. The Christian people is not subordinated to the rhythm of generations. Communication can be faster and more extensive. The Christian people can be a much younger people because it delivers the power of communication to young people, without necessarily going through the old. Hence, change, evolution, adaptation to the signs of the times could and should be much faster in the people of God than in any other people.

Yet, this is not exactly what is seen in practice. The church's action, including evangelization, is not entrusted to young people but to the clergy which concentrates all powers and all functions and only allows for assistants. The clergy is a particularly closed bureaucracy in which power belongs to those who are oldest. Today almost all bishops are over fifty, and contemporary popes have almost all been old. Certainly some older people maintain a spirit of creativity and accept risk, like John XXIII, but that is not common. At 75, a member of the clergy generally has the theology learned in the seminary fifty years previously. The church is a gerontocracy. Most of the younger clergy do not have any decision-making responsibility, and they have to wait a long time before having access to functions of responsibility. Moreover, they are situated within a system that is so strict that they have little freedom. The ecclesiastical system is set up to administer the past and discourage any desire for change. It is not set up for evangelizing, and hence there is very little evangelization and there is no point in multiplying spiritual appeals for evangelization if the structure is not made for it. There is no point in exhorting priests, as though the problem were moral conversion. Priests are blocked in a closed system that forces them to do what they do and does not allow them to try anything else.

Moreover, as a privileged class, the clergy by nature does not like change and is afraid that in any change it might lose some of its privileges. The church is not only a gerontocracy, but a caste society, an aristocracy, and hence renewal through the action of younger generations is much more difficult. It is not impossible because a fifty-year-old bishop may be more inclined to change structures than one who is seventy-five, but the difference is not great. Numerous forces in the church militate against change.

If that were all the problem would not be so serious, but there is also the Roman Curia. Any administration tends to stay the same and resist any change. Officials change but the administration stays the same regardless of the individuals occupying it. Its stated purpose is the common good of the society but it is hard to make that really happen. Left to itself the administration serves itself, its conditions of life, future, self-maintenance. In a struggle going back to the eighth century, the administration has accumulated so many privileges that today not even the slightest change can take place in the church without its consent. It struggles unceasingly to preserve its privileges, and has centuries of experience of spotting and eliminating dangers.

Feeling threatened at Vatican II, the administration decided to destroy the force for change, and it succeeded in removing any force that it regarded as harmful or threatening. Charles Maurras (leader of the reactionary Action Française) used to congratulate the Roman church because it had succeeded in removing from Christianity the dangerous leaven of the gospel. Similarly, it can be said that the Curia has succeeded in removing the gospel poison from Vatican II. The only thing left are some texts that are dead, meaningless, good for quoting in official documents.

Officially the Curia is at the service of the pope, but popes come and go while the Curia remains. An administration can completely paralyze a pope. If he resists, the response is to create a passive resistance that discourages even the most courageous. The Roman administration devotes all its efforts to preventing any change in the church and annulling the effect of generations. Because it can appoint bishops, it can choose those whom it knows are not going to want to change the way things are. Today it manages to do this almost perfectly, and when it makes a mistake it is only on unimportant bishops.

The Roman administration has successfully imposed an ideology of stability, and has spread the idea that the primary claim for the Catholic Church's glory is that it never changes and no one can force it to change.[22] It remains unchanging in a stormy world. That ideology brings conviction as well as subjection. The normal play of generations thus disappears, and indeed the church does not change. The upshot is that the people of God disappears and is replaced by an inert mass, as could be seen in the twentieth century. In the final stage everything disappears, as in contemporary Europe, the final stage of centuries of decline. The people of God was snuffed out at the very moment when Vatican II recognized its right to exist. The people was in its death throes, even while the clergy and hierarchy tried to close their eyes. Many still undoubtedly have their eyes closed, dreaming of the multitudes of the seventeenth century that no longer exist.

If the people no longer exists, neither is the faith truly passed on with all its human incarnation. Transmission of the faith is a free, personal act coming from God's freely given gift. However, it becomes a human reality. Young people receive the faith not alone but to a great extent in their family, neighborhood, environment, i.e., in a Christian people, in the people of God. If the people disappears, the faith is no longer transmitted. That is what is going on in Europe. Parents have become so passive that they no longer transmit the faith to their children, and the neighborhood is just as indifferent. No one talks to them about this anymore, and young people grow up without hearing a witness of faith. All religion has been emptied from their world. Rather than a people there are only individuals who still have religious feelings but are so lifeless that they no longer have any strength for speaking to their children.

Catechisms, religion courses, Catholic schools, sacraments, and preparation for the sacraments all exist. But all of this is outside the context of the people of God and remains inoperative. It passes over the heads of the young people, who do not even perceive it. So-called religious education is limited to a pedagogical technique without content. If education is simply pedagogy, the use of pedagogical techniques to pass on a religious message, the message ceases being faith and becomes culture, and the people of God are not going to be different from any other people on earth. Faith is passed on by people led by the Spirit.

The education of the people of God cannot be bureaucratic, like public education in the West. Christian educators display their faith, not what they know. They give witness to their own faith. They do not impose the garb in which that faith is lived, but let each individual choose the cultural garb. They give witness through the communication of their personality inspired by faith. The church ceases to be church if it simply communicates a pedagogy. There are many signs that the church is disappearing in Europe because the faith is no longer passed on to the younger generations. What is transmitted is a certain pedagogy, which has no content, and hence holds no interest.

Indeed, a young person who received a Christian message but was not integrated into the people of God would be completely unable to express his or her attachment to Christianity concretely and would remain isolated. There cannot be a Christian who does not belong to a concrete community. Any Christian must be connected to the people of God through the mediation of concrete groups in which behaviors are passed on and reformed as in a people. Those who are young cannot do anything but think of reforming this church into which they have been brought.

Being eschatological, the people of God needs continual correction and reform. That can only be performed by the young, even though young people often have to struggle their whole lives to achieve even a portion of what they dreamed when young.

The Puebla Conference had a chapter devoted to the "preferential option for young people." The aim was to take the edge off the preferential option for the poor, by making it one instance among others. Even so, the option for young people was very good and could have changed the history of the church had it been taken seriously, but most Catholic educators did not have that in mind.

The meaning of an option for young people would be to give young people their due place in the church, being a force for reform and change. Certainly the writers were not thinking of that at all. What they intended was to study ways of winning over youth. In any case, the option for young people did not go anywhere; young people have never been given their proper role. They were never taken seriously because any change was ruled out in advance. It may well be that such an option for young people is the only way to refashion a people in the church, by moving away from the religious individualism that has been accepted so readily. But what hierarchy is going to trust young people?

Chapter 6

THE PEOPLE AS ACTOR

Ultimately a people means the poor who seek to govern themselves, free of the lords of the earth, subject only to the Lord of heaven. The concept of "people" is linked to the concept of history, which arose in the Bible, was lived in the past by the Christian church, was elaborated in the course of Western history since the Middle Ages, and was best formulated in nineteenth-century Romantic philosophies, i.e., in the great modern ideologies.

It is no accident that the concept of "people" disappears from consciousness when the concept of history disappears, as is happening today. History is made by peoples. The ancients were not familiar with this concept because for them history meant simply the narration of the past, a narration from which lessons of wisdom and examples for individual and group life might be drawn. This was a past closed in on itself and thus the Christian people is very different from the Greek *demos* and Roman *populus*, both of which are stable realities, fixed structures, regarded as a gift from the gods or sages.

Medieval Christendom was also based on a stable vision of society. It recognized the stability of social orders—clergy, warrior nobility, workers— and assumed that society had the stability of the cosmos described by Ptolemy. In this structure whose supreme value was "order" there was no place for a people.

But the biblical leaven could not be content with such a static vision. Even in the Middle Ages, there began to emerge a vision which sees history as an ongoing journey, ascent, search for something new, the journey of the Reign of God on earth. The key notion is that the Holy Spirit is beginning a new age in which the people will become more active and less dependent on the clergy. With the Spirit the people will build the Kingdom of God on this earth in a way quite similar to the eschatological end. Rather than expecting everything from God, human beings must build themselves on this earth. This idea, which was voiced clearly in the Middle Ages, thus has Christian roots and grew into the contemporary idea of people.

"People" means society becoming responsible for its future and seeking to win happiness and freedom on the earth. This conquest begins with free-dom over the forces of nature, making use of the earth and the energy and resources it provides. But this freedom is sought primarily in relation to all the powers that seek to dominate the people and yet regard them as a threat (landowners, feudal lords, and church hierarchy).

In the people all are free and fundamentally equal in the sense that there are neither dominators nor dominated, slaveholders nor slaves. In principle, all work together and help one another: freedom, equality, and fraternity are theoretically the conditions for a people. Yet those qualities are precisely what must be won, for they are resisted by the dominant who seek to win back what they have lost. The people must defend its rights, its essence. A people seeks to free itself and does not want to receive a freedom won by others, which would conceal a hidden domination. Hence the sovereignty of the people has been present from the beginning. Everything starts from peoplehood.

This people has power—it is stronger than its masters. It belongs to the future, for the future consists of the advent of peoples. This idea was para-mount in the nineteenth century, especially the first half, and reached its peak in the revolutions of 1848. It has been present in Latin America since the period of independence, but it came to the fore from 1960 to 1990, when Fidel Castro and Che Guevara were the heroes, and peaked with Sal-vador Allende (1970-1973) and the Sandinista period in Nicaragua (1979-1990).[1] "The people are the subject" was an oft-repeated slogan throughout the revolutionary period in Latin America. It is not surprising that the topic of the subject has declined at the very time the notion of "people" has gone into decline.[2]

From the outset it seems that there are two sides to the movement of liberation of the people in history and as history. First, the people is made up of lay people who seek to affirm the autonomy of the temporal world, the freedom to develop this world independently of clerical power. The people are the subject in the sense of being the driving force of temporal history, the history of this corporal and material world. That is the source of what will later emerge as "people" understood politically and temporally. Second, the people seeks to exercise agency in the religious realm, in opposition to the exorbitant privileges of the clergy, and seeks to return to early, pure Chris-tianity, and to become people of God. The adversary in the first case is the clergy as master of the temporal world, and in the second it is the clergy as distortion of early Christianity. Lay people seek two autonomies.

The origin of the idea of "people" has been traced to the medieval move-ment of communes, particularly in the thirteenth century,[3] reflecting both sides of the popular emancipation movements. Initially, there are two move-ments which will run through history in constant ambiguity. First there is the demand of lay people in the church who want to be church and protest against a purely clerical church. "People" appears as opposition to the clerical monopoly.[4] The people is made up of laity opposed to the clergy. Second, there is the natural desire for autonomy, which is expressed in the appeals of Aristotle and the philosophers of nature, who insist that the realities of earth have their own existence before their absorption into Christianity. The people takes a stand against religion's domination beyond its own realm. Thus we have laity versus clergy and the natural versus the supernatural.

Hence the commune or popular movement is not simply a movement of secularization, but also a move to return to nonclerical early Christianity. It is important to stress both these elements because the feeling of people—especially of the people of God—cannot be understood without taking this history into account. Both forces are at work throughout subsequent history, interacting with each other.

On the one hand, the people is formed by the movement of lay people freeing themselves from domination by the clergy. The church is of the laity, of the people. The great theologians of the late Middle Ages—Wyckliffe, Hus, Marsilius of Padua, William of Ockham—all drew on this idea, and all were condemned. They are significant because they show that the lay emancipation movement came into ever more intense conflict with the Catholic hierarchy.

But this movement—which is not just of some theologians, but ultimately is of a class that has now learned to read—is Christian. It is rooted in a theology of history: the Reign of God is not Christendom, but neither has it arrived yet. The Reign of God is a reign without imposition, earthly powers, or repression, a reign of freedom and equality. The people are journeying toward their own advent. A people is a subject seeking and making itself, an active subject struggling to fully exist. The true church must be born from it. This idea of a movement toward the true people keeps growing and thus clashes with the hierarchy.

The conflict finally broke out in 1517. Yet the Protestant explosion was still not the advent of the people. Neither Luther, Calvin, nor Zwingli thought of a church of the people. The idea was in the air, but the reformers imposed discipline on the reformation and retained a clergy, one that was in fact allied with political forces. They halted halfway or even earlier in the journey.

But the seed had been sown. Anabaptism took the popular principle all the way. The principle survived in Holland, crossed over to England, and was embodied in the Puritans who won a revolution in England, albeit temporarily. One part emigrated to the United States, where they founded what they thought was the true church of the people, and thus produced the free churches of the United States.

At the same time another development was interacting with the first one. From the communes onward, the idea of autonomy kept gaining ground: the idea of independence of political institutions from the church. Greek philosophy, especially Aristotle and his theory of nature and natural law, would provide the intellectual tools for helping promote the idea of the independence of the people vis-à-vis the church. Thomistic theology accepted this autonomy to some extent and produced a whole theological school that would serenely accept the existence of something natural alongside the church.[5]

The evolution of the issue of the laity went hand in hand with this two-fold evolution of the people. In the Middle Ages, "lay man" meant the opposite of cleric, that person in the church who wants to participate and be recognized as a true member of the people. "Lay man" also meant one who was claiming autonomy in the temporal world and wanted to free temporal life from the domination of the church. Here "lay person" meant emancipation from the extension of clerical power over temporal society. Hence, "lay" was applied in two ways: in civil society and in the church. In civil society lay or laicism meant excluding the church, i.e., clerical domination. In the church "laity" meant those who were challenging and questioning power in the church rather than the outside world. Both meanings developed in tandem, sometimes peacefully, sometimes at odds.

The problem was complicated by the emergence of states at this same time. They also arose in opposition to the church and to clerical power. That is why the incipient state sees itself as lay and invokes the arguments of laicism. It applies the attributes of the people to itself. It becomes a representative of the people, challenging clerical authority along its two lines: political-temporal and religious. From this point onward the people is facing not only the clergy but the state as well.

The state also has two roots. On the one hand it invokes nature, natural philosophy, and natural law, as though it were the rebirth of the Roman republic or the Roman empire. Hence, the kings claim to represent autonomous civil society: politics is autonomous. However, the kings also want to have a messianic mission in the people of God. They want to be the successors of the emperors who were the religious powers.

The kings act on two levels and supply themselves with two series of arguments, thus placing the peoples in a difficult situation. In struggling against the church the people could call on kings for help, but they ran the risk of becoming employees of the king, as happened in historic Protestantism. Or they struggled against both church and king and ran the risk of being crushed, as happened with the Anabaptists. This struggle was successful only under certain circumstances, such as in the United States, because of the absence of clerical power and the weakness of the king's power. Elsewhere, the people could be on the side of the clergy against the state, but that works only if the clergy has significant social weight.

Rivalry between these three forces, clergy, king, and people, has gone on for six centuries. When clergy and state have allied, the people have been kept mute. This is still the case to some degree in some Latin American countries. The people can only raise their voice if they gain power in the state or the clergy, especially if there is rivalry between the two.

If there were a distinction of levels between the power of the clergy and that of the state, if the people received what the clergy and the state promised them, problems would be much smaller than they are. But all three powers see themselves as messianic: the state regards itself as charged with establishing the Kingdom of God on earth; the clergy regards itself as delegated by God to establish the Reign of God on earth and in heaven; the people, as people of God, regards itself as unjustly deprived by the other two of being people of God already present on earth.

Who is the true subject of history? Who constructs the people of God? Who constructs the church? The state, the clergy, and the people all have claimed to do so, but it can be shown that the subject is actually the people. The earthly powers are necessary, each in its proper place, as services to the people of God. Neither the state nor the clergy are saviors. Through the institution of Jesus, the people is saved through the grace of the Holy Spirit, and in no other way. Both state and clergy are servants, but they do not make history. Only the people makes history, which is the journey of its liberation.

PEOPLE: SUBJECT OF HISTORY

The history of the West is the story of the rivalry between the three forces of hierarchy, people, and state. In 1825, Felicité de Lamennais, before he was expelled from the church, wrote the following about the hierarchy:

There is no church without the pope, there is no Christianity without the church; there is neither religion, nor society; thus the life of European nations has its source, its sole source, as we say, in papal power. Any attack against the power of the Sovereign Pontiff . . . is a crime of offense against religion . . . [and] a crime of offense against civilization, against society.

The popes themselves taught this, e.g., Boniface VIII in the bull *Unam Sanctam* (1302):

The temporal authority must be subject to the spiritual authority. If the earthly power errs it must be judged by the spiritual power, but if the spiritual power errs, let it be judged by the higher power. If the higher power errs, only God will be able to judge it, not man. Hence, we declare . . . that every human creature absolutely must be subject to the Roman pontiff.

This doctrine, stated firmly by Boniface VIII and under the influence of Romanticism by Lamennais, was taught for centuries and defended by the

"Ultramontane" party during the nineteenth and well into the twentieth century,[6] and it has fervent advocates even today.

The pope exercises this function in the name of the church. He is the liberator of the church, its servant. He combats emperors, kings, and the state in the name of the people and as defender of the people, who are never far from his mind. The pope is certain that ultimately it is the people who grant him legitimacy. He is there on behalf of the people of God and as their servant. Even if in practice this service is one of domination, it is domination in order to serve. So declared the decree of Nicholas II (1059), which reserved to the cardinals the election of the pope:

> Instructed by the authority of our predecessors and other holy fathers, we have decided and we order that after the death of a pope of the universal church of Rome, the cardinal bishops must together and with the most careful attention seek the most worthy one and afterwards meet with the cardinal clergy; and finally the rest of the clergy and people shall come forward to accept the new election.[7]

Henceforth the role of the people was that of simply accepting, but it was still present, as a remnant of the past and a sign of remorse. The role of the people has now diminished even more. Today the papal election is secret, with the result communicated to the people outside the election hall. There is no longer any sign of an active presence of the people.

The emperor also claims absolute power over the world and over the people of God. Since the time of Constantine, all emperors have regarded their role as all-embracing, simultaneously civil and religious. So wrote Alcuin, a monk ideologist and adviser to Charlemagne, to the king of the Franks who had become emperor. Alcuin first states that two persons have previously been endowed with universal authority, the pope and the ancient Roman emperor:

> In third place comes the royal dignity that Our Lord Jesus Christ has reserved for you so that you may govern the Christian people. It surpasses the other two dignities; it eclipses and surpasses them. Now the churches of Christ rely on you alone, from you alone they await their salvation, from you avenger of crimes, guide of those who stray, consolation of the afflicted, support of the good. . . .[8]

This claim remained in place throughout the history of the empire, and then of kings who claimed this same imperial power, exercised over the people of God, ever in competition with the pope. In the Americas, the kings of Spain and Portugal always acted as heads of the church by virtue of a divine investiture established by the popes. What interests us here, however, is that the emperors and kings always sought to justify their absolute power by delegation from the people, as if their power emanated from the people. Even in ancient Rome, the emperors claimed to have received absolute power by delegation from the people through the Royal Law.[9]

Indeed, the emperors invoked a special title from the Christian people who had conferred power on them, as stated in the annals of the empire of Charlemagne:

> And because the name of emperor had now ceased to exist in the land of the Greeks and because they had a woman as emperor, it was seen both by the apostolic Leo himself and all the holy fathers who were present in that council [i.e., the council held to decide the fate of Leo III and before which he took his purification oath] and the rest of the people, that they ought to name as emperor Charles himself, king of the Franks, who now held Rome itself, where the Caesars were always accustomed to have their residence, and the rest of the places which they held in Italy, Gaul, and Germany. For Almighty God conceded all these places into his hands, and therefore it seemed to them to be just, that he—with the aid of God and with all the Christian people asking— should not be lacking that title. King Charles did not wish to deny their request, and with all humility, subjecting himself to God and to the petition of the priests and all the Christian people, he received the title of emperor through the coronation of the lord pope Leo.[10]

The entire history of the monarchy in Europe attests to these two features: a) the king claims to have authority over the whole country, over the civil people and the religious people fused into a single people, namely, Christendom; b) the king claims to justify his absolute power by delegation from the people, drawing legitimacy from the people which is the sign of God's will; yet he also claims to receive his power from the priests, who have acknowledged his superiority, just as the pope affirms his superiority over earthly sovereigns.

We come to the crux of the matter: modern states have not radically broken away from this model—they are also the heirs of kings and emperors. First, they claim to have a universal role, governing human beings in their totality. They have an ideology—free market, socialist, or fascist— which is the secularized expression of Christianity. States are not simply administrative machinery; they are the saviors of the people and want to achieve what Christendom has failed to do.

Second, they claim to constitute the emancipation of the people, they invoke investiture from the people, and all claim to be democratic. In some manner, they seek to make even the external forms express this popular origin of their power. However, they are not simply government by the people. They exercise total authority, a domination that is the continuation of the monarchy. The people are regularly called on to renew the investiture of the rulers, but what is done is not by their decision. Through ideology rulers are able to convince the people to confirm them in power. That is true in liberal democracy, but some forms of rule are even more hierarchical.

The Declaration of the Rights of Man and the Citizen (August 26, 1791) begins, "The representatives of the French People, formed into a National Assembly, . . . recognizes and declares, in the presence and under the auspices of the Supreme Being, the following Rights of Man and of the Citizen."[11] In Hegel's philosophy of the state, the Spirit is realized in the people and through the people in history. But the people only becomes a historic people through the mediation of the state.[12] This concept has prevailed through history: it associates the state with the movement of history. Even Marxism, which proclaimed the disappearance of the state, ultimately made it the moving force of history throughout the Soviet empire. Fascist states arrogantly claim that their mission as saviors of the people comes from the people. Hitler believed that the Nazi state would give the German people happiness for a thousand years: it would be the achievement of the millennium and the full realization of the Reign of God. What appeared there in a grotesque and aggressive form is still present, in a more civilized way, in the minds of many rulers of states in the modern age. They have never satisfactorily defined their relationship with the people, or with the people of God, for they do not want to surrender their messianic aura.[13]

Modern secularization has not been complete because the state has claimed a saving function and has expressed its ideology through religious signs that are secularized but are still identified with the clergy. They also claim to come from the people, the people of God which is said to have conferred on them a saving mission. Modern democracy is a secularized form of the people of God. Both clergy and the state have claimed a messianic mission: they seek to be saviors of the world. They invoked investiture from the people, and ultimately investiture by God, but such investiture has been an illusion or deceit: no one replaces the people.

This brings us to postmodernity. In recent decades there has been a strong critique of the state and its ideology and power of domination, and a demystification of the state's role as savior and of its institutions. We might have expected this critique to have been a liberation of the people, but unfortunately that has not happened. What has emerged is not the people, but the individual.[14] Margaret Thatcher said that she knew only individuals, not "the people." Indeed, she announced the advent of a new age: a policy of reducing the functions of state, restricting them more and more. With the messianic ideology of the state gone, what is left? Only the state as police, guardian of order, reduced to its function of sole wielder of violence.

In this instance, the concern is not for the advent of the people but for the market. The critique of the state was not the product of popular movements—quite the contrary. Under the circumstances, the humiliation of the state would not have been possible—and would not have issued in its dismantling—had it not coincided with the advent of economic globalization. It was the new supranational economic powers that wanted to destroy the state: the financial groups that engage in worldwide economic speculation, the multinationals that control most of world production, submitting everything to the law of profit and capital accumulation. In all of this there is no people; only the consumer exists. Not everyone is a consumer, only those who have access to money, which makes it possible to consume. Never has there been such a wholesale destruction of the people—the impression that populations are being offered happiness and freedom notwithstanding.

Moreover, the critique of the state leaves one with a suspicion, namely that it is not about the reduction of all states, but of all except one: the United States. The critique is not aimed at the United States, which as the power of world domination is above any critique. The critique is aimed only at social policy in the United States, anything that hinders the freedom of large corporations. But the large corporations need and demand the help of the American state to open world markets for them. For that they need to destroy and make other states harmless. That is being done, albeit not always as fully as desired.

The United States has an ideology that is both civil and religious. It regards itself as the only really Christian power, the one intended by God to bring about the happiness of the world. It is considered the great savior, especially by those who have economic power and are in the ruling class. Consciousness of being the power intended by God to rule the world was arrogantly manifested in the rejection of the Kyoto environmental accords.[15] There are no prospects of the United States doing anything to help other countries in need, unless profits are to be made.

The historic character of the people is illuminated by its biblical foundations. History in the Western sense comes from biblical eschatology. We now turn to the eschatological foundations of the people in its various meanings.

THE PEOPLE IN ESCHATOLOGY

Leaving questions of Israel's historic origins to historians, what has been decisive for peoplehood, particularly in the West, has been the Bible's description of Israel. From the outset Israel is eschatological: it is, but is not yet. It is people of God, but not yet. It is called to be what it is from the beginning. It knows that it will never be what it is, except through a final intervention by God who called it, as if God wished to force it to go to the limit of its possibilities, while recognizing its incapability.

The people of Israel is hope and eschatological reality always on the way. Why this never-ending journey? Because the people is ever absorbed by the forces of inertia, it lets itself be assimilated into its environment, it dissipates in the midst of all the world's populations which do not have the same hope.

Israel begins with the patriarchs, and they are the paradigm. Ever on the move, migrants, with no stability, a pilgrim people with no land of their own, the patriarchs are the image that Israel pursues from the beginning to this day, ever struggling in the midst of dominant forces, seeking a foothold in history that will allow them to live. Abraham has to give in to the Pharaoh but he survives. Jacob is saved because his son Joseph, through the forces of fate, has been a slave in Egypt, and after a series of unforeseeable events is able to save his family from famine.

When Israel is in danger of being assimilated by Egypt, Moses takes it from the land of slavery and thrusts it into the unknown, into the danger of the desert. For forty years the people live on the road, with no assurance, no base, no ground in which to take root. Before entering into Canaan, the people are frightened at the site of the Canaanite cities and ask: how can we win? They enter Canaan in unending battle, then battle the Philistines to defend the land won. Other struggles follow. With the kings the people are deceived by apparent security in stability; at last the people of God will take firm hold. But this is when the people of God is most in danger of falling apart. A long struggle of the people against the kings begins. Under those circumstances the people is constituted by the prophets and a small group of their disciples who dare to confront the king's power. The historic books of the Bible portray Israel as always in a struggle as people of God in the midst of a wide range of adversaries. The most dangerous were those within, such as the kings.

With exile the people again become more authentic, but at the cost of losing all their possessions. Yet exile is an enormous temptation: how can a small flock resist the psychological pressure of a huge empire? The people appears in its purest form just when it needs to preserve itself while confronting a total power. Cyrus appears as savior. Israel returns to its land, but only to fall back into domination and corruption. Such is the situation in Israel when Jesus is born.

In the time of Jesus, the people are dominated by imperial power, the priests and the temple, the scholars and the wealthy. The temple should be the sign of the freedom of the people celebrating the true God against idols, but it has fallen into corruption; the law ought to guarantee the freedom of the people, but it has been turned into an unbearable yoke. The land should belong to everyone, but there are rich and poor, and the poor are like Lazarus. All the signs of the people have become signs of domination.

Where are the people? In Jesus and in the disciples who are willing to return to the journey of the patriarchs. Like the patriarchs, they have no home of their own. The people of God is on pilgrimage again (cf. 1 Peter) and finds itself ever in diaspora.

The first Christian generations were conscious of being the true Israel, the true people of God. After confronting the opposition of those who are ruling Israel, Christians have to confront the Roman empire. From the three hundred years of resistance to the Roman empire, they recall the memory of the martyrs who represent the true people of God, but this did not take place without difficulty. Alongside the martyrs were the "traitors," those who denied the faith, and were much more numerous than the martyrs. They created the problem of the *lapsi* (the fallen), who wanted to be reconciled to the church. The struggle against the insidious penetration by the whole context of the dominant civilization was never-ending.

Constantine was celebrated as the new David or the new Solomon by the theologians of the empire, like Eusebius of Caesarea. Many accepted the conversion of the Roman emperors as though it would inaugurate an era of peace and prosperity for the people of God, but history repeated itself. The empire became the biggest problem of all, bringing the corruption of the people. Christendom was celebrated for fifteen centuries as though it were the peace and tranquility of the people of God, as a sign of the Reign of God on earth. But as with Israel and the temple, God's worst enemy was found to be within it. The people of God had apparently triumphed in the sacred empire, the clergy, official legislation, in the imposition of Christianity as obligatory religion, but actually the true people of God was hidden beneath all of this panoply, in movements of return to the gospel that reappeared each generation to question the established system of the supposedly Christian society.

The people of God is always present behind the official façade of the people. Normally it is a minority, as in ancient Israel—the prophets whom God stirs up in every age. The true people of God is in the struggle for the people to really become people of God.

How to recognize the presence of the true people of God, a people like other peoples but different, a people that is the soul of other peoples? The sign of the people of God is that it acts to free, build, increase, and develop the people. Of course everyone says that—all the powers claim to be serving the people, but the reality is otherwise. Worldly powers are ambiguous. Certainly they bring some benefits to the people, because nothing on earth is absolute evil, but while they promote the good of the people, they also promote their own benefit, and often that is what comes first.

The clergy promote the good of the people but they also promote their own as a social class. The issue is not individual behavior—individually the members of the clergy are almost always selfless, but when the issue is one of class, the priestly caste, they defend class privileges tooth and nail. The clergy defend the good of the people but in a way that does not jeopardize their own power. Few times in history have the clergy spontaneously given up any privilege. When it did so, as in the case of some Latin American bishops who turned over the lands of their dioceses to small farmers, they were rebuked by higher authorities. Their sin was defending the rights of the people over the rights of the church. Rome has always been resistant to giving up any of its power, most notably in the case of the papal states, which a number of popes defended with every possible military and political weapon, when it was obvious that these states were a scandal, among other reasons because as a head of state the pope had to engage in violence.

States promote the good of the people, but they also promote their own good, the growth of their power and might in the midst of other states. Modern history attests to endless wars, in which millions of human beings have been annihilated and have endured unspeakable suffering, solely because of the ambition of some states.

* * *

Historically, the Christian people has had to struggle for its own existence against civil or temporal powers and against church powers. It has never had a peaceful life or lack of problems. Without retracing the history of these struggles we will note some facts. We have already noted the medieval communes, where a wide range of works of solidarity and Christian charity were developed, with men and women devoted to serving their neighbor. These were the precursors of a welfare society where all are provided for. The communes were able to keep their distance from bishops and from kings and princes but were unable to preserve their independence indefinitely.[16] The Italian cities also struggled but they likewise fell into the hands of the aristocracy. The many popular movements between the thirteenth and sixteenth centuries were unable to resist the power of the kings and the Catholic hierarchy. The sole exception was Switzerland, where the cantons were able to gain autonomy, probably because of their poverty.[17]

The Protestant Reformation aroused great hope, but it was soon extinguished when the leaders of the movement surrendered to the princes or created authoritarian republics, as well as retaining a clergy like the old one, to whom the people were subject. But Protestantism opened the way for a more freedom-oriented conception of the Christian church, e.g., the Anabaptist and Puritan lines led to the American colonies, which proclaimed their independence. This was the first time that a people rose up against the king without interference from a clerical church. For the first time since Switzerland, a people had the opportunity to establish itself as people. The people become a people when they take on their own destiny collectively, and emancipate themselves from any higher power (religious, political, military, racial).

The people is expressed, for example in the U. S. Declaration of Independence:

> We, therefore, the Representatives of the United States of America, in
> general Congress, assembled, appealing to the supreme Judge of the

World for the Rectitude of our Intentions, do, in the Name, and by Authority of the good People of these Colonies, solemnly Publish and Declare, That these United Colonies are, and of Right ought to be, free and independent states.

Likewise the United States constitution (September 17, 1787) begins, "We the people of the United States. . . ." The people takes on its destiny, defines the rules for its common life, and decides on how to choose its rulers. Thus "people" means history, in the sense of Christian eschatology. The people journeys through obstacles toward its own fulfillment. It is aware that civil and clerical powers are necessary but it also knows that these powers tend to take it away from its mission.

The greatest contemporary challenge is to understand that the dominant forces tend to destroy the people. They do not need peoples; they only need the consumers who make up a vast market. The people is an obstacle because it stands for tasks other than those of a sheer globalized market. The dominant forces need an atomized world where everyone is nothing but a consumer, and where money can circulate freely, and peoples do not raise barriers. Individualism is so strong that the sense of peoplehood, the eschatological consciousness of being on a journey in which the people of God seeks itself in all the peoples of the earth, is tending to disappear.

Some declare "the end of history." But the history of the West is eschatology. What the powerful fear is precisely eschatology: the constant presence of this people, repeatedly repressed but ever coming back, journeying tirelessly toward its fulfillment. If there is no more history, there is no more people, and everything stays as it is. Time becomes the endless repetition of the same gestures where the only difference is quantitative, rising and falling currencies and stock prices.

Despite claims that history is no more, the people are there—hidden again, but present, and their presence will be made known. The powers will not prevail. Appearances notwithstanding, the people are still persevering and journeying.

PEOPLE AND FREEDOM

What does a people seek? Freedom. How does it seek freedom? Through freedom.

A people is not made up of slaves. Greek cities and the Roman republic were not democracies or peoples, because only men—not women, slaves, or foreigners—from traditional families had the rights of citizens. Despite the emancipation of slaves and women, in certain regions the process of constituting peoplehood is still very weak. Large numbers of human beings have no access to freedom whatsoever. This is not surprising because seeking freedom demands the possession of minimal living conditions and minimum social independence. A person who can only survive cannot think about freedom. One has to overcome the deeply rooted fear experienced by poor people around the world.

The starting point is freedom of thought, which has not been allowed in many civilizations and even today is repressed in many parts of the world. Since the eighteenth century, freedom of thought has been the basic issue in the entire movement for democracy in the West, the culmination of a movement which started in the eleventh century, though it was always marginal to established society. The struggle for freedom of thought was aimed at the entire political and social system of Christian society. Because the clergy, and especially the hierarchy, were the bearers of the official ideology, the battle was aimed primarily against their control over thought.

One of the worst tragedies of Christendom was that for centuries the hierarchy was absolutely opposed to freedom of thought. It was completely blind, unable to understand what was happening, and invoked increasingly senseless arguments against freedom of thought. It failed to see that freedom of thought was born within the people of Israel and the Christian people. This was one of the reasons why the Catholic Church lost almost all of Europe, and if it continues in the same way it will lose the rest. Asking forgiveness is not enough; mistakes need to be corrected. When the movement for freedom of thought triumphed for Europe in the French Revolution (it had existed since the seventeenth century in England and the United States, beyond the reach of the Catholic Church) the hierarchy reacted by solemnly condemning freedom of thought. In 1791 Pope Pius VI wrote to the archbishop of Aix on the Civil Constitution of the Clergy, which he said allows people to "think, say, write and even have published anything they want about religion." He ridiculed the assembly's claim that this "monstrous right" should flow from the "freedom and equality that are natural to all human beings." In 1834 Gregory XVI called freedom of conscience "error, or rather madness . . ." which leads to the "ruin of religious and civil society," and yet is going so far that some claim that it is "of great benefit to religion."[18] There is no need to multiply texts of this kind. Only at Vatican II did the hierarchy accept the religious freedom which is the basis for freedom of thought. Without personal thought there can be no subject and no people.

"Sapere aude" (Dare to know) was modernity's slogan. Being a citizen entails having the courage to think for oneself, i.e., not thinking as one's family or leader thinks; one cannot let fear of the powerful keep one from thinking.

* * *

In early Christianity, evangelization meant awakening to freedom and beginning to think freely. Times have changed, to the point where evangelization paradoxically means imposing a closed system of thought.

Yet freedom of thought, freedom to think against preconceived ideas, against what the authorities think, and even against the laws of kings and princes, arose not in Athens—Socrates did not have the audacity to criticize the laws of the city—but in Israel with the prophets. They were the first who dared to challenge, refute, and accuse the established authorities and the majority of the people who identified with their oppressors. The prophets, admittedly few, were the first free thinkers.

The long history to the point where many began to think freely was never separated from its origins in the prophets. It is true that the prophets were persecuted not only by the authorities but by the mass of the people who abandoned them in times of danger. We can assume that in their hearts many of the poorest agreed with the prophets, but did not say so out of fear. This still happens today: many disagree with the powerful but do not have the courage to admit it, because they would have to pay too high a price.

Let us not deceive ourselves. It is easy to criticize heads of state because they no longer represent authority. But criticize the owner of the company where you work or the professor on whom you depend for a test grade? It is difficult to take a stand against fashions, against the idols of the moment or mainstream media opinions. The prophets of Israel opened the way to dissidence, and a great deal can still be learned from them.

Today if we ask Catholics whether they define themselves as a people made up of free, active, and autonomous subjects, the question would strike most of them as strange. That is not their idea of themselves. Catholics are regarded as obedient, conservative, submissive, not thinking for themselves but thinking with the church, i.e., like the hierarchy. Not thinking for oneself is regarded as a virtue. For those outside of the church it would be absurd to define Catholicism as a freedom movement—they would point out that all emancipation movements in recent centuries have taken place against the church hierarchy, which ceaselessly attempted to curtail thinking.

Yet if we look at the early church, at Jesus and the apostles, we see something else. Jesus comes on the scene as a pure representative of free thought. Unencumbered by self-interest or personal hatred, he says what he thinks, what he feels, what he wants, with utter simplicity and aware of the dangers. He knows that what he says goes against the official truth defended by all the authorities of Israel. He knows that speaking the truth is the first step of freedom; it is the very act of freedom. The apostles follow the same path: it is better to obey God than men, they tell the authorities of their people, even though the apostles are uneducated and powerless, the kind of people who remain silent in the presence of authorities and never dare to contradict them.

This was the age of the martyrs who solidly witnessed to the value of freedom of thought and word. Control over thinking began later when the church was "converted" to the empire, and it has lasted for fifteen centuries. Catholics forgot the ages of freedom. Being a Christian meant submitting to the religion of the empire. For fifteen centuries being a Christian could mean accepting the religion of the empire, Christendom, one's parents—or accepting the gospel of Jesus Christ. But these two aims could clash; and then the people of God stood with the rejected of the people.

Other freedoms depend on freedom of thought. "Uniform thought" little by little forms a prison that does not allow for taking any initiative, applying any plan of action that is not accepted by the hierarchy—which means the pope, because the bishops also are not free to take any significant initiative either. Theologians have recently shown how for the hierarchy truth has increasingly become a set of propositions stated with fixed words. It is as though God has given humankind a code of statements and entrusted it to the hierarchy. The hierarchy's mission is seen as protecting and defending this deposit against distortions and attacks by the people of God.[19] The hierarchy is increasingly seen as magisterium, i.e., as guardian of orthodoxy and single teaching power, the *ecclesia docens*. Teaching means the magisterium, and what it teaches is always the same set of propositions.

The extent of the magisterium has grown enormously, especially since the nineteenth century. The magisterium increasingly claims to speak the official word of the church on everything human. There is no more room for a Christian to say anything original, because almost everything has been said by the documents of the magisterium.[20] When new issues arise, it has to give answers that are true, and so the body of revealed truths keeps growing. In the twentieth century, the documents of the magisterium expanded to the point where very few can read everything published by the Vatican.

All these truths make it possible to condemn the actions of clergy and lay people who are not in agreement with the Holy See's strategy. Anyone taking initiatives will always run into contradiction with some text of the magisterium, and can be condemned. A good Catholic must keep quiet and obey. In the name of truth, the Holy See cuts off initiative because the magisterium is better at condemning than communicating. It starts with the assumption that any Catholic is a possible heretic. Simply writing makes one a suspect.

Certainly there have always been free voices in the hierarchy, the clergy, and the Christian people; the people of God has always been active. In all generations there have been free persons who attacked the falsification of the gospel in the name of the "truth." Many have been persecuted by church authorities, such as Bartolomé de las Casas (d. 1566), who had barely taken office in his diocese when he was expelled by landowners who felt threatened. There was the case of Montesinos and the Dominicans in Santo Domingo, who criticized the horrors of the conquest, and were imprisoned and sent back to Spain, where they were harshly punished for having challenged the authority of the conquerors.

Centuries later some are rehabilitated and even cited as proof that the church has always been present in the just causes of the liberation of the poor, and concerned with social justice. Some have even been beatified and canonized. But when they were condemned, expelled, and martyred by the church itself, they constituted the true people of God; they were free.

Free Christians have often been treated as heretics. That is why Catholics have to learn from the separated churches, which have usually been expelled from the Catholic Church by the hierarchy for freedom of thought. What they wanted was not to be separated but to think for themselves. Rather than having a dialogue, the Catholic hierarchy thought that the evil had to be "cut out at the root," i.e., they already knew it was an evil. Expulsion meant condemning freedom of thought.

Indeed, modern democratic revolutions have been carried out in the name of God and Christianity (the "Revolution of the Saints" in seventeenth-century England). An entire book has been written on "Europe, mother of revolutions," showing that modern revolutions are rooted in Christendom and in Christianity.[21] Even anti-Catholic and atheistic revolutions have been carried out in the name of a Christianity that had already been rejected by a magisterium closed to any freedom.

It is no coincidence that Vatican II, which highlighted the "people of God" in order to explain the church, was also the council that accepted religious freedom. There is no people without freedom and freedom exists only in a people. An attack against one of these ideas assaults the other. We may conclude that behind the rejection of "people of God" in the past two decades is a restraint on freedom.

PEOPLE MEANS COVENANT

The people of God is a communion, but it must be kept in mind that this is so through covenant. Contemporary spiritualistic movements tend to defend communion as an emotional union. The hierarchy tends to defend it as common submission to the pope. Communion may also be understood as people being absorbed into an encompassing totality, a cosmic, quasi-organic community. It can also be understood as uniformity of thought or action.

Again our starting point is the people of Israel, the people of the covenant. The Bible speaks of this covenant in different ways. The traditions are garbed in the traits of the priestly or Deuteronomic author, but the initial significance can still be recognized. The twelve stones that were the memorial of the crossing of the Jordan (Jos 4) or the altar built "as a witness between us and our descendents" (Jos 22:16-18) signifies a covenant. This covenant is sealed by God, not by any human power. God's presence in the covenant is a warning that no other human power may usurp God's place and undo the covenant.

The image of the twelve tribes itself represents the covenant. The tribes are equal and have equal rights. They make the covenant voluntarily; no one is forced. Moses himself offered a sacrifice to conclude the covenant, and "built an altar at the foot of the mountain, and set up the twelve pillars, corresponding to the twelve tribes of Israel" (Ex 24:4). The covenant is not simply a commitment between God and each person, but a commitment of the people to itself, a commitment that constitutes the people and is consecrated by God, a commitment to unity around God's law.

The theme reappears in the New Testament, at the Last Supper, when Jesus speaks of his blood poured out, the blood of the new covenant. This covenant is made with the twelve apostles, the successors and representatives of the twelve tribes. Jesus sets them up to govern the tribes of Israel. The supper is the sacrifice that seals the covenant as in the time of Moses. They will form a people, the people of the new Israel, confirmed in the law of God. This law is what unites the tribe; God's law is freedom, love in freedom. What unites the tribes and makes the people of Jesus is shared pursuit of freedom in love.

In instructing his followers about the relationship among them, Jesus always uses the model of the covenant: "You know that the rulers of the Gentiles lord it over them, and their great ones are tyrants over them. It will not be so among you; but whoever wishes to be great among you must be your servant, and whoever wishes to be first among you must be your slave" (Mt 20:25-27). "The greatest among you will be your servant. All who exalt themselves will be humbled, and all who humble themselves will be exalted" (Mt 23:11-12). These texts mean that relations among the disciples will be relations between equals, and no one will be above the rest. Jesus understands relations between the disciples in terms of the covenant model.

In early Christianity, communities are always governed collectively: the apostles travel together; the communities are directed by colleges of presbyters. All the churches are equal and relate to one another as equals, even though the Jerusalem community has a certain privilege of honor. The theme of the equality of the churches and of the covenant between the churches runs through the patristic period, although certain churches in large capital cities are given a preeminence of honor.[22] To this day the Eastern church maintains this image of covenant between equal sibling churches.

In the West the theology of unity expanded to the point where it completely displaced the patristic tradition. The principle of unity came from Greek (especially neo-Platonist) philosophy as the imperial political ideology. The popes held onto the ideology of Rome and pressed it into service for their universal power. The definition of the pope's role was raised to the point of being the unity of the world, of the church, and of the peoples, a role that had no basis in Peter's mission in the New Testament.

When the pope was made synonymous with the unity of the church—and placed above it—the theme of covenant became irrelevant. Churches were no longer equal or interrelated. The church of Rome was above them all and claimed to govern them. The idea of the universal church as institution rather than covenant was born. In that universal church the head is the Roman church, and all the particular churches are parts or fragments of this universal church. Gradually the name "church" was reserved for the universal church, headed by Rome, and the particular churches were given the administrative term "dioceses," and they become mere administrative subdivisions of the Roman church. This theory, created in Rome and imposed on all Catholics, held sway until Vatican II. It has reappeared in the pontificate of John Paul II, despite all the talk about collegiality in which the Roman theory is taken for granted.

The rebirth of the ecclesiology of the first thousand years with the idea of collegiality (another way of saying "covenant") was a surprise in the Vatican II texts. We will later return to the hopes born of the council.

* * *

The idea of covenant has passed into the daily life of the peoples of Christendom at least since the eleventh century. The notion that a people is a covenant has always been present at the origins of communal life: a people is formed only on the basis of an agreement between free citizens. There is no covenant without freedom, and without a covenant there is no freedom, because a solitary human cannot gain freedom.

What about the people of God? The new Code of Canon Law recognizes freedom of association, after almost all states in the world have recognized it, but the principle of covenant is still reduced to a minimum. In its second millennium, the church was organized at almost all levels around the monarchical principle. The effort has lasted a thousand years. The upshot is that everything has been centralized around an absolute boss: pope (universal church), bishop (diocese), pastor (parish). New communities and new initiatives keep appearing, but the system keeps working to reduce everything to centralization, and hence nothing escapes monarchical power.

The parish is the form of integration where all Catholics experience this. What is typical of the parish is that all powers related to it are in the hands of a priest, who decides by himself as a sovereign. After the principle of collegiality was introduced at the council, attempts were made to set up parish councils, but they do not have decision-making power. Their members are generally chosen by the pastor, and they are there only as long as they agree with the pastor—who in any case decides by himself. This is not really different from before, when the pastor always sought advisors. Even now when some associations have canonical recognition, a pastor is unlikely to allow the existence of groups that are not under his direct control or direction, as devotional organizations used to be.

There has been talk of the parish as a "community of communities." This formula is being applied with positive results in some places. But its application depends entirely on the pastor, and few pastors are willing to grant sufficient autonomy to base communities. Nothing in tradition, custom, or the official structures helps persuade them to give up their own absolute power over everything that happens in the parish. In most cases, the pastor imposes his style, his program, and his person on communities, which are supposed to reproduce the parish system. That is why so many so-called "base communities" are devoted almost exclusively to traditional activities in the parish with little or no contact with the neighborhood, the outside world, other religious groups, or social programs in the region. If the parish meant the organization of a community of autonomous communities, it could be aimed at the world for the sake of evangelization. This is where the covenant principle most urgently needs application.

Bishops have generally proven to be more "collegial" than parish priests, more sensitive to the covenant principle. They try to govern with the consent of the priests, or at least most of them, even though nothing in canon law forces them to do so. The council seems to have done a lot to develop episcopal spirituality (e.g., based on the Medellín and Puebla documents). Spirituality for priests has developed less, and it remains stuck in the past, because seminary formation reproduces what has been traditional since the seventeenth century in Europe.

The problem is that the diocese is an artificial unit, an administrative boundary. Canon law regards the bishop as called to administer a region more or less arbitrarily drawn on the map of the country. If he gets together with the priests it is around his power, or to administer the region; there is no object of common concern. Of course, everyone says that their common concern is evangelization, but that evangelization is abstract, in words, without any specific object, and naturally it is inoperative. In practice, evangelization means administering the diocese. Some bishops on their own go out to engage the society in which they live, but they do so as a personal calling, not by virtue of their function.

The real unity that ought to constitute a particular church should not be decreed by some office in Rome, but simply embrace the city. The church exists for the city, to evangelize the city. That comes before administering existing communities, which should be continually invited to send out missionaries so as to be the Christian presence and message in the city. The diocese does not feel responsible for the city, and so it does not act in the city as city. It takes refuge in the tranquility of parish communities, turning them into private enterprises oblivious to what is going on in the city.

Leading the particular church—which means the church in the city—along with the bishop is a council guided by a number of advisors. The particular church encourages, nourishes, and supports evangelizers who are witnesses to the Christian message throughout the city. Cities have to be made into true cities. The church has an indispensable leavening role. It cannot run away from the chaos, trying to survive by itself.[23]

Standing at the head of the church of the city, a single man cannot decide everything, even if he has the final word. A single man cannot be sensitive to everything that happens in the city. He has to be joined by all kinds of people with many capabilities. A bishop, now dead, once told me that learning about the city was never a problem. Every day he used to go to the city square to buy a paper, and there he would find the whole city, and he learned everything that was happening. That is no longer the situation in today's cities. His excellency the bishop would be unlikely to find out everything going on in the city in the city square.

If we think of the church worldwide, episcopal collegiality was one of the burning issues of the council, and we know its fate since then.[24] The council defined the theological principles, but did not go into the applications, and so they have never been applied. Roman synods are merely parodies of collegiality, because the conclusions are written by the Curia before the assemblies take place and what the bishops intend to say is irrelevant. If there is no real collegiality in the episcopate, how can we imagine there will be collegiality between local churches? How could they communicate, since they are all alike, faithful copies of the Roman church?

The small reforms in the Curia have only served to further centralize all power, and to extend control over all Catholics, particularly bishops. Episcopal collegiality has been reduced to a community of feeling. Collegiality means everyone together obeying the pope. The bishops conferences that have not been reduced to silence and to purely administrative functions are constantly the object of continual destabilizing maneuvers, as has been happening in Brazil since 1970. The Episcopal Council of Brazil (CNBB) has had three dynamic presidents, and all three have been punished. CELAM (Latin American Bishops Conference) was so humiliated in Santo Domingo (1992) that it is now virtually useless.

The people is constituted by covenant between communities. The church is called to be people of God. There is still a long way to go. It must free itself from being dominated by the monarchical principle which comes from the empire of neo-Platonic philosophy, and it must return to the gospel. Everywhere there are seeds of hope, the beginnings of exchange, the beginnings of equality between autonomous communities. Many feel that the idea of service highlighted by the council needs to be interpreted in the sense of a covenant between equals, and not in the imperial sense which is that of dominating in order to serve.

Chapter 7

PEOPLE OF THE POOR

Since Medellín (1968) and Puebla (1979) the Latin American church has asserted more clearly that the poor occupy a special place in the people of God, that the poor are a characteristic of the people of God, and that the true church is the church of the poor. Bishops conferences have spoken in these terms and a number of church movements have felt legitimized by this teaching.[1]

This was the context that gave rise to the CEBs (Christian base communities)[2] which many regarded as embodying the church of the poor. They arose within the poor and were recognized in the church independently of the parish system although that was not made explicit. CEBs were set up by priests or sisters linked to the parish who understood parishes as associations of communities, and so they gave each community sufficient autonomy vis-à-vis the parish. However, that autonomy depended on the goodwill of the pastor; when clergy were transferred the communities lost their support.

CEBs were recognized by the Latin American hierarchy but had no canonical status and were viewed with suspicion by Rome, which imagined that they were a Marxist intrusion of class conflict in the church. As soon as the poor are seen as real actors, it looks like class struggle; the poor are supposed to be well-behaved and grateful.

Over time it has become clear that the CEBs were not the church of the poor, but only a basic step toward the poor. Despite the current resistance by the clergy and the desire of many to go backward, we must go even further.

The CEBs have become parish-oriented and hence have lost contact with the poorest.[3] Those participating in CEBs were poor: not the poorest, the excluded, but rather those poor who had attained a minimally stable life. Rather than advancing toward the poor, the CEBs became enclosed within a certain cultural level, an elite among the poor. As happens in church history, institutions founded for the poor or by the poor rise on the social scale, and the poor are left behind. For the CEBs to go back to their origins they need to return to the poor and start over with the lowliest of the poor.

Insofar as the CEBs adopt parish activities, they are no longer of interest to the poor. CEBs have responded to the poor and continue to do so somewhat, but they are in danger of falling into formalism. They can end up like a number of religious orders that were founded to serve the poor, but after a century became part of the bourgeois culture.

However, the current low regard among the clergy for the CEBs is not because they fail to serve the poor, but because the clergy has gone back to ignoring the poor. The institutions now in vogue are the "movements," almost all of them middle class and with a certain standard of living. They have nothing against the poor, but simply ignore them.[4]

In this respect they are in tune with the dominant neoliberal model. During the age of the "welfare state," the official political line held that redistribution was necessary so that the poor would have a basic living standard, but neoliberals argued that help for the poor should be suppressed because it is counterproductive; instead of helping resolve the problem of the poor, aid fuels it; rather than prodding the poor to get out of poverty it encourages laziness.[5] Cutting social spending has been the prevailing line since Reagan in the 1980s.[6]

Other countries are pressured to do the same. Whenever a country is in a crisis over making debt payments, the IMF prescription is always the same: cut social spending. Brazil has been a good pupil, and some (Chile, Argentina, Central America) are even better. To keep up appearances, the government classifies as social spending some expenses that really serve the interests of the wealthy.

During the 1990s, international agencies changed their line. As poverty in the world increased, they began to speak of the struggle against poverty as a priority for all nations, but in practice they continue to recommend cutting social spending, and impose policies that lead to greater poverty. More recently their rhetoric has improved a little: they have discovered that poverty comes from inequality so they now call for a struggle against inequality. But the policies imposed by the IMF, World Bank, and WTO are still increasing inequality. Their statements are sheer demagoguery to lull the growing worldwide opposition.

The fact is that in the past fifteen years real interest in the poor—not just by those in authority but in public opinion in general and the Catholic Church in particular—has waned alarmingly. That is a sign that we are headed in the wrong direction.

IN SEARCH OF THE POOR OF JESUS CHRIST

Who are the poor of Jesus Christ? In the time of Bartolomé de las Casas—about whom Gustavo Gutiérrez has written a wonderful book subtitled *In*

Search of the Poor of Jesus Christ—it meant the Indians.[7] The gospels show us Jesus seeking out his poor: he sends his disciples out to the lost sheep of the people of Israel. Who are those lost sheep today? No doubt the same as those who appear in his speech in Matthew 11: the blind, the lame, lepers, the deaf, and the poor, who include all the other categories. In the gospels these words of Jesus are highlighted, and hence they are very much alive in the mind of the first community, and they are the basic guideline for the behavior of the first disciples.

The author of the Acts of the Apostles highlights the role of the rich in the community, showing the help that they provide by making their wealth available to the needy. The rich have a place but they are to serve the poor who are the center.[8] From Paul's letters we know that his communities were poor. He is aware that some are rich but the condition for being a Christian is to share, and to make their property serve the needs of the poor.[9]

In the early centuries the church was of the poor. It could not be otherwise, because it was a legally prohibited religion and liable to be persecuted at any time. That was not the ideal situation for attracting the rich, though there were notable examples of martyrs from rich families. According to Origen, the pagans ridiculed Christians for their low social level.[10]

The apostles went out in search of the poor of Jesus Christ. Paul's strategy of working to earn a living in the cities where he wanted to evangelize is very significant. By choosing to do manual work, Paul went to live and work in the poorest neighborhoods. He did not use the method of philosophers and vendors of pagan wisdom, which apparently were imitated by some Christian missionaries, i.e., Paul's adversaries, who went to preach in public squares in hopes of being hired by the city's rich to teach their children. Paul went looking for the poor, not the rich, and he sought not the wisdom of the pagans, but the pure wisdom of God which is found among the poor.[11] For the early Christians, the example of Christ, who became poor, was enough. They believed in God's power because for them God's power was not with the power of the rich.

The Jewish scriptures spoke of a poor Messiah, but that was one strand among several in Judaism. It was difficult to resist the pressure of pagan peoples. Earthly power was always interpreted as a sign of God's power. The powerful believed God was on their side, and was behind their power and possessions. Such was the theology of Deuteronomy. Loss of power was interpreted as reproach and separation from God, e.g., Job's false friends, who are by no means an exception but simply reflect the wisdom of all peoples. This is still the theology of the powerful in the United States. It is also the basis of the prosperity theology spread so successfully by neo-Pentecostals in Brazil today.[12]

The disciples of Jesus were able to pick out the Bible texts that speak of a poor Messiah. The church then went in search of the poor of Jesus Christ spontaneously, because they were poor people seeking other poor people.

There was no need to talk about the church of the poor, because it was of the poor.

After the break that changed everything in the history of Christianity, the poor were still in the church but they were no longer representative, and the church stopped speaking the language of the poor. This was the time of temptation, seduction, and danger. Henceforth the rich would occupy the first rung, with the emperor on top, then his officials, the generals, the representatives of imperial power in all cities; last but not least the clergy, starting with the bishops. From now on, the clergy would be a privileged class: the church was increasingly identified with the clergy, and hence was no longer of the poor.

The theologians of the imperial court heralded the privileges granted by the emperors starting with Constantine as a great victory of Christ. Mosaics and paintings depicted Jesus as emperor, Jesus the richest of men because he was an emperor. That changed everything: the poor son of Joseph of Nazareth became emperor of the world. The church shared very concretely in his "promotion": bishops were treated as senators, and the clergy became a class enjoying various political and economic privileges, as well as the honors bestowed on it. The churches became wealthy with donations.[13] The emperors had magnificent churches built and in a few centuries the church owned half the land in the empire.

Christians were facing a dilemma. Indeed the emperor's word was an order. They had little opportunity to examine the situation and choose freely. When the emperor called the bishops to Nicea, he gave them no choice; they had to go. Thus, without recognizing it, they were integrated into the empire. Many must have thought this was a unique opportunity that opened up the gates to the entire world. The writings of Eusebius of Caesarea, the ideologist of the Christian empire, attest to this almost delirious enthusiasm. It was as if Christianity had conquered the empire; apparently few realized that the empire had conquered Christianity. St. Augustine, an African, pointed out that Rome was a den of thieves and that the much vaunted empire was nothing but a huge act of banditry. Even so he was unable to cut his ties, and when the Vandals invaded, he urged Christians to defend this empire.

Many were amazed to see their own religion becoming the center of the culture and social life of the empire, which they saw as the entire world. Many were enraptured: Christians could now show that Christianity could transform the world and make it the image of God's Reign. The Christian empire would be very different from the pagan empire. The poor would have a place in the Christian empire. Indeed, for fifteen centuries the church— clergy and lay—has undertaken many works of charity. But the church stopped being the church of the poor.

From then on, Christians, led by the clergy, were responsible for running the world. That was unexpected and it changed the way they saw things. It is easy to have beautiful theories when you are in the opposition, but holding onto them when you are in power is something else. For fifteen centuries Christians have felt responsible for the direction of Christian society, the world with which they are familiar. One of the great concerns of Christendom was what to do with the poor, and not abandon them as pagan Rome did. The clergy decided to help the poor, albeit unevenly. In this task they had the help of millions of devoted, self-sacrificing women: almost all the work of helping the poor was done by women, whether they had taken vows or not.

The church was no longer the church *of* the poor: it became a church *for* the poor.[14]

CHURCH FOR THE POOR

We cannot minimize the admirable work of missionaries, priests, sisters, and lay men or women, who have plunged into the shantytowns of large cities and formed communities of poor people, miniature churches of the poor. But we cannot forget that they are a minority, an Abrahamitic minority (Archbishop Hélder Câmara). They are generally a church for the poor, doing work that helps the poor. Insofar as the church simply helps the poor, it is not identified with them. The hope lies with the minority that breaks with the Christendom model and commits itself to the poor. This minority is preparing the future of the church, because there is no future for it anywhere else.

The countless works of charity performed by the Christendom church cannot be dismissed. In the midst of the chaos caused by the Germanic invasions into the Roman empire, the bishops often ended up being the only authorities, and they had to take over governing the cities. With everything else collapsing, they had to handle serving the poor. The bishops were the first to organize the distribution of food and medicine and care for poor sick people, and burial for those who died. They took on the role of "fathers of the poor."[15]

Throughout the ages of Christendom the works of practical charity to assure the survival of the poor multiplied. Hospitals were open to everyone; all the poor felt that they were members of the community. They were taken into consideration, albeit at a very low level. Legions of women created a civilization in which the poor were welcomed, although the needs often went beyond their capabilities, e.g., during war, epidemics, or natural disasters. Even so, Christian history is full of examples of men and women who stood up to plague or cholera, sacrificing their own lives to aid helpless victims.

Although the church was aiding the poor, the very situation of Christendom created two limitations. First, because it was associated with a kind of hierarchized society made up of very different classes and orders, the church could help the poor but it could not transform the condition of the poor, because it could not change society. Second, criticizing society would have meant questioning the privileged position of the clergy in society. There were always protests against this fundamental inequality, but they were always the work of dissidents, heretics, the underground. One could not criticize the established society publicly without running the risk of being condemned for attacking the power of the church.

For these two reasons, the church could be church for the poor, but not church of the poor. The very idea disappeared from theology: care for the poor was primarily the task of women, but it dropped out of official awareness. The church was not of the poor, it was not the people of the poor. After numerous condemnations of the spiritual Franciscans and their spiritual heirs, the topic of poverty itself because suspect. It would have seemed entirely pointless in ecclesiology, which dealt with the hierarchy and its powers.

With regard to the situation in Latin America, Octavio Paz shows how in Mexico, the missionaries were able to give the Indians a new reason to live. When the entire Indigenous world collapsed, their gods had also been shown to be impotent. By baptism the missionaries brought the Indians into a new world where they had a place: they were sons of God and sons of Mary, equal to the Spaniards. Their self-esteem could be restored. They were on the bottom, but they had a place in colonial society—a place that they partly lost in the liberal world that followed.[16] What happened to the Indigenous in colonial Mexican society may be compared to their fate in the North American colonies, where they had no place and could be exterminated.

The works of mercy as they existed in Spain and Portugal were transferred to the colonies, alleviating poverty, albeit without questioning the system of the conquest. (Some missionaries, religious, or lay people doubted the legitimacy of the colonial regime, but they were immediately arrested and expelled and spent the rest of their lives in the prisons of the monarchs.)

Did the poor always patiently accept a "church for the poor" and its alms? All the popular literature of the time (songs, pageants, theater) was a continuous protest against the wealth of the clergy. Most did not want to leave the church, because they could be burned at the stake. From the eleventh to the sixteenth century (during the Protestant Reformation), almost all heresies and movements condemned by the hierarchy were calling for the church to be poor and of the poor. For five centuries protests were raised against the wealth of the clergy[17] with a great deal of support, especially among the poor. The movements of the poor led by these heretics were destroyed but they kept coming back.

This shows that in their minds the poor had a feeling of belonging to the people of God and the conviction that the people of God was of the poor.[18] Externally, they had to act as though they accepted the system, but internally they did not accept it, and they kept the flame of the true church, the true people of God, burning. Unfortunately, they repressed their feeling for centuries and only heretical theologians dared to challenge the authority of the hierarchy and were thus condemned.

St. Francis brought about a major shift that has had a powerful influence in subsequent centuries down to our own time. St. Francis went out to the poor not simply to help them—as he did early on when he was rich—but primarily because he recognized the presence of Jesus in them. That is why he proclaimed and showed respect for the dignity of the poor in everything he did.[19] He became poor with the poor, not for ascetic reasons as the monks before him, and not to flee the world, but precisely to be in the midst of the world, where Jesus was. He became poor to be one of the poor, to imitate Jesus, to be with Jesus in the company of the poor. This was something new and this stance aroused such enthusiasm that many youths found the truth of the gospel in this approach. They discovered, as St. Francis said, that "the gospel comes not on horseback, but on foot."[20]

The Franciscan leaven has been present in the church ever since then, not always in the religious institutions that traced themselves to him, but in the entire church. Within the Franciscan movement there have been many reforms, many returns to the true Franciscan spirit. The most extraordinary (and most "Franciscan") of the Franciscan adventures was the mission of the well-known "twelve" in Mexico at the start of the conquest. The mission reached Mexico City on June 18, 1524. Their spirit was to follow St. Francis as radically as possible. Their poverty brought millions of Indians to ask for baptism. They were so different from the conquerors that the Indigenous recognized them as their true brothers.[21]

The Franciscan intuition has been taken up at different times and has entered the true Christian tradition. Even so, each of these servants of the poor had to face resistance from the structure of Christendom. St. Vincent de Paul was a heroic voice in the midst of the haughtiness of the ascendant kingdom of France, in the midst of terrible poverty created largely by the wars that were the glory of the monarchy. He founded the Daughters of Charity, and gave them a rule that would never have been accepted by the hierarchy, and hence he could not accept their solemn vows as religious. He told that them that they would have "for monastery, the houses of the sick; for cell, a rented room; for chapel, the parish church; for cloister, the streets of the city and the wards of hospitals; for enclosure, obedience; for grating, the fear of God; for veil, holy modesty."[22]

St. Vincent is said to have influenced Bossuet's famous sermon on the eminent dignity of the poor.[23] Bossuet's words are worth citing because they show that at the height of the absolute monarchy and the Catholic Counterreformation, the consciousness of the true church was not forgotten:

> Building a city that would be the true city of the poor could only be something of our Savior and of the politics of heaven. This city is the holy church. If you ask me why I call it the city of the poor, I will answer through the following proposition: the church in its original plan was built only for the poor, and they are the true citizens of this happy city

that the scripture calls the City of God. Even if this teaching seems strange to you it is nevertheless true. . . . In its foundation the church of Jesus Christ was an assembly of poor people, and if the rich were welcomed into it, they gave their property away upon entering it and placed it at the feet of the apostles, to go into the city of the poor (which is the church) with the seal of poverty.[24]

The French Revolution brought the end of Christendom, the old regime based on the three traditional classes of clergy, nobility, and everyone else. The idea that human society is made by human beings and not by a divine determination entrusted to privileged classes came to prevail. Society could be changed and brought in line with reason and ethics. The challenge of fashioning a new society was posed. At this time, the industrial revolution was creating a new kind of poverty, that of industrial workers. Urban poverty compounded the poverty of the countryside.

The confluence of these two facts gave rise to socialism in the nineteenth and twentieth centuries. Socialism became the religion of the poor, the Christianity of the poor, the largest separated church of all time. For intellectuals socialism may be a scientific theory of economics, a politics, a philosophy of history, but for the poor, socialism was the new religion.[25]

The hierarchy failed to see or hear or understand or recognize the signs of the times. It was completely occupied with defending the vestiges of Christendom, its last privileges, its remnants of wealth and power, so it failed to realize what was happening in the world.[26]

Some prophets (Frederic Ozanam, Bishop Ketteler of Mainz, Lacordaire) did discover that now the problem was the causes of poverty, human responsibility for poverty. Some priests and lay people pointed out the challenge and the route the church should take, but they were not heeded. We need only cite what happened to Ozanam's legacy: they attributed to him a caricature of charity: the St. Vincent de Paul Society. Obviously his appeal was not accepted.

In 1877 a French worker named Claude Corbion wrote an open letter to Bishop Dupanloup of Orleans, one of the leaders of the French bishops, and said, "Your Excellency, you have asked us, 'Who will tell me why the people have abandoned us?' Well, we have abandoned you today because you abandoned us centuries ago. And when I say abandoned us, I am not saying that you have denied us the 'comforts of religion.' No, your priestly zeal prompted you to pour them out, even back then. What I mean is that for centuries you have given up our temporal cause and your influence has been aimed more at blocking our social redemption than serving it." Bishop Dupanloup was intelligent, and had at least discovered that the people were leaving the church. Many others could not even see that.

Some did insist that the church should stand with the poor, be identified with them, and so found its true mission. Toward the end of his short life

Emmanuel Mounier wrote: "The poor are not infallible but they are at the heart of the problem, and we reject any consideration that does not take the viewpoint of the poor into account."[27]

This background is helpful for grasping how John XXIII was not understood when he spoke of the church of the poor, or that Cardinal Lercaro was not followed except by a small group of a hundred bishops. The appeal was heard in Latin American, however, at Medellín. That this should happen in a church that before Vatican II was completely asleep, living peacefully in feast days, rituals, parish routine, and celebrating itself, was a miracle of some bishops aided by priests and lay people who were committed to the cause of the liberation of their oppressed peoples. We may point to Manuel Larrain, Hélder Câmara, Leonidas Proaño, Ramón Bogarín, and Sergio Méndez Arceo, to mention only those now dead.

At Medellín the bishops returned to the eschatological idea of people of God as it is in *Lumen Gentium*. The people of God is in gestation; it is hidden in a society that calls itself Christian, but it is far from carrying out its mission, which requires that the church move toward poverty.

> This commitment requires that we live a true biblical poverty expressed in authentic manifestations, clear signs for our peoples. Only a poverty of this kind will let Christ, the Savior of human beings, shine through and uncover Christ, the Lord of history.[28]

The chapter on the poverty of the church refers to the people of God, although the text speaks primarily of the poverty of the hierarchy and the clergy. The entire people of God is called to this same vocation:

> We wish the Latin American church to be the evangelizer of the poor and one with them, a witness to the value of the riches of the kingdom, and the humble servant of all our people. Its pastors and the other members of the people of God have to correlate their life and words, their attitudes and actions, to the demands of the gospel and the necessities of Latin America.[29]

DEFENSE OF THE POOR

Poverty is usually not easily detected, but it is there. Some make the effort to discover it. When they do so, they have a further step to take: defending the poor. Once the church's ministers discovered the poor, they discovered how the poor are exploited and humiliated in their private life, their work, and their public life. Law and justice do not exist for the poor. One need only approach the poor to verify that they are robbed, their work is taken away, and they are humiliated and left abandoned. If they are killed, the killers are almost never punished; if they are robbed, the thief is never found. If they are accused and thrown in jail, they are likely to be held for years before being put on trial. Yet the powerful can be assured of almost guaranteed impunity. Faced with this situation a Christian is disconcerted and discouraged. How to take on so many cases?

One discovers that what is called "social sin" or "institutionalized violence" takes place in the form of millions of particular sins: global and structural oppression comes to bear in millions of cases of local and particular oppression. One likewise finds that the poor have no defense. How to defend the poor? Medellín broke away from five hundred years of complicity and took on the commitment to defend the poor.

There is no law allowing or ordering the church to take on the defense of the right of the poor; it does so by the will of God. It is God who grants authority to defend the rights of the poor—for our God is God of the poor, the liberator of the poor, and there is nothing more obvious in the theology of the Bible. If God is the defender of the poor, God's prophets will undertake their defense. This will not be easy. A price will be paid for defending the poor. Anyone who dares to defend the poor is attacked, condemned, rejected by society.

Those who criticize the oppression of the poor are breaking the solidarity with their social groups—even with their own families. When Bishop Manuel Larrain of Chile carried out a land reform on his diocese he was condemned and rejected as a traitor by his upper-class landholding family (three of his ancestors had been presidents). When Bishop Leonidas Proaño of Ecuador carried out land reform on the diocesan lands, he discovered there the torture instruments used by the diocese's administrators to punish Indians who did not produce enough. Because he had done justice for the Indians, he was denounced in Rome. When Cardinal Silva first became archbishop of Santiago, Chile, he also carried out a land reform on church lands. He was accused of misusing church property. The two canons who denounced him were immediately rewarded by being made bishops.

These are just some examples drawn from the lives of people I have known. The same thing happens in the lives of thousands of clergy or lay people who dare to take up the cause of the poor. Indeed, they are breaking with the established order. In the name of what? Only something higher than society can justify, something that is transcendent. It is God who gives authority to defend the poor, even by attacking the unjust social order. God is thus revealed as God. Bartolomé de las Casas invoked God's authority to defend the Indians. He could speak in the name of God, this God whom the oppressors also invoked, albeit blasphemously.

Puebla recalls the memory of the early evangelizers who defended the Indians on behalf of justice: "Antonio de Montesinos, Bartolomé de las Casas, Juan Zumárraga, Vasco de Quiroga, Juan del Valle, Julián Garcés, José de Anchieta, Manuel Nóbrega and all the others who defended the Indians against the *conquistadores* and *encomenderos*—even unto death, as in the case of Bishop Antonio Valdivieso" (8).[30] All of them were troublemakers, and were persecuted, as has happened also with the bishops who have followed their example. Serving as the "voice of the voiceless" was the slogan adopted after Medellín and Puebla. The Puebla document states:

> We see that national episcopates and many segments of lay people, religious men and women, and priests have made their commitment to the poor a deeper and more realistic one. This witness, nascent but real, led the Latin American Church to denounce the grave injustices stemming from mechanisms of oppression. (1136)
>
> The Church's prophetic denunciations and its concrete commitments to the poor have in not a few instances brought down persecution and oppression of various kinds upon it. The poor themselves have been the first victims of this oppression. (1138)
>
> We will make every effort to understand and denounce the causes of poverty. (1160)

Today even the International Monetary Fund, the sanctuary of the total market, recognizes that poverty is increasing because social inequality is increasing, but it does not change the thrust of the economy. Everyone knows that the continual increase of the foreign debt makes it impossible to pay. Nevertheless, paying the interest impedes any effective social policy.

The poor are not in a position to know why they are poor. They tend to think the fault is theirs. They are not familiar with the social or economic mechanisms that have led to their situation. The dominant society has become so complex that a huge part of the world population is prevented from understanding why it is that way. They do not know what to do. They are disoriented, immobilized, and feel powerless. Indeed the current globalized system does a great deal of advertising to show that there is no point in resisting—nothing can change, it's all inevitable. It promises that all problems are going to be solved by themselves in the future. So who can take up their defense? Who can speak, explain, open the consciousness of the excluded? Should this be the church's job?

Society tends to look at the poor as mere objects who can be neutralized through services, not as subjects of rights. But the Christian gospel as proclamation of good news consists precisely in awakening the awareness of rights in those who are unaware that they have rights. The first step is to defend these rights. By defending the rights of the poor, Christians show the poor that they have rights. By thus becoming aware of their rights, they become citizens with dignity. They feel like children of God, worthy of respect.

Many are willing to help the poor, but they rebel when the poor claim rights. This notion of rights is fundamental, but it has not always been recognized in the church. Indeed, the fact that the rights of lay people in the church are so few and so limited is not helpful for developing an awareness of rights.

Puebla says, "Action by the church is also needed so that the displaced and marginalized people of our time do not become permanent second-class citizens. For they are subjects with rights and legitimate social aspirations" (1291). Many such texts were produced, because the tasks of defending and teaching rights were carried out with great effort during the military dictatorships. Today, however, now that the appearance of democracy has returned, and faced with the capitalist economy's self-propaganda ruling out any alternative, people are intimidated and often silenced.

The church no longer experiences human rights violations as it did under the military regimes. Sensitivity to the social rights of the poor is not so strong. Official propaganda claims that democracy rules and that all rights are defended and promoted thanks to social policies and the integrity of the courts. The church allows itself to be taken in by such language. However, one need only go through the cities or the countryside to see the reality: the poor are as oppressed now as they were during the military regimes, and democracy has still not reached the poor. Hence the church's responsibility is more urgent than ever. Defending the rights of the poor is still a task of the people of God.

THE CONSCIOUSNESS OF THE POOR

We have seen that the first result of publicly defending the rights of the poor is that the poor themselves are awakened to their own dignity and freedom. After that first step, other steps may be taken to help the poor to awaken their own consciousness. In Brazil after forty years of practices deriving from the Paulo Freire method, there is no need to insist on the importance of consciousness raising in the life of a people. Paulo Freire himself was an educator, and he created a new educational method for stimulating consciousness raising, which was then adopted, at least officially, by documents of the Latin American church.[31]

But education is not everything. Experience has shown that consciousness raising proves to be harder than anticipated. Teaching, speaking, education through the word can help but they do not bring about a radical change of consciousness. Only acting can convince and change behavior. When poor people see that they can do something, that they are capable, they become convinced that they are human agents like others, capable of struggling for their dignity.

The experience of the Movement of the Landless (MST) and similar movements in the Brazilian cities shows that getting land is what changes the consciousness of rural people. Standing up to attacks by hired gunmen or the police—or both together, as usually happens—teaches people to overcome fear. A person feels that this experience leads to a new ability, the ability to affirm oneself. That is where the awareness as a people is born. Otherwise, this is unlikely to happen—such is the meaning of the MST pedagogy. Consciousness-raising courses alone do not have this effect.

What paralyzes consciousness is fear, as those on top are well aware. They know that fear has to be fueled by demonstrations of force, that they must intimidate and create the impression that the only remedy is to submit. Torture in police stations serves to instill fear in the poor. The powerful know that when fear is overcome, a new consciousness emerges.

There is still a long way to go before such a consciousness takes shape. Fear still reigns: that is why the poor elect so many corrupt leaders—fear of reprisals. That is why drug traffickers are so powerful. Fear intimidates and discourages the poor and takes away their will to struggle. The humiliated cheer for those who humiliate them.

The church can play an important role in freeing the poor from fear. The example of bishops, priests, religious, and lay activists who have overcome fear and denounced, confronted, and rejected intimidation—and have often been killed—has unquestionably changed the mindset of the people. That is why the memory of the Latin American martyrs is so important. The example of church people is worth a great deal because religion still occupies an important place in the culture of the poor. Their basic motivations still come from religion. If religion provides courage and constancy and helps overcome fear, it can make an important contribution.

Yet for centuries religion has served more to stifle this consciousness than to awaken it. For centuries the poor were taught that it was God's will that they submit, not resist, not be insubordinate. They were offered the example of Jesus who did not resist those who crucified him. Jesus was the example to be followed in all the crucifixions of daily life. The poor felt enhanced by resignation to their humiliation. They thought that their dignity lay in suffering and degradation.

This message of the crucified was the ideological version of the passion of Jesus, and it was told for centuries. This message was better than nothing: at least it gave a sense of self-worth to those who were stripped of all worth in society. But it was not the gospel message or true Christianity. God wants the poor to be members of his people, with full rights, and wants this people to be the image of the world renewed.

The power of religion can be seen in Pentecostal preaching. Through the strong word of the pastor, Pentecostals are able to free people from alcohol and drug dependencies, smoking, and other vices. They are able to provide such a strong religious motivation that people break their dependency on a vice. Someone who had given up, thinking that he would never be free of his vices, succeeds. Religion has given him a new consciousness of his worth and his ability. Once he thinks he is capable, he will actually be capable.

The problem with Pentecostalism is that it springs from individualism, American individualism in particular. Conversion is strictly individual; individuals are saved by themselves. Once converted they enter a community that separates them from the broader human community around them. They do not reach consciousness as a people, or they lose it if they already had it. For these converts, the world is divided into those who are saved and those who are not. There is no longer room for the people. "The people" means "everyone else," those who still live in sin and are not saved. God calls human beings one by one and has no message for the whole.[32] Still, what is positive about Pentecostalism is that it succeeds in overcoming fear and enabling timid people to speak publicly, overcome their timidity, and to go out to others to present the gospel.

THE PEOPLE OF THE POOR

John XXIII wanted something more than helping the poor, defending their rights, doing consciousness-raising, and awakening them toward their own liberation. He wanted a church that would be constituted by the poor themselves united in a common faith, a common hope, and a constructive covenant. This idea seemed so unreal that most of the council fathers did not pay attention to him. It would have been inconceivable, and they could hardly attribute to a pope an inconceivable idea.

> When we talk about the poor, we are talking about something *collective*. There is no such thing as an isolated poor person. The poor belong to social groups, races, classes, cultures, sexes. That is precisely why the irruption of the poor is so tough and aggressive. If it were simply a matter of individual poor people, there would be no problem. But since it has to do with classes, races, cultures, and the condition of women, tension and conflict are entailed. Something very important is at stake in all this: the identity of the poor people.[33]

During the ages of Christendom, it would have been impossible for the clergy to understand the idea of a church of the poor, except in the sense of the aid that the church gives the poor (an idea still found in *Novo Millennio Ineunte* 49). In Christendom the church includes everyone, all social orders, all conditions, and naturally the clergy out in front—in front, under the hierarchy. The poor have a place there, namely the place they have in overall society, i.e., last place, as recipients of charity from the most fortunate.

It is not surprising that when Christendom seemed to be mortally wounded, some prophetic voices arose to recall that the church does not need the powers of this world and that it is of the poor. One of these was Father Julio

María when Brazil went from being an empire to a republic (1889), and church was separated from state. After the French Revolution came Lamennais, Buchez, Lacordaire, and others, and there were yet others when the Third Republic drew apart from the church (1880-1890). However, the dream of Christendom had not expired and many are still attached to it: for them the poor would be a "poor" consolation. They thought that the benefits of Christendom could still be recovered. That has been and in many cases still is the mindset of the clergy. For them a church of the poor is inconceivable, even incompatible with Christianity.

But what about the poor themselves? Do they reject this idea of a church of the poor? The awareness of being people of God has never entirely disappeared from among the poor. It might be repressed by social pressure, submission to priests, the fear of clashing with the official view always repeated by the clergy. It might appear to be hidden and even to have disappeared for centuries. But whenever an alternative to the Christendom model arose and the poor were told that they were the people of God, a large mass of poor people rose up and joined. Deep down they have always wanted a church of the poor, but history never gave them a choice, and the hope remained latent until a prophetic voice was raised.

We have already noted that between the twelfth and fifteenth centuries the poor rose up to hear the voice of the *humiliati* of Lyons, the Waldenses, the Albigensians, and the Hussites. Whenever there appeared a church that wanted to return to the origins and embody the gospel message, the people were roused and followed. All these movements were ultimately crushed, but at least people had experienced some years of hope. For conventional Christendom, many of these were simply heretics taking advantage of the poor, but some more perceptive observers recognized that the poor were not attached to the heart of the established church, but belonged only because they had no alternative. When they had an alternative, they went from the established religion into the prophetic church.[34]

Until the revolutions of 1848, all popular movements were Christian, all inspired by the awareness that the church of Jesus could only be the church of the poor. From that point on, the popular masses changed their minds, having seen that the clergy was not with them. The clergy maintained its alliance with the ruling classes and bourgeois governments, as though Christendom still existed. It never listened to the calls from the poor. That was when the great schism of modernity took place: the break between the church led by the clergy and the popular masses, especially the working class. The Christianity of the working class found another "church": socialism.

Initially, socialism's adherents were limited to a few intellectuals, but after 1850, and especially after 1880, socialism acquired a popular character. It entered the milieu of the people and was adopted as a "new church," or rather the true church, the church of the poor: the people of God was present there as people of the poor. At first workers wanted to be socialists and Christians at the same time, and being socialist meant returning to authentic Christian religion. However, the clergy took it upon itself to exclude them. The hierarchy condemned socialism as though it were an ideological doctrine, without considering what the people were thinking. Workers had to choose, and had no alternative but to leave the church which did not accept them.

The hierarchy thought condemning was the solution, but condemnation was one of the greatest mistakes of the popes in recent centuries. The main mistake was making formulas of faith more important than millions of human beings, as though the mission of the church were to define formulas of faith.

Thus, the people left the Catholic Church. They had found another "church" that they regarded as more authentic because it was more truly the church of the people. The awareness that the people of God is poor and that the poor are the people of God has always been present in the popular consciousness of socialism and to some extent constitutes the essence of socialism for the workers.

There are many episodes in the history of socialism, and its coloration in each country is different. There is no socialist orthodoxy because socialism is not set up as a fixed practice or doctrine. It does come from a common assumption, however: the true people is the people of the poor, and society must change to give access to this people of the poor. Hence, the problem of poverty is not solved by individual measures, but society must be transformed as a whole. If, as intellectuals thought, private property of the means of production is the main obstacle preventing the participation of all, private property must be suppressed. However, that was not the essence of popular socialism, which was and still is where it has managed to survive, the deep feeling of socialism: to bring about the dream of Jesus Christ, who was of the poor. This is not the place to examine the varieties of socialism, which may in no way be confused with Marxism. Marxism never made its way into the socialist movement in Anglo Saxon countries.

Initially, socialism was practically indistinguishable from workers' associations. It became the official or unofficial ideology of labor unions and the basis of anarchism. When socialism took the form of political parties toward the end of the nineteenth century, it began to adopt a more precise ideology. Socialist parties were the work not only of labor leaders but of intellectuals, almost all of them from liberal or radical traditions, and in Latin countries they were virulently anticlerical. They broke away from liberal movements but retained the same hostility to the ancient regime and against the conservative church.

Even so, the separation between socialism and religion was not inevitable.[35] Some Catholics spoke in the same vein. For example, in 1812 Felicité de Lamennais wrote that factory workers were treated like "machines" and that they were "forced to be prisoners in factories for a piece of bread." "Their need has made them your slaves," he said to the owners.[36] Gregory XVI condemned Lamennais and L'Avenir. Lamennais broke away from the church but his colleagues continued the fight, even with the limited means left them by the pope.

Research during this time was revealing the dire conditions of workers to all, especially to the church, but the church, relying on support from conservative peasants, did not move and did not feel challenged. In France, Charles de Coux, A. de Villeneuve, Gerbert, and others denounced the vice of capitalism well before Marx. Buchez, Ozanam, Maret, Leveneux, Corbion, Pierre Leroux, and others who wrote in the newspaper *L'Atelier* were active in labor and called for a Christian socialism. Socialists themselves referred to the gospel, e.g., Louis Blanc's *Socialist Catechism* begins, "What is socialism?" "It is the gospel in action."[37]

In the 1848 revolutions, socialism was Christian. Workers invoked the name of God and of Jesus Christ, as the God of the poor and oppressed. Everything was still possible. Almost all the revolutionary leaders invoked the gospel; Marx was an isolated voice without a social base. Socialism and Christianity could have formed an alliance; or rather, socialism was still Christian, at least for the masses of workers. It would have sufficed to not excommunicate it. *L'Ére Nouvelle,* the paper of democratic Catholics, said that the revolution was not only allowed by God but was one of the "most honorable, deepest and most fruitful movements that the world has ever seen."[38] Priests were active in revolutionary clubs and bishops said nothing. In the elections to the constituent assembly, three bishops, three vicar generals, six priests, and Father Lacordaire, OP, were elected. Bishops encouraged the priests to run. But that fervor did not last. Most of the members of the constituent assembly were political rightists and they opened the way for the bourgeoisie, which wielded almost unimpeded control for the next forty years. Terrible repression was unleashed against the labor movement.

Throughout the nineteenth century, bishops' documents denounced the poverty of the workers and appealed to the conscience of the rich and powerful, but their voices were not recognized by the working masses, who no longer believed in the spontaneous generosity of the bourgeoisies now reveling in their conquest of the world. Labor organizations were regarded as subversive and illegal, and the clergy adhered to the law. In condemning popular organizations in the name of charity, the hierarchy insisted on unity and patience. The clergy generally lamented the dire poverty of the workers, called for charity from the owners, but it regarded working class movements as subversive. Only after *Rerum Novarum* did Catholics begin to accept labor unions, and even then with some resistance. In any case, by then the break with the working class was completed in France and in Europe as a whole.[39]

The popes had ruled out any possibility of accepting socialism. In practice, consciously or unconsciously the clergy allied itself with the triumphant bourgeoisie. The few priests and lay people who wanted to be socialists were condemned or completely marginalized. The clergy chose the winning side.

The posture of the church in France was formulated in a famous speech of Count Montelambert in the National Assembly on September 20, 1848, after the revolution had been defeated:

> The church says to the poor: be resigned to your poverty and you will be rewarded eternally. This is what the church has said to poor people for over a thousand years, and the poor believed in it until the day when faith was ripped from their heart, and the horror of the social situation immediately set in.[40]

The clergy became hostile to socialism and to the now semiunderground workers' movements. Historians estimate that around 1860 the bulk of the working class was no longer willing to put up with so much aggressiveness from the clergy and broke away. That was when socialism became an increasingly secularized "parallel church." Over time socialism lost its religious and prophetic character. What is the connection between the breaking away of the working class in the nineteenth century and the complete secularization of European society at the close of the twentieth? Who knows? However, it is interesting to note that in the United States, where there are many popular churches and there was no clerical Christendom, secularization has not occurred to the same degree. Religion is more resistant than in Europe.

In any case, the poor of the First World have no awareness of being a people. Advanced capitalism diversifies social classes and levels of life. It avoids large concentrations of workers and has reduced manual work. It also has huge propaganda machines, especially television and other means of advertising, whose effect is overwhelming. Thus far it has not generated any effective response. The poor are aware that they are excluded but have no hope of being a people. Or hope is so constrained that it seems to have disappeared again.

Socialism arrived in Latin America later, entering Argentina and Brazil in the late nineteenth century, and later in Chile where industrialization was delayed because of the large landholders who feared losing control of the country. In any case, after 1930 socialism grew in all countries, but it had no contact with the clergy, which would never have had anything to do with anything so solemnly condemned by Rome. With greater openness to the world stemming from Vatican II, there were two major moments of encounter between Christianity and socialism in Chile (1971-1973) and Nicaragua (1979-1990).

In Chile socialism had been around since the beginning of the century and was split into the Communist and Socialist Parties. The Communist Party was very dependent on the Soviet Union and it had a vague program that was subordinate to the fluctuations in Soviet orientation. Even so, it sank deep roots among the workers. The Socialist Party did not accept the leadership of the Soviet Union and had certain anarchist roots, but it claimed to be radically revolutionary and determined to nationalize productive property. It was also rooted in the working class. These two parties can be said to have embodied the European model. For the working class they were a true "church," the church of the poor. They helped to unite the people of the poor. Catholic institutions had some presence in popular milieus, but they did not really embody the people of the poor because, deep down, the poor were not accepted in Catholic society.

The Allende government included Catholics who had broken away from Christian Democracy (Christian Left and MAPU). These Catholics claimed that Christian faith and the socialist program of "Popular Unity" were in complete harmony. It is noteworthy that this aspect—socialism as the people of the poor—was not very much on the minds of the Christian intellectuals who were active in the Popular Unity.

Documents of that period said that socialist revolution was the only possible route for Latin America in order to escape from the existing state of dependence. People believed that the Allende government was opening a new history, the history of the establishment of socialism in South America. Anyone who sought liberation had to join the process.[41] The emphasis was on socialism as a historic necessity.

In 1971 a group of eighty priests published a document declaring that they were supporting the Allende government in the name of their Christian faith. Here the emphasis was on the moral value of socialism as humanly superior to capitalism. "Socialism is not simply a new economy, but it must also generate new values, that will make possible the emergence of a society of greater solidarity and fraternity, in which workers will assume their role with dignity."[42] The accent was prophetic: socialism promised a more humane society.

Significantly, these Catholic intellectuals invoked theoretical arguments. They did not join the Popular Unity movement out of fidelity to the people, or because the people were present in this movement. This was a sign that Catholics were in fact not present in the people and were not allowing themselves to be guided by popular sensitivity. They were too theoretical.

On July 19, 1979, the Sandinista Front took power in Managua, Nicaragua, after the flight of the dictator Anastasio Somoza. Enrique Dussel wrote that this represented a "new phase of church history," as the question of religion was posed "in a positive, innovative, revolutionary manner," as a result of the "revolutionary stance and active participation of thousands of Christians in the 'war' against Somoza. Both before and after the revolution these Christians have taken an active part, many of them belonging to [Christian base communities] or Christian institutions."[43] As in Chile, the whole accent is on the revolutionary movement, an elite or vanguard movement, and on the participation of Christians in this movement. The people are the object that will benefit, but still the object—not the active subject. Indeed, in Nicaragua the people were even less the primary protagonist of the revolution than in Chile.

It is true that in the final stages before the Sandinista movement took power the people rose up against Somoza in a number of regions in the country. That was when the National Guard got out of control and began to kill indiscriminately. When the people rose up with the Sandinista Front their attitude was not revolutionary—they were defending their lives. The Sandinistas were later able to mobilize a major portion of the population, but not the majority, as shown in the elections. The protagonist was the revolutionary movement. The people would win their liberation, but it was clear that it was the revolutionary movement that would liberate the people.

At first this might seem to be true of any revolution but in fact there have been revolutions in which the people participated overwhelmingly—1848 in Europe and the 1871 Paris Commune, the Russian revolution, at least for the industrial workers. In this case Christians committed to the Sandinista movement wanted to liberate the people and so they did something new, as Dussel says, by joining the revolutionary movement. This was certainly an important step because it was a sign of a break between one group of Christians and the ruling classes and established power, but these Christians were still not the people of the poor becoming the protagonist of its own liberation.

The fact is that peoplehood is achieved only when the people becomes the subject or agent of its own liberation, and then are born as people of the poor and enter into history. Until that moment the people is still not structured so as to act in history—it is rather project, prophecy, proclamation. The vanguard acts in the name of this people, but it anticipates the future, because it has not been a vanguard chosen by the people. The situation derives from the huge separation in the Third World between the world of the poor and intellectuals able to form revolutionary movements.

The participation of Christians in the revolutionary movement was justified on the basis of love for the poor. It was assumed that Christians were not the poor, who would not need to love the poor. One of the most perceptive representatives of Christians committed to the Sandinista revolution observed:

As the concrete mediation of love for the multitude, the revolution was able to become the highest value for authentic Christians. . . . The revolutionary process could now become the maximum Christian value because it represented the one and only approximation to the historical version of the food given to the hungry person and the cup of water given to the thirsty person. So the revolution, as the high road to the new human being and the new society, became a cause that gave meaning to life.[44]

At that time there was a great deal of talk of the "irruption" of the poor, particularly by Gustavo Gutiérrez: "The presence of the poor is making itself felt first of all in the struggles of the common people and the new historical awareness associated with those struggles."[45] Events have shown that this "irruption" took place only in part, and in fact there were various aspects. A new really strong and active consciousness emerged among the Indigenous. Indigenous peoples have proven to be the most united, the most aggressive, and most full of initiatives almost everywhere in Latin America. The "irruption" of the Indigenous is unquestionable, but it does not extend to the rest of the poor.

The Indigenous have a very strong collective identity, and have a common cause, the resurrection of their people, which has been humiliated for centuries but not destroyed. The mestizo masses, who make up the vast majority of the population, have not reached the same level of consciousness, and are not very involved in popular struggles. Blacks are little in evidence, and certainly do not have a collective consciousness, because they do not find a common cause. Legislation already condemns racism so there is no point in struggling to enact laws. The problem is changing the mindset of whites, but that does not take place through a decree or even through political, let alone military, means.

In socialism the people of the poor was seeking itself. Popular groups helped make the revolution and at the same time it seemed as though the people was being created by the social revolution. Nevertheless, to this day the secularized dream of the people of the poor is still hobbled and very limited. The Indigenous movement, for example, is more a return to the traditional Indigenous community, and finds it hard to formulate the principles of a new society; thus it has no influence in the majority world. Some are nostalgic for a people of the poor that would be the church of the poor. However, the church that sought to be of the poor has failed, and they are seeking to realize the church of the poor outside the church.

The hope for a "church of the poor," a "popular church," lasted for about twenty years after Medellín. The term was commonplace and was even used by the hierarchy. It was very much debated around Puebla (1979) but was not taken up by the bishops because the pope had prohibited it in his opening speech. Puebla incorporated the pope's warnings and without condemning the formula, hedged it with so many reservations that it practically ruled it out.

Nevertheless the heirs of Medellín kept recalling the idea or utopia of a church of the poor.

The people's church, according to Puebla, should be understood as "a Church that is trying to incarnate itself in the ranks of the common people on our continent. . . . The people's church is the vocation of the entire church, which is called to be constantly reborn from within the poor, who are the privileged of the kingdom. Thus we are not speaking of a church that is parallel to the institutional church, but rather one that responds to the most basic gospel demands."[46]

In view of Puebla's restrictions after the pope's address, the notion that prevailed was the conversion of the church to the poor. The theme of "People of God," of the poor, was in vogue after Medellín for about twenty years, but gradually became more limited. The "preferential option for the poor" falls far short of the hope of the poor; it does not become the church of the poor.

It should be recognized that a thorough conversion of the church to the poor is inconceivable at this point. If we consider church-going Catholics, it is obvious that the vast majority are not poor, or they are poor people who are still part of the old rural mindset, and culturally are still part of Christendom. What Medellín and Puebla wanted was a beginning, a turn toward a church of the poor.

Deep down, the poor themselves have never lost the conviction that the church should be theirs, that the people of God was the people of the poor and that some day this dream would become a reality. Given the inertia of the institution they kept quiet, and the idea became latent, but it reappears whenever there is a historic opening. Such occasions have been less frequent lately. When the church begins to approach the poor, the hierarchy immediately reaffirms the priority of the status quo, allowing some to opt for the poor with the assurance that nothing significant is going to happen.

When new movements arise among the poor and seem to be the incarnation of the true church, the poor go over to them en masse. Isn't this what is happening with Pentecostalism? The Pentecostal churches are much more of the poor than the Catholic Church. The Catholic Church is not really rich, but it looks rich because its culture is the culture of the rich. There is a demonstration effect: the hierarchy insists on showing signs of power and wealth, even though it does not have power and wealth. That is enough to drive the poor away.

By way of illustration, Paul VI had a great deal of confidence in Archbishop Hélder Câmara, and their friendship went back long before Montini was elected pope. One day Paul VI told Hélder to write whatever he wanted about reforming the church. After some time Hélder decided to write, and he began by congratulating the pope for having announced in a meeting with Roman nobility that he was no longer going to distribute titles of nobility, nor would he regard himself as the head of a nobility. In the same spirit he congratulated the pope for having given up the tiara, a symbol of empire. So, Dom Hélder continued, why not consider that it is kings who live in palaces and have ambassadors in other countries? Why not give up the palace, and live in a more modest house, not a poor one, but one more accessible and comprehensible to ordinary people? Why send ambassadors to governments that aren't always Christian or even respectful of human rights? He said he was sure that the pope could easily find people in each country who would be willing to serve as liaison between the local church and the Holy See.

The reply came not from the pope but from Cardinal Villot, the secretary of state, who said that we are no longer in the first century, i.e., the church had accumulated property and power that it needed and had to protect. The church could no longer be as Jesus founded it.

Yet sometimes a persecution comes along and takes all this weight of the past away from the church. Christians go back to living as they did in the early days, persecuted, and the hierarchy loses all its privileges. Under those circumstances the church not only survives, but the persecuted Christians come to the conviction that they are now really rediscovering the gospel of Jesus. That was the case in the communist world for seventy years, but when persecution stopped, everything went back to normal.

Hope is nourished when there are groups—few or many depending on time and place—that embody the signs of the people of the poor, the church of the poor. In Latin America the hope of a church of the poor was stimulated by the Christian base communities (CEBs) which developed and spread starting in the 1960s, in some countries sooner, in others later. The first experiences in Brazil date from the 1950s (Bishop Medeiros in São Paulo de Potengi, and Father Helio Campos in Fortaleza). Elsewhere in Latin America the first experiments were started in San Miguelito, Panama City, by priests from the archdiocese of Chicago. Base communities reached their high point in Brazil between 1975 and 1985. At that point they leveled off and they have been on the defensive since then, with the return of democracy and the renewal of relationships between the clergy and the ruling classes.

For a time it was hoped that the CEBs would provide a model for the future church. Some dioceses were reorganized based on CEBs, giving the impression that the whole church would be a constellation of CEBs. As could have been expected, the times were not yet ripe. Traditional parishes continued, and religious orders generally continued to serve the upper classes in schools and universities. The "movements" that were likewise of the bourgeois culture were on the rise. In the 1990s, almost everywhere in Latin America, the clergy were more interested in middle class movements than in grassroots pastoral work.

The CEBs were shown to be what they actually were: a popular minority facing a church predominantly tied to the middle classes, though it kept talking about the preferential option for the poor for some time. Even the term had disappeared by the time of the synod of the Americas (1997). The poor went back to where they have been for so many centuries, the object of charity of a church united around its bourgeois base.

However, the dream does not disappear. The movements often have a twinge of conscience and seek to bring the service of the poor into their ideology and their activities. That may be a positive sign and a statement of conversion. Thus far, however, this aspect remains quite secondary in their concerns.

In conclusion, John XXIII raised the issue of the church of the poor and an aspiration of the conversion of the church. History has shown that the church cannot be people of God unless it is church of the poor. The two go together (as shown by their suppression in Santo Domingo and at the Synod of the Americas). The people of God is the people of the poor, and it is the privilege of the poor that they make up the people of God. The wealthy are admitted if they place their wealth at the disposal of the poor.[47]

Chapter 8

THE PEOPLE WITHIN OTHER PEOPLES

The people of God lives within other peoples, like them in many ways, yet different. It exists only within them; isolated from other peoples it does not exist. One cannot be a Christian without being a member of another of the earth's peoples.[1] Vatican II calls it a "messianic people" to express its specific condition and the role it plays within other peoples.[2]

The people of God is different from other peoples, in its temporal condition, its visibility, its human reality. The council says, "This people possesses the dignity and freedom of the daughters and sons of God, in whose hearts the Holy Spirit dwells as in a temple. Its law is the new commandment to love as Christ loved us (see Jn 13:34). Its goal is the kingdom of God" (LG 9). If that is the definition of the people of God, it is clear that it is not identical with the concrete, institutional reality of the Catholic Church. Only a modest minority in the church fits that description to one degree or another. It may be said that the people of God subsists ("*subsistit*") in the church, but is not identical with the church, if we take the church in the sense of the visible institution of which we are members. That definition likewise enables us to see that the people of God also finds members outside the limits of the Catholic Church and of the Christian churches as a whole.

This people of God is situated on the same earth as other peoples; it does not have land of its own, but is made up of people who belong to other peoples—it is a people among peoples. It is composed not of a combination of other peoples, but of minorities in other peoples who come together, independently of geographical borders, to form a people that does not have the same visibility or structure as other peoples, but is still a true people. It does not replace or absorb other peoples but influences them.

In Latin America it is hard to imagine the Catholic Church without Christendom, which still affects how Catholics see and think. Catholics think that Brazil is completely Catholic. Upon rational reflection that is clearly untrue but it remains in the unconscious. In the clerical mindset the hierarchy can still speak on behalf of the whole country. The other churches are regarded as a kind of appendix, conceivably useful to the Catholic Church in confronting the overall society.

In our imagination we have no other image for representing the church in the world. In Europe the ideology of secularity serves to represent the situation of the church.[3] Its official status is that of a private association, but it is really more than that. Separation is not complete; even in France, the most secularized and secular nation, such ties still exist. It is neither Christendom nor separation; the future status is between the two extremes of this hard-to-define situation. It is impossible to define it legally, but that does not mean that something that is not legally recognized cannot really exist. Secularism contains aspects of the Christian tradition, and the "disenchantment of the world" (Gauchet) is not yet complete.[4] Such is the situation in Europe.

Latin America does not even have a framework of words for expressing the situation of the church in the various countries. Religion unquestionably occupies an important place in the culture of Latin American peoples. As an institution, the Catholic Church is highly respected: in public opinion it is the most highly respected institution. It is significantly present in the media, and almost all governments seek support from the Catholic Church—not necessarily the bishops conference, but Catholic religious symbols—contrary to European governments, which try to keep their distance. Yet little or no attention is paid in public or private life to what the hierarchy or clergy say. The church has significant symbolic influence, but little or no influence on people's behavior, legislation, or the socioeconomic system. There is no term for such a situation, or at least none has been discovered thus far.

The people of God has a universal mission in the midst of the other peoples. It is a "messianic people" that may even seem to be a little flock but is a "seed of unity, hope and salvation for the whole human race" which God has gathered as the church so "that it may be for each and everyone the visible sacrament of this saving unity. In order to extend to all regions of the earth, it enters into human history, though it transcends at once all times and all history" (LG 9).

We thus come up against the issue of inculturation, which has been a hot issue since it was accepted in the 1975 synod and incorporated into *Evangelii Nuntiandi*. The relationship between the people of God and other peoples is broader than inculturation, but that issue cannot be evaded. There are two meanings to inculturation: 1) the church changes cultures to bring them into its own culture, or at least to make them compatible with it; 2) the church is changed so that the peoples it seeks to evangelize can understand and accept it. In principle, the two meanings are not necessarily contradictory but in practice they are hard to combine. Roman documents emphasize the first to the practical exclusion of the second, whereas the primary concern of missionary movements is to change the shape of Christianity so that others may live it.

WHAT THE CHURCH RECEIVES FROM PEOPLES

The council turned things upside-down when it distinguished the people of God from other peoples, clearly stating that the people of God does not have its own land and hence is within other peoples, and thus broke away from the Christendom framework. Christians must accept their situation as participating each in his or her own people. Loyalty to one's geographical people is a duty.

For fifteen centuries a Christian society was both the church and a geographical people: the population of Europe, the western portion of the Middle East, and later the Americas. This people interacted with other peoples, defended itself, and conquered other lands. In the culture of this people, the Christian religion occupied a privileged place and sometimes almost all the space (e.g., in Spanish and Portuguese colonies in the Americas). There was no other culture for religious culture to penetrate: science, art, feast days, clothes, space and time, social relations, events in private or public life—everything was consecrated by religion. There was no act that was not sanctified by religion, including eating and drinking and the lawful exercise of sexuality.

The break signaled by Luther's doctrine of two kingdoms and separation between the church and the earthly kingdoms was not very decisive because the modern states stemming from the Reformation brought back the Christendom pattern, albeit limited to a single people. Even after the French Revolution and the gradual secularization of society that it produced, relations between church and society remained close, regardless of the recognized legal status of the churches. Only in the second half of the twentieth century did secularization take a more radical form, not in terms of church and state but of the relationship between the church and society as a whole.

Throughout all these centuries, the Catholic Church continued to act as if Christendom still existed, seeking to determine laws, condemning ideologies, and publishing documents as though all nations were listening. This could happen because even though modernity won over the bourgeoisie of the city, the rural masses were little affected by the political and cultural changes. Modernity came into the countryside only in the second half of the twentieth century, primarily through television, which brought city culture to the country. Thus the church could maintain the illusion of Christendom, and did not seek to devise any other way for peoples to relate to the people of God. That is why many were unable to understand the change wrought by Vatican II.

Vatican II announced the end of Christendom, but it could not change established mindsets nor did it have any other model to present. The lack of a model caused an identity crisis, which John Paul II has resolved by closing the doors and windows and returning to the Christendom regime, albeit artificially: he receives acclaim from everyone, but practically no one does what he says. The problem may be suppressed, but it will return more forcefully in the future.

Actually, Vatican II arrived four centuries late. What it says about the relationship between the church and the world had already been said by the most realistic and wisest Catholics in the sixteenth century in a rational response to the Protestant challenge. In reply, Rome pursued religious confrontation for four centuries with the illusion of defeating all the "errors" through condemnation. The fanatics on both sides, Protestant and Catholic, won out.

Had the moderates like the Erasmians prevailed, history would have been different. Peoples would have moved much more quickly and peacefully toward their emancipation without the wars of religion and the struggle between the conservative church and the progressive and secular state. Confronted with the Protestant schism, the hierarchy should have created another way of being present in the world, but it would have needed great clarity to respond to this challenge. It was so imbued with the spirit, ideology, and advantages of Christendom that it was unable to critique it, and to recognize that Christendom was not to be confused with Christianity. That would have meant recognizing that the enemy was right.

Rather than needing lay people, the hierarchy thought it could resolve matters by itself by insisting on formulas of faith. Four centuries of war have ensued, with millions of people killed, destruction, hunger, mass poverty, and many other terrible consequences of the wars of religion. Accustomed to seeing everything in Christian society as grounded in Christianity, the hierarchy was unable to discover everything that was non-Christian in it— not necessarily anti-Christian but simply non-Christian—hence not essential to the people of God and therefore changeable.

Then came the revolution of Vatican II with John XXIII who sought to listen to what the people of God was saying. With him, and by listening to the voice of lay people who had been speaking for four centuries, the hierarchy became aware that their relationship to the world could and should change. Certainly it was still far from seeing all the difference between what could change and what could not, between the biblical core and what had been shaped by history, between what came from Christianity and what came from other cultures. But being willing to listen was the first step.

The challenge is still open. Now that the church is no longer identified with Christendom and the multiplicity of peoples has been recognized, the church has to create another way of relating to the peoples. This is a unique revolution in history. For three centuries the church lived as a persecuted minority and then for fifteen centuries in a Christendom regime where church and people were coterminous. For the first time in history, the church needs to invent a way for the people of God and the peoples of the earth to relate.

In order to discover what the church can and must change, and what it may create, the aspects of Christendom that were not essential to Christianity must be determined: everything that has been "received," voluntarily or not, consciously or not, from the culture of the peoples of the Middle East and Europe. The church will thereby discover the full extent of its freedom and all the room open for its creativity.

In speaking of what the church has received from peoples and cultures, *Gaudium et Spes* speaks as though everything were positive and final, and does not consider the issue of the relativity of what it has received. As with the inculturation being discussed today, the inculturation of the past was positive or negative, favorable or unfavorable, necessary or superfluous to Christianity. Moreover, inculturation only goes part of the way—it does not touch on the issue of political and economic relations, which are as important as the cultural relationship.

Furthermore, the way inculturation is discussed seems to assume that the church is completely autonomous in deciding its situation in the world; it fails to take into account that the church is dependent on many forces in history that it cannot control. The church may engage in the inculturation that peoples accept, but it cannot simply apply its pastoral plan as it conceived it. It can prepare an inculturation program, but events may change everything. Economists may plan economic development but facts will force them to change; economic forecasts are rarely correct. Similarly, pastoral planning may often turn out to be mistaken, but that should not prevent pastoral reflection. The council said:

> In this way it is possible to create in every country the possibility of expressing the message of Christ in suitable terms and to foster vital contact and exchange between the church and different cultures. Nowadays when things change so rapidly and thought patterns differ so widely, the church needs to step up this exchange by calling upon the help of people who are living in the world, who are expert in its organizations and its forms of training, and who understand its mentality, in the case of believers and nonbelievers alike. (GS 44)

The assumption is that the church takes the initiative in the exchange and guides it as it wishes. That is not really how things happen. Some in the church may react immediately with the first contact, but the hierarchy delays. By the time the hierarchy recognizes the change it is over and there is no way to undo it. Moreover, different forces are always at work, and how they work may depend very little on the hierarchy's decisions. For example, in Brazil and elsewhere Black slaves had to be baptized, but their Christianity was quite different from that of their white masters, closer to *Candomblé* or *Macumba* than to the catechism. They received this religion not from the clergy but from the *pais-de-santo* and *mães-de-santo*. When the bishops tried to step in they encountered stiff opposition and realized that they were unable to influence the religion at their own will.

The council states: "The church is not unaware how much it has profited from the history and development of humankind." However, it ignores how much it has been manipulated and distorted by the history and development of humankind. Not everything supplied by history has been positive. The church has often let itself be guided more by history than by the gospel, and its religion has been based more on the history of religions than on gospel inspiration. When it ignores this past, it is prevented from knowing how much it has to change if it wants to respond to the demands of evangelization in our times. The council continues:

> The church learned early in its history to express the Christian message in the concepts and languages of different peoples and tried to clarify it in the light of the wisdom of their philosophers: it was an attempt to adapt the gospel to the understanding of all and the requirements of the learned, insofar as this could be done. (GS 44)

The question is: was it the church that adapted the gospel to the capacity of the peoples, or was it the peoples who adapted the gospel to their demands? In the emerging amalgam, especially in Christendom, was it the gospel or traditional popular religion, or possibly certain philosophies or wisdoms, that came out on top? Who should have given in? Who was in charge? The answer is not so clear.

Certainly, the church needs to be aware of all that it has received from the cultures of the peoples in which it has lived. Many things may have been positive at first but later became an obstacle. Stances contrary to the Christian spirit entered into Christendom because it was impossible to resist them, e.g., the notion of holy war or the inquisition. By discerning what was right and what was mistaken in the past, we can be better prepared to deal with the future.

Let us cite just a few particularly eloquent examples of the reception of culture by the church from Greece and Rome. What it received is incalculable and until recently it was all regarded positively, as progress, improvement, a providential instrument for strengthening the church and making it more suited for evangelizing the world. The time for discernment has now arrived. For some time, Protestant and independent writers have taken a critical look at this whole inheritance the church received, and have not seen it as wholly positive. Catholic apologists have opposed this historic revisionism, feeling that it would lead to revising many ancient institutions in the Catholic Church which they wanted to maintain. But that is just what we have to do: revise obsolete institutions.

The church received its conception of truth through philosophy, especially from Plato, for whom truth exists in ideas outside human beings.

Human beings receive ideas directly through illumination of the mind. Whether it is through ideas (Plato) or through abstraction from a sense experience (Aristotle), the important thing is that the truth is in concepts and their interconnection. Knowledge of the truth grows through deduction, which is the surest means for reaching truth (a manipulation of concepts starting from primary truths). Truth is stated in propositions: a statement is true or false (principle of contradiction). Everything becomes simple because it can be stated in simple, evident propositions.[5]

This concept of truth was applied to Christianity, which was presented as a "truth," that is, a doctrine stated in clear and true propositions, through clearly defined words. Being logical and coherent, Greek thought has all words defined on the basis of the system. The same thing was done with Christianity. The variety, multiplicity, and complexity of biblical images was eclipsed by a system with clear and simple propositions, the whole of which was said to be the truth, Christianity being this truth. Attaining salvation entailed accepting this truth. Since the truth is evident, no one who does not recognize it can be justified. Denying the truth may be regarded as a crime and is always sin. The concept of truth, associated with salvation, produces heresy and inquisition.

Based on the Greek philosophical perspective, a human discourse was defined as capable of speaking pure and simple "truth." In the gospel Jesus says he is the Truth, but in the Hellenized world, truth, as elaborated by the clergy, became a doctrine about Jesus. This conception of truth led the church to define Christ's revelation increasingly in formulas like those of the philosophers. Christianity became primarily a doctrine, and naturally a doctrine beyond discussion because its foundation was God's word.

If the official doctrine is saving the truth, denying that doctrine not only constitutes error, but a crime: it is heresy. Battling heresies came to occupy a disproportionate place in the life of the church. In the second millennium concern about heresy has grown unceasingly. Heresies have expanded the function of the magisterium, which has the mission of combating them. This struggle against heresy is a historic memory that is now associated with the church, to the point where the only thing some people know about it is the power of the inquisition.

To what extent was Greek philosophy perhaps a trap? Indeed, philosophy made possible a rationalization of the Christian faith that would not have been possible anywhere else in the world. But it also exposed the church to a great danger. St. Paul wanted nothing to do with philosophy out of fear of contamination. During the patristic period, the monastic movement as a whole was also opposed to philosophy. The condemnation of Origen was a key event, recalled for centuries. Scholasticism arose in the West, however, and theologians thought that they could control philosophy and make it a servant of faith: *philosophia ancilla theologiae*. But was philosophy really the *ancilla*? In practice, what should have been the servant became the master and theology was dominated by scholastic philosophy.

Scholasticism used Greek philosophy and thus offered the church a powerful instrument of control for battling heresy. It offered a clear and coherent formulation of doctrine. It facilitated the work of the inquisitors, offering them a complete catalog of all truths. Scholasticism developed without significant opposition from anyone defending the biblical and patristic tradition. Thus the hierarchy could be regarded as the depository of all truth, capable of judging and condemning. John Paul II has asked forgiveness for the condemnation of Galileo, for which scholasticism must take the credit, but he does not seem to be very sensitive to the snares of the theology of scholastic "truth" that led to Galileo's condemnation. Galileo was not condemned by bad theologians; his condemnation was simply an application of scholastic principles.

Evangelization itself was conceived as teaching the catechism. Being a Christian meant, first, not being a heretic and knowing the truths of faith. Doctrine had a priority over the action of charity. Today the concern for truth considered as a set of propositions is still prevalent in evangelization.

The most serious consequence was that this conception of truth divided Christians into two categories, which until recently were called the "*ecclesia discens*" and the "*ecclesia docens*," that is, the learning church and the teaching church, pupils and teachers. The teachers are the hierarchy, with priests as assistants. The learning church is lay people. They must remain silent and the clergy must speak; their word is always right, because priests know and lay people do not. Lay people will always be suspect of heresy, and so over the centuries they have learned to be quiet.

The theology developed in the scholastic schools, based on the Greek notion of truth, is an esoteric knowledge reserved for specialists. Lay people became convinced that Christian doctrine was so esoteric that only the priests understood it and others had to accept it blindly, the more blindly the better.

The people of God was divided, i.e., it ceased to feel and exist as a people, as Christianity was transformed into a set of formal propositions. The people was now made up of the ignorant guided by a knowing clergy. This does not come from Christian origins: it was a deviation that has caused immeasurable disasters in the history of the church, and it is particularly at the root of the great apostasy of the educated classes in Europe from the end of the seventeenth century to the late nineteenth century. To the educated, Christianity looked like the imposition of a doctrine, an obsolete doctrine, in the name of the power of truth.

Another legacy from Greece was spiritualism. It did not come from the classic Greek arts which extolled the human body. That legacy was forgotten and suppressed when the Roman empire became Christian. It came from the philosophers who placed all human value in the soul or spirit. The body had no value of its own but was merely an instrument (food is to sustain life, sex is only for reproduction). The body must be disciplined to provide the services demanded by the spirit. Control of the spirit over the body became the center of Christian perfection. Those ideas are not in the Bible, but in Greek philosophy (e.g., Stoicism).

With the inculturation of Greek spiritualism, Christian life became a matter of mortifying the body. The lives of some saints showed how much bodily suffering one could endure. They valued such mortification as participation in the passion of Jesus, even though the gospels do not say that Jesus inflicted these sufferings on himself for ascetic reasons; they were inflicted by others.

Spiritualism lasted until the twentieth century and the great bodily revolution of the 1960s: body, health, beauty, activity, harmony, and therapy became the center of culture. This movement included the sexual revolution, which is still unfolding. It was—and still is—a vigorous reaction against the disciplining of the body prominent in various past cultures, including the culture of Christendom.

A huge cry of protest thus arose in response to centuries of bodily and sexual repression preached by the church and transmitted through Catholic education. Naturally the great revolution of the body produced a huge cry of indignation blaming the church for repression of the body. This repression has no basis in the Bible, but was incorporated into Christian morality under the influence of philosophy. Did the church adopt philosophy or did philosophy adopt Christianity to serve as the vehicle for its wisdom?

Hellenism influenced Christianity through its conception of truth and its ethical spiritualism. Today it is clear that this legacy burdens and commits the church to things that are not really Christian and are no longer recognized as cultural values. This inculturation—which is at least obsolete if not exaggerated and dangerous and the source of many evils—should be a lesson for us.

From Rome the church received the structure and the very conception of power as empire, monarchy, domination. During its second millennium it was organized increasingly along the lines of Roman imperial law, culminating in the power of the pope as absolute monarch. When the Roman emperors became Christian, the empire already had a religious character. Christianity had to shape itself to some degree to the religious content of the empire. The emperor was the mediator between God and human beings, and the Christian emperor continued to be the primary mediator to whom the bishops and the entire Christian system submitted.[6]

The empire was not a people; it was fifty peoples brought together under the emperor's authority. The church was also transformed into a power structure in which the bishops were the emperor's delegates, each in his own province. The emperor was charged with maintaining peace in the world as the pope was in the church. When certain churches representing certain peoples rebelled (e.g., Egypt and Syria) they were regarded as schismatic churches, and heresies were attached to them. Only the emperor's church was orthodox. This structure reflected imperial theology. In practice there were controversies and problems because the patriarchs did not always submit passively, but as a rule everything operated in accordance with the imperial framework. Upon examination, it is clear that the teachings of the Monophysites and the Nestorians could have been reconciled with orthodoxy had there been goodwill, but political motivations prevailed: anyone who did not submit to the empire could not be orthodox.

History unfolded differently in the West, where the legacy of Rome was not lost but rather transferred. The Western emperor failed to achieve the same prestige as his Eastern colleague because he inherited a congenital defect: the imperial crown had been given to Charlemagne by the pope, who thus was situated above the emperor. After a fifty-year struggle between pope and emperor termed by historians the "Gregorian revolution" (Gregory VII), the pope became like an emperor, claiming supreme authority above the emperor, and hence above the kings and princes of Christendom.

Power in the church was gradually organized along imperial lines. For centuries the popes sought to reserve the appointment of bishops to themselves, finally succeeding with the 1917 Code of Canon Law. Once appointed by the pope, bishops became delegates of the pope's imperial power. Henceforth everything operated as if the church were subdivided into districts like imperial society, or like the state today. The clergy was completely subordinate to the bishop, i.e., to the pope, with no rights or privileges. The 1983 code suppresses the last guarantees of whatever modest autonomy had remained. Lay people are purely passive. The pope creates a diocese or changes diocesan boundaries without asking the inhabitants. The bishop appoints a pastor without even asking the parishioners, just like the emperor appoints officials or army officers. Lay people are as passive as in the Roman empire; their role is to obey.[7]

None of this was in Christian origins. It was taken up by the church, using a political instrument that it found in the world where it took root. Was this a fortunate inculturation? Did it help evangelization?

A particular kind of evangelization did take place, top-down evangelization, the Christendom model, which was almost the only one in the evangelization of the Americas. In the eyes of history, however, can we say that it was a victory for the church, which could use the empire for evangelization? Or was it a victory of the empire, which could use the church for its own power? We could ask the same question in our present situation.

The Roman Curia, representing a thousand years of conquering power, still thinks that evangelization is top-down, with the help of human powers, starting with political power; it is a faithful depository of imperial theory, and it is amazing to see how it almost always manages to choose agents whose psychology and personality fit this model. The Curia knows how to administer, and continues co-opting identical people who adapt themselves to fit their role as shapers of power. A nuncio once told me, "The church cannot evangelize without the help of the government." For him, evangelizing means conquering, as it was throughout the history of Christendom.[8]

There may well have been no other way to evangelize. (Even so, let us recall that strong voices were always raised in protest, e.g., in the mendicant orders from St. Francis to Bartolomé de las Casas.) Today, however, we must recognize that the legacies of both Greece and Rome are primary obstacles to evangelization. Within the system created by these legacies, it is impossible to evangelize current Western culture. It is radically impossible to evangelize Asian peoples who live in very ancient civilizations, which do not accept the model of domination. It is radically impossible to evangelize the Indigenous peoples of the Americas and African peoples, who may possibly submit because they are fascinated by the church's power, but their inner soul cannot be reached this way.

The ideology of Christendom assumed that everything taken in throughout history was good. Everything added on was seen as positive, and it was all of a piece with true Christian tradition. Today we are more cautious. Anything new brings advantages and disadvantages. In history there is no final solution but we can at least be prudent and not simply accept everything that history has brought us.

Thus, the people of God must ever be seeking itself, striving for its own authenticity. This is a people made up of persons who belong to their peoples by birth or adoption. Its members bring their entire way of life, the entire culture, politics, and economics of their nation, and likewise their entire religion. Even if subjectively they want to be converted, they continue to bear most of what they have acquired in their people and continue to acquire through a shared life. Even if they strive to be pure Christians they are always only partly so, because they are still pagans in many aspects of their life, especially religion.

The problem is that they are not always conscious of this dependence. They regard as gospel something that entered into their subconscious and actually comes from elsewhere, e.g., General Pinochet, who said: "As the gospel says: 'Everyone for himself and God for all!' " He was sure this was in the gospel, not because he had read it, but because it was in his subconscious. He was convinced that whatever he thought must be in the gospel. That is a great barrier to change.

The people of God exists only as project, intention, trial, basic option; it is always in the process of being made. It is not a steady advance or continual growth. There are advances and retreats; it does not follow a straight line. Accidents of history, strategic errors, mistaken options can cause detours and lost time.

Under Christendom, people were unaware of the historicity of the human condition. Had they studied the Bible more they would have discovered this historicity, but they read the Bible with the eyes of Greek philosophy which hid much of its message from them. They thought that the people of God was identified with Christendom, as a finished product. They thought that the church as it existed was what Jesus intended. While the hierarchy and theologians defended this orientation, the opposite conviction was common among the lower classes and heterodox theologians, namely that the church was being corrupted and needed reform *in capite et in membris*. With Christendom gone, we now know that people of God means journey, goal. We know that we are on pilgrimage toward that people.

One extraordinary sign stood up against the Christendom model of the second millennium, so marked by these legacies, and condemned and unmasked it and stripped it bare: Francis of Assisi. He stood opposed to the entire Christendom system, and went to the extreme in his life-option precisely so that it would constitute a complete condemnation. In opposition to the education of the clergy, he did not want his companions to have even a single book, and preached the gospel that he had not learned in school or books. In his testament he says he has received everything from Jesus, not by way of the pope. In contrast to the clergy's imperial power he had nothing: no money, no house, no horse. He never spoke ill of the pope, bishops, or priests, and indeed spoke well of them, but his whole person was a tremendous condemnation.

What is remarkable is that for six hundred years almost all Christians have identified with him; they have recognized that this was the gospel message and that everything else was dust, fiction, a phantom, empty. It was hard to follow the message. St. Francis was the response of Jesus to the edifice of Christendom. Many popes, bishops, and priests knew that, but they did not have the courage to give up what they had and to follow Jesus' advice to the rich young man. They did not dare to apply this gospel episode to themselves.

This tells us a lot about what the church receives from peoples. We have here a warning not to accept poisoned gifts.

Although Vatican II critiqued the cultural legacy of Christendom, it generally did so discreetly, so as not to offend the conservatives. The contrast between restored biblical teaching as a standard and historical embodiments is not always clear. This will certainly be a task for a next council: to say clearly what is purely cultural, a changeable product of history, and what comes from Jesus, and to clearly say what should be changed because as a cultural legacy it is now obsolete and counterproductive.

INCULTURATION

In recent decades inculturation has become a priority, sometimes the number one priority, in Third World churches. We are not going to deal explicitly with this vast issue,[9] but we may present some considerations in the light of the theology of the people of God that we are seeking.

Until recently, inculturation was not assumed consciously in the history of the church because there was no awareness of the historicity of the church itself, which was accepted by the clergy—in principle—only after Vatican II. *Evangelii Nuntiandi* (1976) was the first document that officially brought the issue into church discussion. Some processes in previous church history might have been inculturation in a way, but they took place almost unconsciously. When the church brought people into Christendom it did not think it was engaging in inculturation. Thus inculturation is a new challenge, and we have little experience of how to do it. This lack of experience is likewise apparent in almost all studies of inculturation, which insist on its necessity but do not provide concrete examples of where it has been accomplished.[10]

We know that there was an inculturation process in Africa, specifically in Ethiopia where a completely Black Christian church started in the sixth century, but few scholars and missionaries have studied it. The Nestorian church was inculturated not only in Syria, but far away in Asia, where Nestorians got as far as China, but this is not well known. Within the Christendom of the Roman empire, matters were controlled and increasingly centralized. The imperial ideology was not inclined to accept diversity. With the formation of the Roman subculture, especially in the last two centuries, all Catholics are asked to be alike, everyone in the whole world bound to the Roman subculture.

Two types of inculturation may be identified in the West: one for the ruling classes, essentially the clergy, and another for the world of the people, especially in the countryside. In the educated classes (the clergy and later a small urban petite bourgeoisie) there was an encounter with Greek philosophy integrated into scholastic theology and an encounter with the monarchical system of government inherited from Rome, as we have noted.

In the world of the people, the missionaries found different forms of polytheism, full of magic. A letter from Pope Gregory to the missionaries in England gives us a very good idea of what happened. The missionaries destroyed the idols and put the saints in their place, thereby giving rise to the veneration of the saints which is essential to popular religion in Christendom. The saints were the former pagan gods under other names, and their worship was slowly purified of the grosser forms of paganism, without ever risking a break. Those devoted to the saints believed they were perfect Christians, and the clergy never sought to question this kind of Christianity, which Protestantism ultimately condemned and eliminated. What happened in Latin America with the gods of the Indians and the Orixás of Blacks was simply the continuation of the traditional evangelization process.

The result was not really an inculturation but a juxtaposition of two religions. Catholics submitted to the obligatory rites imposed by the hierarchy. They did so more out of obedience than conviction, because they understood little of the rites which were so far from their own way of expressing themselves. Alongside this quasi-formal religion, they continued to practice their traditional religion of the saints, which replaced the gods that had been toppled. The aim of this worship was first of all health, followed by protection against the dangers of war, natural disasters, and perhaps other important concerns such as getting a marriage partner; St. Anthony was the great marrying saint, obtaining fiancés for millions of anguished young women. The missionaries did not create problems as long as the peasants submitted to the sacraments.

This popular religion was marked by feast days, and the saints are a reason to celebrate feast days. They were not very different from the feast days celebrated in the Americas a thousand years ago, or in the East five thousand years ago. That does not mean that they were worthless. Ancient polytheistic worship always had a great deal of value, and it organized the lives of farming peoples from the creation of the earliest human settlements. However, there is not a great deal of difference in value between a patron saint's feast and the feast day of an ancient god; it may look different, but deep down little has changed. Hence, it should not be cited as an instance of inculturation.

This does not mean that under Christendom the people were not Christian. However, their Christianity was not connected to religiosity, or rituals, or beliefs. Feast days are essentially social events, and Jesus is something else. The message of Jesus is not based on rituals, but on everyday life: love for neighbor, caring for the poor, the sick, children, the old, in patience, in seeking peace, in human relations, in sacrifice for the sake of others, in short, in living the gospel. These things may be experienced even without participation in feast days or religious rites. The two things are quite far apart, and thus evangelization has little to do with religiosity and feasts or saints; they are two different areas of life. The people was evangelized to a greater or lesser extent: more when it could find figures like St. Francis; less when it did not have that opportunity. In any case, evangelization in itself is something other than inculturation—which is itself a result of evangelization.

In the past the church came into contact with other peoples and cultures in the foreign missions. The Jesuits raised the issue in the sixteenth and seventeenth centuries, but they were condemned. The Catholic hierarchy was convinced that the Roman subculture was the universal truth, and hence comprehensible to all human beings. If there was anything in other cultures that was incompatible with the code of beliefs or Catholic morality, it had to be stamped out. Only after 1950, as decolonization began, did missionaries discover that other peoples had their own cultures which had their own values. Thus began the problem of mission, and more recently of inculturation.[11]

We are at the beginning of a truly human encounter, as a dialogue with the other great religions of humankind. It is something new and will occupy us well into the new millennium. In the Roman empire, Christianity did not encounter any great religion, but simply the vestiges of a decadent polytheism which was scorned by Greek and Roman intellectuals. The church encountered a philosophy and a law, but not a religion. Today it has to accept the encounter with major religions and their imposing concomitant cultures. This is a completely new task, and we do not have anyone or anything to help us, and must proceed with care.

It is not clear why the Roman Curia is so afraid of the first attempts at contact with the religions, as if it knew and had proven advice to offer on this matter. Both the Curia and we know next to nothing about this, and hence we have to pay attention to all experiences. If inculturation were to occur, in the sense of integration between Christianity and another religion, it would be unprecedented in the history of the church. We can imagine the scope of the problem we face. Church documents generally do not seem to be aware of the problem; they give the impression that it can be resolved with some decrees by Roman congregations.

Indeed, inculturation does not take place by decree, nor by decision of the evangelizers, because it is done by each people. Inculturation is unpredictable. It cannot be said ahead of time whether a people will open up or not, whether it will accept something from Christianity or not. Dialogue may or may not take place, but no one can decide when—certainly not because a missionary wants to. Obviously it will only become feasible after a long and deep shared life; at some point a mutual compenetration begins between Christianity and another culture. In this area any so-called pastoral plans are useless.

Furthermore, relationships between persons or peoples are primarily subconscious, and no rational decree can change the unconscious from one day to the next. Hence, evangelization takes place mysteriously, primarily in the unconscious, when communication takes place between persons. Culture operates on a more external level. People first have to be on the same wavelength.

Another task that is quantitatively less important, and perhaps more difficult, also requires attention: the encounter between Christianity and the so-called primitive religions, that is, those that are less complex intellectually, but more complex in terms of the subconscious. They have no theology, but do have gestures, rites, traditions, and myths. They are primarily African and Amerindian, but they also exist in Asia and Oceania. Here we face a vacuum. Thus far there have been two procedures for dealing with these religions, both by Christians who were bearers of a more developed civilization and were in the countries as superiors or invaders. Primitive religions were sometimes regarded as sheer idolatry, and the starting point for mission was to destroy all external signs of polytheism, with the conviction that these religions would not survive the destruction of their religious objects. This first approach was used extensively in the Americas. In the second approach, the missionaries did as we have seen: they replaced the idols with Catholic saints, and the saints became consecrated idols. This approach produced a juxtaposition between polytheistic religion and Christian religion, but no mutual compenetration.

If we want to begin a dialogue with so-called primitive religions, the traditional religions of rural people, it is going to take a very long time. One has to put aside one's entire Western education and begin to live with the people to the point of feeling like them. Westerners want to understand right away, to judge and see how they can utilize what they know. Attempts to understand and to judge will have to be put aside. The aim is to share life so as to see if it is possible to communicate with the deep soul of a people. Superficial shared life is easier, because these peoples learn the more conventional answers from Westerners, and because they cannot express what they feel in terms of Western rationality. One who seeks to do this will have to spend a lifetime doing it, and in the end will probably find out that he or she has understood very little. Things will become clearer after a few generations.

For thinking through the relationship of the church and other peoples we need the concept of "people of God." "Communion" does not express what that relationship is. The church cannot simply be said to be the communion of all peoples, nor can it be said that it integrates the communion of peoples. The notion of "communion" cannot account for how relationship occurs in history.

As the set of relationships between the people of God and existing peoples with their religions and cultures, inculturation involves a great many complex processes. The relationship is as complex as the peoples themselves, because it has to take place in all levels and dimensions: space, time, education (physical, psychological, and intellectual), training, preparation for faith, hope and charity, moral virtues, language, bodily and intellectual expression, ways of thinking, acting, loving, modes of social relations, organization of communities, and communication.

One suspects that an ecclesiology of pure communion leads to including in the church of God only the spiritual, that which is of a disembodied soul. From this standpoint, it may be thought that everything is solved with a good emotional relationship, with gestures of friendship and statements of agreement in a community of spirits, rather than through inculturation. The people of God would not receive anything from peoples as peoples; everything that comes from the people would be beyond evangelization. That would simplify things: Western-style human relations would suppress the diversity of peoples. No importance would be given to diversity: all human beings would be regarded as pure equal souls.

WHAT PEOPLES RECEIVE FROM THE CHURCH

Gaudium et Spes offers a brief but thorough summary of what the church brings to the world and to peoples. First, says the council, it gives meaning to life, an insuperable meaning, in response to human yearnings (41). This is a wonderful program and it says what the church ought to do, and what it does sometimes—but things are harder in practice. Today the Roman subculture is so isolated that for many people, as the expression goes, it is providing wonderful answers to questions that no one is asking. Before responding to human yearnings it is important to know what they are. They cannot be just in the minds of theologians, let alone just in the minds of Curia officials.

This consideration of the meaning of life comes from Christendom. Indeed for 1500 years the church provided all of society and all individuals with a complete view of the world and of life, a plan of action and an organization in which all could find support. In principle it offered a complete response to the problem of life; in fact it supplied the questions, instilled them in the population, and then presented the answers that fully satisfied the questions asked. Even so, historical documents show that this worldview and its program of life were not always accepted peacefully and happily.

In any case, the church no longer owns the questions. For most baptized people living in the former lands of Christendom, the church does not offer what it claims to offer. This is also true of the urban population in Latin America which no longer finds in the church the answers it seeks.

Many feel that it is a repressive and domineering force that seeks to impose itself on their consciences and obstructs freedom instead of promoting it. That may be regrettable, but it is how things are. This certainly does not come from the gospel, or from Christ or from official documents or teaching, but from how all of this is presented in the church today. But it is important that the council has recalled what the church ought to be, because it thus shows the way to conversion.

Second, the church "announces and proclaims the freedom of the daughters and sons of God, it rejects all bondage resulting from sin, it scrupulously respects the dignity of conscience and its freedom of choice, it never ceases to encourage the employment of human talents in the service of God and humanity, and finally, it commends everyone to the charity of all." Finally the church proclaims human rights (41).

Some will find this passage somewhat ironic—in view of the history of Indians and Black slaves of the Americas, for example—when it speaks of respecting the dignity of conscience. Actually the council is saying what the church ought to provide, not necessarily what it actually has provided and provides now. Indeed, the greatest reason why a growing mass of people in what used to be Christendom reject the church is precisely the lack of respect for dignity of conscience and freedom of choice, because the church wants to govern the entire life of human beings and society on the basis of demands drawn from the gospels by the hierarchy against the resistance of people's consciences. Unfortunately, many decisions by the Holy See in the past twenty years have only reinforced this conviction in the minds of many, including those who want to remain in the church because they believe in the possibility of conversion.

In the next paragraph the council considers the help that the church strives to provide to human society. The church:

- is able . . . to initiate action for the benefit of everyone, especially of those in need, such as works of mercy and the like . . .
- acknowledges the good to be found in the social dynamism of today, specially in progress toward unity, healthy socialization, and civil and economic cooperation.
- calls upon its members and upon all people to put aside, in the family spirit of the children of God, all conflict between nations and races . . .
- wants to help and foster these institutions insofar as this depends on it and is compatible with its mission. (GS 42)

This has to do with all human institutions created to improve their condition.

Here also some may note that in the past two centuries the church has promoted primarily its own institutions, such as schools, hospitals, cultural and leisure centers, while not promoting others, on the grounds that they were not in accordance with its mission. The church created a network of institutions that made up a kind of parallel society, and was not much interested in how other institutions were doing. For example, in Brazil religious orders were very concerned about their own schools, but not about public schools and universities, as if these could not receive anything from the church.

What the council is saying would be a radical change of strategy, but it is proposed for future generations in the church. Vatican II seems to say that a particular phase of the church's action in the world, namely the period when the church organized society in various nations and had control over a major portion of the population, sometimes as much as half, as was the case in Holland, Belgium, Germany, Ireland, Italy, Spain, Portugal, and Quebec, is now over. Today there is a tremendous reaction of the population against these isolated institutions and against the temporal power they give the church.

The new program would mean helping and promoting institutions common to all citizens. Rather than guiding society, the church would devote itself to furthering the freedom and dignity of every human being in each institution, using persuasion rather than the power of its institutions. These principles are a declaration of intentions, rather like political party platforms that state principles but are never implemented.

Efforts were made right after the council, but after a few years it was clear that little had changed in the system of church institutions, and that the overall strategy had not changed. The network of establishments in education, health care, and social assistance is so strong that no one even considers changing them. Little has changed and *Gaudium et Spes* remains on paper. Indeed, the other council documents support the traditional institutions, as if the principles stated in *Gaudium et Spes* had no implications. No doubt most intended to go on as before but with other intentions: human dignity, freedom of conscience, human rights, helping community institutions, and so forth would be a statement of intentions and that would be fine as long as nothing had to be changed. Putting the principles into practice would entail a step that many regard as impossible.

* * *

In order to learn what the church gives the people, rather than looking for what it should offer, it is better to examine history to see what the church has actually given the peoples thus far. That would require gathering all the information on the influence of the church in the lives of peoples in the past, and certainly is material for many volumes of history. By way of example we want to recall what a great canon lawyer and historian of canon law, Jean Gaudemet, wrote about the Christian influence on Roman law after the so-called conversion of Constantine. After insisting on the difficulty of uncovering Christian influences, because other factors were involved and in many respects Stoicism was in agreement with Christianity on social morality, Gaudemet examines some aspects in which it can be argued that there is a Christian influence.

Most importantly, Christianity changed family morality. The law became more demanding with regard to breaking engagement or divorce, impeded remarriage, protected the interests of children of a first marriage, prohibited leaving newborns out to die, trafficking in children, and other abuses in the use of the *patria potestas*.

The church accepted slavery but it corrected certain particularly odious aspects: prohibiting the branding of slaves on the forehead and the dividing of slave families. Emancipation by the church was legally recognized. The church achieved the prohibition of gladiatorial games and prostitution. But it does not seem to have corrected the harshness of the criminal code or changed economic structures. Initially Christians went along with the practices of Roman law on marriage, but soon a body of legislation, increasingly original and different from Roman law, was created. This process lasted over ten centuries, ending after the Council of Trent.

The church fathers had no hesitation in accepting the principles of Roman law on slaves. They did try to soften the weight of slavery by defending slaves against the excesses of their masters and encouraging emancipation. In the course of the fifth century the number of slaves declined, partly because the Romans could no longer defeat their enemies and bring prisoners back as slaves, and partly under the church's influence and efforts toward emancipation. Economically, the fathers and the councils condemned charging interest and also commercial profit which entailed buying cheap and selling dear. Thus they prepared legislation restricting circulation of money and freedom of trade.

In short, it can be said that the church struggled against cruelty in customs and in favor of emancipation of slaves and respect for their human dignity, at least at a basic level, and it also struggled against usury, defending the poor and encouraging aid for their needs. At that time, any other kind of action in a society as strong as Roman society was impossible. Some more demanding groups wanted a more radical stance toward the vices of society but they did not win people over. The bulk of the hierarchy was unwilling to criticize Roman society as a whole, because it was part of it.[12]

There is another example in what the West usually calls the Middle Ages, the period between the tenth and the sixteenth centuries.[13] Christianity, especially through monks and friars, created a new society based on the development of agriculture, livestock, and artisanry. 1) It created the rural world that survived in Europe until the mid-twentieth century, when it began to disappear. The monks did physical as well as intellectual work, exalting the virtue of manual work, thus breaking with the old Greco-Roman tradition. The church went back to biblical sources to encourage farm or shop labor. 2) The monks improved the land and crops, harnessed water and wind for energy, and bred animals for field work and transportation. 3) They also helped peasants get land, defend their rights against the power of the privileged, and develop their own markets. 4) The rise of cities served not only for economic activities, but for freedom of thought and protection of individuals against the nobility, including the bishops.

All agree that the church laid the foundations for Western civilization, with a linear conception of history that led to a search for progress rather than stability. In other civilizations (Islam, the Hindu world, China) progress occurred by chance or by the effort of a few, rather than of society as a whole. The mindset of temporal and material progress was introduced by the church, particularly by monks and friars (the hierarchy acted more as a brake, insofar as the clergy had a privileged status in the social order).

How did the church progressively lose political, economic, and cultural leadership from the fourteenth to the eighteenth century? How to account for the rise of the modern states that claimed to work more efficiently than Christendom? How to account for the rise of capitalism which broke down the workers' defenses and handed them over to be exploited by capital? How did Western culture come to be ever more critical of the cultural legacy of Christendom? In a way, we might say that this has been and still is the primary topic of Western historiography, as well as of sociology or cultural anthropology. In any case, in the Middle Ages the church was active in creating a civilization which is the foundation of the modern and contemporary West.

Historians recognize that the profound change represented by modernity owes a great deal to the Christendom that it replaced. Science itself with its concern for improving the human condition arose in a Christian environment. The search for truth came from the Middle Ages which had received it from the Greeks, but Christianity desacralized the world: there is no room for science in a world of magic, and hence other cultures whose conditions might have been equal or superior to those of the West (Islam, China, Japan) did not develop the scientific spirit. The medieval Christianity of the West gave birth to modernity in terms of science, against the resistance of theologians and the hierarchy—who were not the whole church.

Modern politics and the modern state are rooted in Christian inspiration: the rule of law (which limits the power of rulers and submits them to higher ethical norms), democracy (which limits the power of kings), separation of powers, citizen participation—all derive from medieval Christendom. They draw some inspiration from Greek democracy or the Roman republic, but the latter subordinated citizens to the state and did not recognize the absolute value of the human being, as Christianity does.

The modern economy starts with a Christian concern: the struggle against poverty, on which the early generations of economists were focused. In the nineteenth century, the assurance that capitalism was the only way to multiply wealth to make it available to the poor masses caused the concern for poverty to decline in society and disappear from the horizon of economic liberals, but socialism did serve as a reminder of the purpose of the economy by proposing an economy entirely based on combating poverty. That is a Christian purpose.

The starting point for these institutions of modernity was a concern for achieving the goals of Christianity. The churches were accused of having deviated from their origins and from the goals justifying their existence. Only by way of exception was modernity anti-Christian—it was anti-clerical and anti-ecclesiastical.

Why this opposition? The only reason is that from the fourteenth century onward, the pope, the Roman Curia, and the clergy in general rejected all proposals and suggestions from lay people supported by theologians or scholars (and occasionally by bishops and even some popes such as Pius II, who could not change the direction of the church institution). In the sixteenth century the church condemned not only the entire Reformation movement as a whole, but it rejected and marginalized Christian humanism, which was a way of living as a Christian in the world of science, the state, and the economy.

Starting in the fourteenth century the hierarchical church took an increasingly closed stance toward every step taken by lay people. Over time, it came to accept, albeit without enthusiasm, what was developed by the lay world: science, the state and democracy, human rights, freedom of citizens, the modern economy (including some aspects of socialism). But it was always at least a century late, and after many condemnations. This rejection, followed by a resigned acceptance after several generations, ultimately led to resentment and hostility against the Catholic hierarchy and clergy. From that time, the hierarchy engaged thousands of theologians in a huge enterprise of apologetics, wasting an immense amount of energy in the defense of a lost cause. The church directed all its energies into the struggle against the rise of modernity, rather than seeking and developing all that was Christian in the movement. A terrible expenditure of energy, for nothing.[14]

In short, the church's major contributions to the world were made before the fourteenth century; since then, the church has been more concerned with itself. Feeling itself under assault, it established a defensive organizational system that only served to prompt more criticism. Instead of responding creatively, the church—that is, the hierarchy and the clergy, who were increasingly regarded as being the church—devoted itself to justifying and preserving the past. To justify itself, it continually had to point to the achievements of the past, but society was expecting new achievements in the new setting.

To be sure, we cannot say that during these six hundred years Catholics have not made any contribution to the world. Some Catholics, including priests, have been writers, musicians, painters, but these have been fewer and fewer over time.[15] As Western culture went through an intense period of development, the participation of the people of God continued to decline, and the hierarchy seemed oblivious, as it cultivated its past and saw no further than the faithful flock. The outside world was blamed: society had prevented the church from contributing more to culture and progress.

The council sought to open a new era in the history of the church, one in which the church becomes more concerned with its contribution to the fate of the world, its earthly contribution. It now accepts that its mission is not simply to save souls for heaven, beyond this world, but that it also has a meaning for this earth. Hence the question: what does the church contribute? In the next chapter we will consider the church's action in the contemporary world.

Chapter 9

ACTION OF THE PEOPLE OF GOD IN THE WORLD

Despite its retrieval of the people of God, when Vatican II turned to issues of practice, it went back to a radical distinction between clergy and lay people, as if this were constitutive of the church. It discussed not the action of the people, but that of the hierarchy and of the laity, as theoretically distinct and separate in practice.

One of the problems with this distinction, which arose out of a particular social context, is that the action of lay people remains individual or personal. It is not connected organizationally, and hence is not very effective. Those who should be on the front lines of the battle take refuge in generalities. The doctrine of the people of God must be taken all the way: the church's action is that of a people, a united collective action.

SEEKING THE ACTION OF THE PEOPLE OF GOD

The distinction between the magisterium which provides principles and lay people who apply them (often enough contradictorily) suppresses the people of God. This distinction comes from a modern individualistic culture which has no shared projects or goals, and no reason to organize any common action. The church, however, does have a common objective: the liberation of the poor. Lay people cannot act together toward that end if the hierarchy is not out in front.

Jesus used various metaphors to define the way his people act in the world: light of the world, city on a mountain. The well-known letter to Diognetus renews these metaphors when it says that the church is in the world as leaven. But such metaphors may be further specified: of what does the church's action in the world consist? How does the people of God act in the midst of the peoples of the earth? How is it to be leaven?

The church has never explicitly clarified what its action in the world is. It customarily speaks as if its presence or action in the world were not an issue, or as if simply being in the world and performing its traditional (e.g., parish) functions constituted acting in the world. But such a presence might be more a lack of action than positive action.

Gaudium et Spes, which remains quite vague, stresses the distinction between church and world. Henceforth the church intends to respect the proper autonomy of the terrestrial order, and Christians are willing to collaborate. About the church's function it says, "The impact which the church can have on modern society is due to an effective living of faith and love, not to any external power exercised by purely human means" (42). The decree on the laity does not go much further:

> It is the task of the church as a whole to make women and men capable of establishing the proper scale of values in the temporal order and to direct it towards God through Christ. Pastors have the duty to set out clearly what is the purpose of creation and the use to be made of the world, and to provide moral and spiritual helps for the renewal of the temporal order in Christ.
>
> Lay people ought themselves to take on as their distinctive task this renewal of the temporal order. Guided by the light of the gospel and the mind of the church, prompted by Christian love, they should act directly in this domain and in their own way. (GS 7)

Clearly at that time the concern of those who wrote the document was to make a distinction between the role of the hierarchy and that of lay people. What concerned them was the relationship between hierarchy and laity, not the content of the mission. They conceived that relationship as understood in Catholic Action: the hierarchy defines the principles and lay people apply them. Popes Pius XI and Pius XII did not want to be committed to the lay people but they wanted lay people to be subject to them. This was the most that could be achieved at that time.

The problem has become evident in Latin America. The bishops call for action and offer principles. Lay people go into action, often prompting opposition from the established powers. The bishops step back and remain silent, and do not support lay people, even if they do not condemn them. Lay people feel frustrated and to some extent betrayed. This process occurred repeatedly between 1960 and 1990. Lay people no longer want to go into action without the support of the hierarchy. They are no longer willing to be prohibited from continuing when they begin to disturb the ruling classes. They would rather leave the church behind and act in independent organizations.

The Puebla Final Document is the most fully elaborated document of the Latin American bishops. Two fundamental themes stand out: the defense of human rights (motivated by the military dictatorships at that time) and the option for the poor, which involves the entire people of God. The themes are basic; the problem is how to apply them in practice.

Human rights are defended by condemning violations and by proclaiming a society of justice. The option for the poor leads to denouncing oppression and announcing a society in which the rights of the poor will be respected.

The most explicit text on how to act comes toward the end of the document:

- The Church bears evangelical witness to God as present in history; and it awakens in human beings an attitude of openness to communion and participation.
- In its own sphere, it establishes organisms of social action and human promotion.
- Insofar as it can, it steps in where public authorities and social organizations are absent or missing.
- It summons the human community to re-examine and give new direction to international institutions. . . . (1284-1287)

Yet evangelization is always conceived as the expression of words and doctrines (Part 2, chapter 1.2) and especially the church's social doctrine (Part 2, chapter 4.2). "Liberating evangelization" goes no further than stating the doctrine. This is Roman doctrine: the church should remain on the level of principles and thus never get down to details, to the specific, never question concrete situations or persons. Of course, a church that does this will never encounter opposition. The doctrine will be received respectfully by everyone, including those who violate its precepts in practice, and everything will stay the same. Pure doctrine not applied to cases does not lead to action. Archbishop Oscar Romero was killed precisely because he did not remain in the realm of principles.

Medellín's timidity in this regard might seem surprising because among the bishops were some who went much further than simply reminding people of general doctrinal principles. This timidity is probably a result of the pope's desire to rehabilitate the church's social doctrine, as stated in his opening address.[1] Stating the doctrine so forcefully amounted to rejecting other forms of action. On the plus side, the social doctrine states principles; on the minus side, it goes no further.

The Puebla document falls short of the practice of the most committed and most evangelical bishops at that time (Oscar Romero, Leonidas Proaño, Samuel Ruiz, Hélder Câmara, and many others). The assembly was unwilling[2] or unable, or did not realize that it was confirming a practice that was much more timid, more within reach of all, but less effective, less efficient, less evangelical. If Jesus had only taught the principles of morality he would never have been crucified. It will be precisely on the basis of the practice of some Christians more committed to the gospel that we can devise more concrete directions for the contemporary world.

However, we must first of all situate action in the current context because each mode of action depends on the situation of human relations at a particular phase of the evolution of humankind. The world is now different from what it was during the period of military dictatorships. The prevailing phenomenon is the globalization of a profoundly individualistic way of life. The great capitalist forces are imposing on the entire world an individualistic model of life, which gives capital free rein. Everything is subordinated to the growth of capital, and the corresponding model of human being is the model of the consumer. That is the great challenge. Can the church's response be reduced to simply stating its social doctrine? The hierarchy would then state general principles condemning this system in such a way that no one would feel it touched them, not even the IMF. There are also lay people, but lay people in isolation cannot do anything against such gigantic forces; they do not represent the church's effective power. The very knowledge that the hierarchy is not backing a particular practice by a group of lay people would be enough to conclude that it has no value and is not the action of the people of God. So is the action of the church limited to principles that in practice are innocuous? Where does the people of God come in?

A further concern arises in Latin America. The hierarchy is said to state the principles and the laity to act—each individual, or each group, in accordance with their conscience. But is that really how it is? Where does the hierarchy draw this social doctrine from? Apparently, we are supposed to think that it has been prepared directly by the pope or some of his secretaries, a doctrine "dropped down from heaven," because there is no mention of the process that led to this doctrine. The hierarchy takes care that the people involved in writing are not made known. The official theory is that it all comes from the pope and no one else is involved. Yet everyone knows that this is not the case. The social doctrine actually comes from many lay people, but there is no way to find out just who they are. Secrecy raises suspicion: what are they trying to hide?

The suspicion is that the social doctrine really comes from a relatively prudent and open Catholic bourgeoisie which regards moderate capitalism as the only solution. What is the basis for choosing these lay people who—whether Christian Democrat or liberal—create the atmosphere in which this moderate capitalist social doctrine is prepared? Were the Christian people consulted? Might it be possible to influence the selection? What are the criteria justifying why certain figures are always consulted and others not?

Anyone who has observed the history of CELAM up close can determine what the criteria are and will assume that the criteria in Rome are similar. However, we need only know who has been consulted to know what the church's social doctrine is. In practice the church's social doctrine is the doctrine of a party. Naturally, such a doctrine can be used against other parties.

As a rule, few people from the popular milieus are consulted, whereas many from the traditional conservative bourgeoisie are. The pope's signature does not change its real content.

Must the hierarchy be limited to stating the principles of doctrine? Can it not also risk becoming involved in ongoing history? The history of Latin America has a great deal to teach in this regard.

What should the action of the people of God be? It is defined by the signs of the times. The great sign today is the widespread individualism of the current globalization system. This individualism is not completely new. Its roots reach far back into the past, but it has now come to a point of previously inconceivable radicalism. This is the field of action for the people—action, not principles alone. Action for the people gathered around their pastors, not just for lay people in their own niches while the hierarchy remains in splendid abstraction.

CONDITIONS OF ACTION AS PEOPLE OF GOD

As Gregory Baum has said, the church can operate in either of two ways: administration or mission. The church either acts for itself, to consolidate or increase its power, size, extension, or the church evangelizes—that is, it addresses the peoples in order to be at the service of their life, freedom, and salvation, offering them the gospel of Jesus. It works either for itself or for others.

An option must be made. Of course, the two systems are not entirely closed. There will always be a need to administer the Christian families who are part of the flock, and there will always be a concern for mission. The issue is the emphasis, the priority, since everything else takes its direction from that priority. A church completely directed toward the world runs the risk of abandoning its faithful, and a church aimed solely at administration degenerates, because it loses its reason for being.

Thus far the direction is in favor of administration, despite statements pointing the other way. Some persons, groups, and institutions are devoted to mission, but the system as a whole is devoted to administering the church as it exists. Vatican II said that the nature of the church is essentially missionary (LG 17, *Ad Gentes* 2). But to say that means opting in the other direction. Papal documents since then have continued to affirm the priority of mission, but the system of administration remains in place, and so nothing changes. The popes want a church to be missionary without changing, but the church as it is does not allow for mission to take place; simply wanting it to be missionary does no good. The parish cannot be missionary, except in a marginal way or in words alone. Nor can the diocese be missionary because it was conceived to manage parishes. It is made up of parishes and all efforts are devoted to parishes, despite the proliferation of supposedly missionary bodies, which as a rule stay on paper, and in any case are not independent enough to be missionary. The chancery office is not a favorable vehicle for mission, nor could it be. Even the missionary institutes administer established missions, but they do not engage in missionary work outside. This is how the established system wants things to be.

The council itself was not consistent. After stating that the church is essentially missionary, it wrote a chapter on the hierarchy, chapter 3 of *Lumen Gentium* in which the mission of the bishops is entirely defined around the function of administration. When it comes time to say what bishops are to do, mission is forgotten, and everything is the same as before—as if theory could operate on its own. Reading chapter 3 of *Lumen Gentium* makes it clear that the church is not missionary and that the bishops are not missionary. Why didn't they complain? Because they realized that when they got back home everything would continue as before?

I myself scandalized people when I wrote that Dom Hélder was a model bishop for the third millennium.[3] He was accused of being a very poor administrator—a completely false accusation because his priority was people outside. Consider the case of Bishop Jacques Gaillot who is sui generis: he scandalizes the "good Catholics" in his diocese for the very reasons that society pays attention to him. He gives priority to those outside, and those inside protest. Could not some bishops be missionary, just as some bishops are army chaplains, officials in the Roman Curia, and ambassadors for the Vatican state? Readers are probably familiar with other examples from the recent history of the church in Latin America. Anyone who has gone through San Cristóbal de las Casas could tell many stories.

In the first half of the twentieth century it was said that the hierarchy and clergy would stay inside and lay people would act outside; the hierarchy would administer and lay people would be missionaries. True, it was also said that priests would train the lay people. Such was the theory of Catholic Action, which at the time was a step forward, and perhaps the only approach conceivable given the condition of the church.[4] But the method could not take hold in Latin America. It fell apart. The place for the bishops and priests is out in front of the laity. In the previous system, lay people were out on the front lines,[5] while the clergy remained peacefully in the sacristy. The clergy gave orders from afar, often without knowing what was really going on.

The irrationality of the system became clear when bishops appeared who took their position on the front line, and the people followed them. This is the normal situation. Otherwise the hierarchy becomes separated from the people when it comes time to act. Lay people were abandoned just when things became most difficult in public life.

Certainly Jesus never intended to confine the apostles to governing the Christian communities. They were primarily missionaries sent to the peoples, and Paul himself believed that it was not his task to baptize because he had another more urgent task. He was not content to teach lay people how they must act; he himself was out in front in the midst of the world. The position of the hierarchy is to be out in front projecting the gospel in the world, not taking refuge in internal life. Otherwise, lay people become disoriented. They need to see concrete signs, to know what to do, and only prophetic charisms can show that way. The apostolic ministries are primarily a charism of apostolate. Latin American experience shows that many thousands of lay people act when the bishop acts, they commit themselves when the bishop is committed, and they do not do anything if the bishop takes refuge in merely providing principles. Indeed, it is interesting to see how Pope John Paul II as pope was out in front of the Polish people's battle against the Communist regime in Poland. He did not shrink back in administration but went out to the battlefront.

In Latin America the people certainly expect the bishop to be out in front of all the church's activity, because he acts much more by his presence and attitudes than by his doctrines or sermons—which in fact only take on meaning within prophetic action. Far from wanting the hierarchy's role to be reduced, the people want it to grow, to be more visible and committed, a sign raised up among the nations.

Lay people, we are told, are to be missionaries and evangelizers, but they have not been prepared for that. They have been prepared to work in the parish or diocese at the service of already-established communities and institutions. They work there under the direction of the pastor, rather than acting on their own. They are not prepared to give witness to their personal faith nor to express personal convictions or attitudes. They are expected to be spokespersons for the parish, to say or do whatever is necessary for the maintenance and advance of the parish. They are lay people in the administration system. For example, if they work in catechesis they do not give testimony of their personal faith, but explain objectively what the church teaches. Yet in mission only personal testimony is valid. An evangelizer must give not what the church thinks but what he or she thinks.

Given their preparation, lay people cannot be expected to suddenly change their whole way of being, and to enter into mission, sent out into the world, into the unknown. Lay people need the security given by the clergy. Otherwise, they become radically insecure. As a proof, one need only compare the average Catholic with the average Evangelical: the difference can be seen from a hundred yards away. The Evangelical is secure, while the Catholic is insecure from the moment he or she is no longer under the priest's protection.

Among intellectuals, lay people are full of doubts: they do not know how to respond to objections presented to them at work or when relaxing. Hence they prefer not to discuss religion when Evangelicals bring up questions. In short, we can observe all the symptoms of the infantilization of lay people that has been noted by various analysts who are not merely naïve servants of the Catholic media (themselves perfect representatives of the model).

There is no mission without missionaries. A missionary is part of the mission system and must be prepared for that system. Strong personalities must be sent out into the world. This strength comes first from the very character of the person, and hence people who have this capability must be discovered. Their natural charism provides the material for the charism of the Spirit. Evangelicals do this systematically; they capture strong personalities.

Nature alone is not enough; missionaries must have as much autonomy as possible. The administration system is based on mistrust: people must be supervised, not trusted. The mission system is different: missionaries have to be trusted or they feel paralyzed. Strong personalities can be formed only by learning from freedom. That means experiencing mistakes and successes, being able to sin and to change, learning from experience. Intellectual formation does not come from assimilating a pre-established system of propositions, but from reflection and dialogue on experiences acquired. Much of this was done in Catholic Action movements, which even though they were strictly controlled were able to take advantage of certain niches when they had intelligent church advisors.

What missionaries are expected to do is to go out to meet the world; there they will discover what they must say and do from within themselves. What they must express in their life and in their word is what the Spirit inspires in them. If they just repeat a lesson, they will hardly be convincing. In the Catholic Church there are many people endowed with these qualities. Parishes and dioceses generally do not know what to do with them; they seem to be disruptive and are not utilized. Evangelicals often go looking for such people, and are able to offer them opportunities.

Missionaries must be in communication with communities, parishes, and the dioceses—but without dependence, because what they do is different and it does not fit into the parish or the parish-bound community. Unless that is allowed, it would be better to stop talking about evangelization.

The first and basic condition for evangelizing is to gain credibility, or to regain it. For we are no longer in the beginning of Christian history at the beginning of evangelization, nor are we in the sixteenth century. Today the church and its past are known. That past has many glorious pages, but there are also many shadows, and the people who were crushed in the past are not so easily forgotten. Gaining personal credibility is the condition for any missionary. The credibility of the people of God must be recovered.

The first thing that must be done is to show respect and understanding, and to dialogue with others, with everyone in the world, especially with sinners—that is, with people regarded as sinners: prisoners, women who have abortions, drug addicts, traffickers, mafiosi, those who are corrupt— as Jesus did with tax collectors, with the Samaritan woman, with the adulterous woman, and so forth. Such an attitude of respect does not mean approval of the sin, but an appeal to human beings in their depths out of a belief that they can still change. Not too long ago the greatest sin was being a Communist. John XXIII gave a powerful sign when he welcomed Khrushchev's son-in-law at the Vatican. Conservatives say that with this gesture he lost a million votes for the Christian Democrats, and that is likely. But what did the loss of a million votes mean, now that the party has gone down in scandal? John XXIII's gesture opened many doors and still stands. When Cardinal Silva set up the Vicariate of Solidarity in Santiago to help and support the families of the "disappeared," the political prisoners, those who were being persecuted, almost all of whom were Socialists or Communists, he gave a sign whose effects are still being felt. That was what allowed Christians and Socialists to come together in Chilean governments since the fall of Pinochet.

The second type of sign is the disinterested gesture. The church is still suspected of always seeking its own advantage in everything it does publicly. That is no surprise because that was the rule Leo XIII gave Catholics: in politics, always seek what is most advantageous for the church. But the missionary sign is when the church does not pursue its own interest.

The third sign is no doubt to recognize mistakes and sins. Pope John Paul II has done so many times in recent years and won sympathy and approval for doing so. It would probably be even more effective if he were to acknowledge errors made more recently.

The dogma of infallibility creates a bad impression everywhere. It is assumed to mean that the pope is never wrong, knows everything, and always does the right thing. That puts people off. Of course that is not what the text was intended to say, but this dogma was proclaimed to the whole world, and that is how it was understood. It is one of the few things that everyone knows about Catholicism. This formulation used to give the impression that the pope was very haughty. Today, if it seems he thinks he is infallible, it makes him look naïve. The way this dogma was stated was a historic mistake, and a missionary mistake, in particular.

If credibility is to be gained, similar mistakes must be avoided. Doctrines and dogmas may not be defined in disregard of how they are going to be received. It is impossible to avoid all mistakes, because there will always be people who will look for ways to criticize or condemn, but they should be avoided as far as possible.

Not all Catholics have to be missionaries—that would be impossible. There are many categories of people in the church with different kinds of behavior. The active ones are always a minority. The issue is knowing which minorities will be chosen by the church as the most representative. Where does the church invest most?

How does the church want to be represented in the world? Today the church looks primarily like a remnant of Christendom, still powerful because there is still a large mass of intellectually backward people attached to it, and because in Latin America it represents the traditional expression of religious feeling. The church is comprised primarily of people who are backward in terms of modern developments, still attached to older forms of culture and life, a large conservative bloc. That is the way it seems in the media, in conversations, in the minds of educated people.

This image persists because the hierarchy's actions appear to justify it. A start could be made toward another image. That would require giving more emphasis, more expression, and more autonomy to other people, other groups, and other minorities. Its image was better during the military regime when the church was more directly involved in the life of the nation. Since then it looks like it is more enclosed in its own affairs. That is terrible for credibility, the condition for any evangelization.

Under the administration system, the people of God as a whole is not expected to have any projection into the world. There is no reason to make options, choose goals, and organize actions around such options. The hierarchy assures people that things are being managed well, and Catholics try to follow their conscience in the world, ever at the disposition of the hierarchy to help where needed.

If joint action by the people of God is to become conceivable, the underlying orientation must be changed. Only by switching to a mission orientation will the church be able to act as a people, everyone together, each in his or her place in the midst of the world. Then evangelization will become a collective endeavor.

It is not enough to say, "We want to evangelize the world," because there is no agreement on what evangelization means, and therefore this expression is not sufficient for defining a collective plan of action. Evangelization must be given historic content. If it does not enter history, it does not do anything, and remains sheer talk. There is a lot of talk about evangelization. This must be quite clear: if evangelization is not engaged in ongoing history, it does not exist. It must define a content that is precisely the response to the explicit or implicit aspirations of the world.

The purpose of evangelization in the world today is to call peoples to really become peoples, journeying within the people of God. Our primary aim is not individual conversions. We think that they will take place if the church is really in tune with the clear or hidden aspirations of the inhabitants of today's world. In order to clarify this purpose, we will now examine the goals that the church set for itself in the past, when it acted as a people.

EXPERIENCE OF LATIN AMERICAN PRAXIS

Pastoral activity in Brazil until the time of Vatican II had drawn inspiration from the 1915 joint pastoral letter of the bishops in the southern part of the country[6] in which all the church's activity was aimed at saving souls individually. After Vatican II the aim was for the salvation of a whole people, the people of God.

Throughout Latin America the emergence of the idea of the people of God led many Catholics to seek dialogue, and then to become involved in their own people, to work together with the world instead of combating it. Latin America was in the throes of transformation, and that discovery was very disconcerting. Previously Catholics thought of the rest of society simply as a force that was out to destroy their religion. They now discovered the positive side of this modern world, and they recognized that Catholics cannot create a world as they would like it to be, but that the world is out there, and it has to be recognized for the way it is.

A minority of Catholics created a new praxis. A portion of the church, led by the Medellín bishops and a group of theologians, prompted the church to abandon its defensive positions and to set out to act on behalf of the peoples that they were discovering. This church discovered itself as people of God in its joint action on behalf of the peoples. It was no longer a matter of individual actions or of actions by particular institutions, but the activity of a whole group, a group action in which everyone joined together in pursuit of a common end.

The church as people is born out of a movement of struggle for the people, for their rights, dignity, and freedom. Hierarchy and laity are not at odds in this action. Bishops and priests have a prominent place within the people, out in front. They sacrifice themselves and die like others, and their presence is a sign of the unity of the people in movement. Symbols recover their value as signs of life because they gather people together into one soul. They are not means of individual salvation, but means of salvation of the people united in action.

The movement for the restoration of Christendom, and a return to the administration model that began in the last years of Paul VI and has taken firm hold in the current papacy, has unleashed a major campaign to discourage the entire practice of the 1960s and 1970s. This campaign highlighted some extreme cases to discredit all the action deriving from the Medellín church.

In a few extreme cases, some Christians took part in armed insurrection movements, e.g., Camilo Torres in Colombia, followed by a few more priests and lay people. The great majority did not think that the existing conditions would legitimate such an action according to the church's social teaching, and that other kinds of action were possible. Later, however, even the Nicaraguan bishops approved the insurrection against Somoza. And many Christians were actively involved with the guerrillas in El Salvador and Guatemala, countries in which everything had failed and all other means were blocked.[7] Such an extreme should not be surprising: Pope John Paul II has beatified two Polish religious who took part in insurrection movements against Russian domination, and has spoken positively about that participation.[8] Certainly the pope did not mean that this was valid only for Poland.

In other instances, Catholics took part in nonviolent movements to transform society, such as Christians for Socialism in Chile, popular movements in El Salvador, Indigenous movements in Guatemala, and movements in Ecuador that claimed to draw inspiration from Marxism. This led to many debates: can Catholics take part in movements that claim to be Marxist-inspired? Events have now rendered such discussions obsolete. Roman opposition caused a great deal of resistance. For some, the accusation of Marxism was enough to condemn people, as Cardinal Obando of Managua did after the Sandinista government took power.

They did not inquire about what this Marxism meant: mentioning the word was enough for a condemnation. In fact, most of the movements invoked Marxism because it was the only ideology that was absolutely opposed to the established system, but that was all. Even today, for many people Marxism simply means opposition to capitalism. But the entire church that was in tune with the Medellín guidelines was rejected due to this Marxism label that was stuck onto it.[9]

When redemocratization came, it was widely misunderstood. Many mistakenly thought that redemocratization was a conquest of the people. The defeat of the huge "Direct elections now!" campaign in Brazil in 1985 should have opened their eyes. Redemocratization was a ploy of the ruling classes who recognized that in the long run the military regime could cause very strong popular reactions if it remained in place. Moreover, the ruling classes no longer needed the military to control the country.

Elections took place, and as predicted the conservatives won handily. Today what is called the democratic system offers certain advantages over the military dictatorship, but it does not constitute a government of the people, it does not allow such a government to emerge, nor has it contributed to the advance of the people. Indeed, redemocratization has caused widespread demobilization. In the church many thought that their role was over and that now they could return to the sacristy and care for the salvation of souls. Democracy would solve social problems and the problems of poverty.

We now know that democratization was a ruse. The people of the poor will never be able to change society along this route. Christians cannot feel relieved by the notion that political action within so-called democracy, with everyone voting their conscience, will now establish justice, with no need for the church to step in. That is an illusion.

In practice, manipulation of the masses through the media becomes inevitable, and those elected do not have much freedom because they are controlled by those who manipulate the media. No one can speak the truth anymore. Governments supposedly elected democratically—i.e., by the electoral circus that we have—cannot do a thing unless they are submitted to high-visibility popular pressure. They will never take steps favorable to the people except under pressure from popular forces. Through the media the ruling elites prevent their own interests from being hurt.

What should be done about this situation? Today there is no need to wait for a majority consensus in order to act, and it does not have to be through elections of representative assemblies, let alone through presidential elections. Today what counts is active minorities, and today they find expression through NGOs (nongovernmental organizations). Especially since the demonstrations in Seattle in 1999, we know that the alternative will come from somewhere else. The people and the struggle for the people must take other directions.

NGOs are an alternative power capable of exerting pressure on the bodies that rule the world nationally and internationally. It is hard to measure their effectiveness, but they are more likely to bring about social change than are political parties looking for short-term results in getting power. Here we cannot focus on each type of NGO in the world, because there are thousands. Not all are suited for collaboration by Christians. Each must be critically examined, but the key point is how they act, and that is what makes them an alternative at this point in history. Many are international because problems today are international and the response must likewise be multinational. Even so, how it is embodied locally is very important.

Each NGO has specific goals, and this is crucial to an NGO's effectiveness. NGOs focus all their energies on a single objective, and that gives them a great deal of power. By contrast, political party platforms are vague and confused; they talk about everything and say nothing because they want to please everyone. This is why their platforms are so much alike. The aim of NGOs is to reach public opinion, that is, attitudes and values. They want to raise awareness of a value. They pursue many causes: ecology, feminism, race issues, Indigenous movements, human rights, protection of children, struggle against the death penalty, healthy agriculture, protection of natural products, struggle against cancer, AIDS, Alzheimer's disease, and so forth. Even if some NGO causes are incompatible with Christian morality (abortion, euthanasia, same-sex marriage), what is of interest is the method. NGOs organize spectacular demonstrations to draw media attention. They use the media because that is an essential channel for acting in contemporary society.

Some organizations of Catholic or Christian inspiration play important roles (the Paz y Justicia network in Latin America or the Sant'Egidio community in Rome). Others are not always supported by the hierarchy. There could be many others, especially if they acted jointly. It is crucial that they struggle for a single objective—otherwise they will tend to become bureaucratized, produce lots of theoretical studies, and be dependent on funding sources.

What might be the role of the people of God in partnership with such organizations or movements? The issue is the action of the people of God, not individual actions, which by themselves are powerless. Nor need all Catholics be involved. What is required are groups of Christians determined to act in society. What would be specific to Christians and to the action of the people of God? We may assume that what is most specifically Christian is authenticity: acting out of love for the people without seeking one's own interest.

What is the goal of the people of God at this moment in history? It is not converting individuals, because that would mean making lots of converts who would soon leave the church because they would not find there what they were seeking. The most important thing is knowing what is wanted and what is being offered to the men and women of our time. This cannot be defined arbitrarily or on the basis of one's personal desires. The goal comes from the signs of the times, which are clear.

First, demographically the Western world is destined to disappear in a few centuries. Already over 80% of the world population is living in the Third World, and the proportion is growing. The sign is that the future of the people of God is in the Third World. Practically everyone is aware of that, but they do not understand the implicit consequences.

Second, the populations of the Third World are living in chaos. Some elites manage to import a Western lifestyle, but the vast majority of the population is just getting by with no idea of where they are going. They have great aspirations and hopes but they do not know where to go. The Christian message is that they are called to form peoples, according to the image of the people of God: people means collaboration and covenant between free and equal people in family bonds. That is the goal.

All peoples will have to achieve peoplehood by themselves. The people of God can show the way and how to journey, if it wants to. Otherwise, it will stay in church praising God while humankind stumbles along with no clear direction. Given the triumphant individualism that constitutes the power of the West but is destroying the traditional integration of the rest of humankind, forming peoples is going to mean a long journey. Certainly anything that can show models of community life will be helpful. The older forms of community are obsolete: they can no longer function within the social model now imposed by the Western way of life. That is why religious communities have disappeared as communities. New ways of living in community must be imagined and created.

Chapter 10

PEOPLE OF GOD AND
THE CHURCH INSTITUTION

Like all peoples, the people of God must be embodied in institutions in order to exist in the world. Initially the church's institutional structures were simple and few: baptism, Eucharist, choice of the group of twelve headed by Peter. Since then the institutional apparatus has grown over time, often unconsciously and in response to situations. The twelve never imagined a structure with a bishop for each geographical area, or the existence of presbyters as distinct from bishops, or a caste distinction between clergy and lay people, or a pope centralizing control, or a model of church from the West spreading uniformly around the world.

But all this has happened, unplanned. The church grew, became more complex, was influenced by its surroundings, and without paying much attention to the New Testament message drew on Old Testament models of priesthood, temple, altar, sacrifice, replacing the institutions of the early church. After the West split from the East, it built a model of church quite different from earlier times. In the twentieth century a new ecclesiology discovered that the resulting institution was no longer appropriate.

Our concern here is the place of the people in the institution, the problems of the current structure, and the challenges for tomorrow. The hopes raised at Vatican II for changes in the relationships between hierarchy and people, bishops and pope, and clergy and people have been disappointed in practice because the council changed the theology but left canon law intact. In the subsequent forty years the Roman Curia has nullified the aims of Vatican II, concentrating control over doctrine and over episcopal ministry and appointments.

A major difference between 1962 and 2002 is that Vatican II represented the concerns of First World churches, whereas the crucial element today comes from the new aspirations of the Third World. Here we will take up first the issues of the hierarchy, then issues of the clergy vis-à-vis the people (not considered at Vatican II, especially because of the prohibition of dealing with celibacy, which remains a taboo), with special reference to Latin America.

DEBATE AT VATICAN II ON THE PLACE OF THE HIERARCHY IN THE PEOPLE OF GOD

Vatican II is widely recognized as a council of transition in an era of transition. It took steps toward the new situation of humankind in terms of its material development, but particularly in terms of intellectual and cultural development.[1] The council could not be expected to give clear and definitive pronouncements in the direction of the church. Few bishops recognized how far-reaching John XXIII's intuitions went.[2] Moreover, each bishop had to deal with the spontaneous reflexes of the theology he had learned in the seminary and the emerging new ideas and hopes. That led to tension as the older view was always present in the subconscious of those who wanted to change. Given the resistance, Vatican II could not be expected to take too forthright a direction of renewal. A new generation, free of ties to Christendom and scholasticism, would be needed.

At Vatican II two models of church were in contention, including two ways of conceiving the relationship between hierarchy and people. In a noteworthy speech at the council, Bishop Emile de Smedt of Bruges noted how the clerical, authoritarian *societas perfecta* model could be traced through church history: Gregorian reform, integration of religious and mendicant orders into papal policy, the subsequent marginalizing of the bishops, the Avignon papacy, conciliar movements of the fifteenth century, Trent, nineteenth-century Ultramontanism, and the popes named Pius, ending finally in the 1917 Code of Canon Law (the first in Christian history).

The perfect society model is top-down, authoritarian, and uniform. The church can only be victorious if it is led by a centralized authority. Both hierarchy and laity must apply the pope's orders to the world. There cannot be various poles, or initiatives other than those of the pope, because that would weaken the whole. The assumption is that the pope has the best information and can best define goals. The result is utter passivity by clergy and laity.

This policy, pursued for one hundred and fifty years, has led to monumental disasters which the Roman Curia does not recognize and the clergy is afraid to express. The pope has asked forgiveness for mistaken behavior by the church, but not for mistaken decisions by popes over the past century and a half. The impression is that these were acts by Catholics who did not submit to the church, when in fact those who committed them were the very ones who were carrying out the instructions of the bishops and the popes.

These mistakes translated into the loss of workers and intellectuals in the nineteenth and twentieth centuries, the destruction of theology by Pius X, enmity with socialism in the twentieth century, the loss of women in 1968, the failure of ecumenism, the destruction of the church of the poor in Latin America, and failure to relate to other religions.

The Catholic Church is really quite isolated. It maintains the illusion that the pope can influence events through his diplomatic power. The Holy See has cut off all efforts at real evangelization that have arisen in the midst of the people of God, under the illusion that evangelization would be done better from the position of the pope's power acting with all the church's social, cultural, and diplomatic force. But disasters are spoken of as though they were victories and no one dares to challenge the official version.

Yet in the twentieth century an older, very early model represented by the "people of God" slowly reappeared. This rebirth came from the confluence of forces from the liturgical, biblical, youth, patristic movements, and from church history. All these movements were in some way a return to the past, and showed the authoritarian line to be not traditional, not in accord with Christian origins, and completely alien to the movement of the Christian people. Converging factors led to a restoration of the ideal of a church from the past. Monolithic centralization spurred the resurgence of the patristic figure of the church of churches, community of communities, communion of communions.[3]

Reading Vatican II texts leaves a strong impression of a utopian movement, of a return to the patristic church, prior to the perfect society model. That the new element would be a return to the past should not be surprising: all revolutions initially present themselves as a return to a pure, mythical past (primitive communism, the Greek city or Roman republic, the state of nature or noble savage). As a first step this was necessary: no one leaps into utter newness. The only way to reject the past is to return to an even older past. For Christianity that past was not mythical but really existed and is normative.

A sheer return to the past, however, would be neither possible nor desirable because the world has changed so much since then. We cannot gaze at the past alone, but must scrutinize the signs of the times with freedom, now that the more distant past has liberated us from the more proximate past. That is why *Lumen Gentium*, which was written before *Gaudium et Spes*, remains abstract and disconnected from reality. It spoke about the church before defining its place or its mission in the world, as though it were something complete in itself, having its own meaning in itself, independent of the history of the world and of its task in this world. It did not use the observe-judge-act method used in Latin America, which had been introduced into the church by Catholic Action.

Thus one has the impression of a disconnect between texts defining the current direction and the utopian texts about the past, and that is why the documents have had little practical effect. In practice it was impossible to return to the past, and there was not enough clarity about the future. Hence Vatican II was followed by a growing sense of disillusionment and a mass exodus from the church by Catholics in the First World, and by the intellectual class in Latin America. It may have been psychologically impossible for the bishops to have comprehended the historic moment and provided a vision for future, but the effect is there. Latin America had Medellín, but in Europe, Asia, or Africa there were no gatherings with an impact similar to Medellín, and hence the utopias, hopes, aspirations, and even the decisions of Vatican II could easily be dismantled.

Anyone wanting to grasp the real situation of the church forty years after Vatican II can read *Novo Millennio Ineunte*, in which the pope expresses satisfaction over the jubilee awaited since the beginning of his papacy. It is evident that the church has nothing relevant to say to humankind about this new millennium: the church is self-satisfied. The simultaneous beatification of John XXIII and Pius IX is likewise revealing. In beatifying John XXIII, the pope was acknowledging that he had been canonized by the Catholic people, with acclaim from all Christians and the entire world. But Pius IX was not beatified by the people. Today he is seen as the pope who consolidated the model of extreme centralization around Tridentine Catholicism in its Roman form.[4] Pius IX has gone down in history as the last defender of the papal states, the last pope to head an army, the pope of *Quanta Cura* and the Syllabus of Errors, the one who sought sympathy as the prisoner of the Vatican, and had nothing to say about the growing desperate poverty of the workers. He stands as a reaffirmation of the centralization model.

Thus there is no point in discussing the relationship between hierarchy and laity in the current context, in current canon law, or in the current interpretation of Vatican II. There is no room for anything new. Under such centralization it is clear that lay people are no longer struggling to defend their rights, and they are leaving. We are heading toward an ecclesial situation in which the hierarchy wields absolute power over a people that no longer exists.

Nor is there any point in discussing the council texts, not only because they are not applied, but because they reflect an atmosphere of a mythical return to the past without reference to the current state of the world. They reflect a Europe that was already in decline and now takes refuge in dreams of material wealth at the cost of human values. Europe has lost its soul and is not going to try to regain it, because it has entered into globalization through the decision of economic elites and the resignation of its peoples, with Rome's blessing.

But there is the rest of the world. Our interest here lies in defining the relationship between hierarchy and laity in terms of the evangelization of the Third World. How are hierarchy and laity together to confront the power of the economically powerful G8 nations? What kind of stand will they take toward the forces converging in opposition to the G8? The Vatican cannot provide principles for such questions.

Lumen Gentium's ecclesiology remained on a formal level because it did not make the promising chapter 2 its starting point. With chapter 3 it went back to the same old way of viewing the hierarchy from an intra-ecclesial perspective. The three functions are conceived from within the church: magisterium for Catholics, liturgy for Catholics, governance for Catholics. The perspective of the people in the midst of the world disappears, as though adopting "people" as a theme did not change all ecclesiology.

This continues to have an impact on how collegiality is considered. Nothing is said about what is expected of collegiality, as though collegiality had meaning in itself, as though the collegiality of the fourth and fifth centuries in the Roman empire could mean something today. The way collegiality was established in the Roman empire was historic and cannot be the basis for the new collegiality expected for the challenges of today's world. The issue is what collegiality brings to bear on the problems of globalization, the challenge of worldwide individualism, and the encounter with the major world religions. What model of collegiality is most suited for this time in history? The key element is knowing what collegiality is for. After all, if it is just for defining some liturgical rubrics or adding some pages to the catechism, there is obviously no need for collegiality; Roman offices can do the job more economically.

Obviously the centralized model is efficient and produces results: namely, the church's diplomatic power with governments. The price for this is the legitimation of the current situation. There is a de facto alliance between the church and current nations, which are bourgeois nations built on the new bourgeoisies dependent on world capitalism. In this society the church can have visible successes provided it does not question society and its structure, e.g., the relationship between rich and poor in contemporary world society. Vatican diplomacy does not question this situation. Any criticisms are superficial and do not challenge the established system. Criticisms go no further than those made by the masters of the world when they relax, and the Vatican assures that no strong challenge can arise anywhere in the church. The whole church is controlled so that there will be no disagreement on the Vatican's worldwide diplomatic policy.

Yet what concerns the Third World is precisely what the church offers the world, its project, its contribution, what the Christian gospel means for the challenges of the contemporary world, where most people are victims of the power wielded by a minority that concentrates all the resources of science, technology, capital, and education. What future is being offered? Is it integration into the model of those on top? Today there is a great deal of concern to bring the local bourgeoisies, weak as they are, into line, seeking to integrate their nations into the world system, even while marginalizing the people and offering them no prospects.

In short, the problem of the Third World is the liberation of the poor. Far from having disappeared, this problem is more urgent than ever. The issue is to learn what structure for the church best serves the liberation of the Third World. What will enable the church to shed light on this path and not be a bloc focused on itself and indifferent to what is happening in the world? Obviously, Roman centralization does little for the liberation of the poor outside of speeches. What might collegiality actually offer?

Especially after Pius IX, the Petrine ministry bolstered the power of the new bourgeoisies, separated the church from the peoples, and sought to reconstitute a new church power after the disappearance of what used to be Christendom. Everything has been done around this power. The church's power is concentrated in the pope's power and serves to reinforce it. The pope is the one who stands in front of a billion Catholics. What matters is not the human situation of these billion people but their numbers, and the discipline to constitute a social and political force. Can the Petrine ministry be said to have been at the service of the liberation of workers, colonized peoples, and the outcasts of society? Judging by the practical effects, should it not be said that the Petrine power has served to close the church on itself, to focus its energies on its internal organization and activities?

That is how we have to think of the bishops as well. What role do bishops actually play? In our world aren't bishops simply the administrators of papal power anywhere in the world? Isn't it their task to set up, assure, and increase the pope's power in their cities and countryside? What qualities are demanded of candidates? Aren't they chosen precisely for this ability as administrative agents of papal power? Of course, church language speaks of evangelization, but in reality, evangelization means bolstering the pope's power.

As things stand now, bishops exist not primarily to respond to the petitions or needs of the local people, but to integrate the local people into the pope's overall policy. If the power of the pope is really for defending and promoting the poor of the world, it is good for bishops to be no more than delegates of the pope's power against the great ruling forces of the world. If that is not the case, the bishops must have more independent power in order to offset this power of the pope and guide the church toward serving the poor everywhere in the Third World.

PARTICIPATION OF THE PEOPLE IN THE LITURGY AFTER VATICAN II

The council emphatically recognized the universal priesthood of the people of God, thereby highlighting what is in the New Testament, which speaks only of the priesthood of Christ or of the people of God. Ministries are never described in priestly terms, as they came to be under the influence of the Old Testament. Acknowledgment of a priesthood of all believers is a revolution, and that is why it has been ignored (e.g., in canon law, which never mentions it and never mentions the "people").

The council began with *Sacrosanctum Concilium* on the liturgy:

> It is very much the wish of the church that all the faithful should be led to take that full, conscious, and active part in liturgical celebrations which is demanded by the very nature of the liturgy, and to which the Christian people "a chosen race, a royal priesthood, a holy nation, a redeemed people" have a right and to which they are bound by reason of their baptism. (SC 14)

The constitution on the liturgy introduces the theme of the people of God and was the culmination of over a half century of the liturgical movement.

However, the liturgy is still being examined as something existing in a timeless realm apart from the world where the church is located. It would have been different had it been influenced by *Gaudium et Spes*. Likewise *Lumen Gentium* could have provided an eschatological perspective on the people of God:

> . . . for the church on earth is endowed already with a sanctity that is true though imperfect. However, until the arrival of the new heavens and the new earth in which justice dwells (see 2 Pet 3:13) the pilgrim church, in its sacraments and institutions, which belong to this present age, carries the mark of this world which will pass, and it takes its place among the creatures which groan and until now suffer the pains of childbirth and await the revelation of the children of God (cf. Rom 8:19-22). (LG 48)

Even with the renewed liturgy, the sacraments do not clearly "carry the mark of this world which will pass." The sacramental liturgy does not seem to take into account the situation of real men and women here and how. The forms seem unchangeable, as though they were not set in a particular time, in a certain people, but rather as if the liturgy lifted peoples above this earth into a timeless world. What might be expected of a further stage of liturgical reform would be that the mark of this passing world be present in the celebration. Lay people would be the ones most suited for bringing the liturgy into this passing world, albeit under the one presiding over the assembly.

The Eucharist is an eschatological celebration (cf. 1 Cor 11:26 and Mk 14:25). This means that the Eucharist points toward the future banquet, announcing the death of the Lord until he comes. This journey is quite real: the death of Jesus continues in the death of his disciples and prophets. The Eucharist cannot be celebrated without referring to the moment of the journey, that is, the death of Jesus in his martyrs and the hope of the final banquet.

The current Roman liturgy expresses this only very abstractly. It is not celebrated in a time and place in the world. The church building is a space whose orientation is away from the world, especially today when it is no longer connected with the life of the city. Interestingly, in practice the clergy and the people make the Eucharist enter into the world, e.g., at the inauguration of the mayor or governor, for a girl's fifteenth birthday or school graduation, and so forth. It is legitimate to ask whether such events are celebrated eschatologically, to connect them to the journey of the people of God toward Jesus who is coming.

In the liturgy as it is now, lay people have a more active formal participation, but there is no content. They can listen, hear the word of God, give preformulated responses, sing, and so forth, but it is not clear what this participation is all about. What does it have to do with our life?

Lay people could point the liturgy toward the life of the outside world, keeping in mind the problems of humankind. They ought to be able to speak up and be involved in symbolic actions, in choosing themes and symbols. To a degree this is being done at the grassroots, often without the knowledge of the hierarchy, or in some cases, with its discreet consent. But this concrete application takes place against the explicit laws of the liturgy, and Vatican II did nothing to point the liturgy in this direction. Hence, such experiences are exceptional. Lay people should be able to put concrete content into the mystery celebrated by the liturgy, for the liturgy is human activity. God does not need praise, whereas human beings are in need, and the whole liturgy is subject to the needs of human beings.

More active and creative participation by lay people in terms of the content of the liturgy would have to lead to a great variety of expressions in space and time, because human beings are very different. However, the current liturgy is completely standardized and controlled by Rome. Only the pope can say what words and gestures may be expressed in the liturgy.

Liturgical participation has failed, at least in the Third World. The issue is not one of form but of substance: lay people do not express their life in the liturgy. They no longer believe in attending mass out of obligation. The liturgical reform went only halfway. One of the priorities of the new pontificate will be to open the way for the people of God, under the guidance of the hierarchy, to develop an expression of the mysteries that will be more comprehensible and better adapted to each culture.

PRESENCE OF THE PEOPLE OF GOD IN CHURCH GOVERNANCE

The church is not a democracy, the pope reminds us in *Novo Millennio Ineunte*:

> . . . the structures of participation envisaged by Canon Law, such as *the Council of Priests and the Pastoral Council,* must be ever more highly

valued. These of course are not governed by the rules of parliamentary democracy, because they are consultative rather than deliberative; yet this does not mean that they are less meaningful and relevant. The theology and spirituality of communion encourage a fruitful dialogue between pastors and faithful. . . . (45)

"Of course": the pope speaks as though he were under higher orders, as though this system were not a system based solely on his decision. The "communion" invoked is the communion of one ordering and the other obeying (officer and soldier), but there cannot be true communion when all do not have a right to deliberate.

If there was deliberation at the council why can there not be deliberation at lower levels over matters proper to those levels? Why are money matters, such as a parish or diocesan budget, restricted to clerics?

Within these limits, it is admitted that the people can help the hierarchy, and hence parish and diocesan councils have been set up. But the issue is not who makes the final decision. Even under democratic governments, the power of a president is such that congresses do not make the ultimate decisions. The real issue lies in the lack of discussion. There is no openness to dialogue, arguments are not presented, no time is allowed for debate.

Church assemblies or councils are more or less superficial, because the issues cannot be discussed seriously. Decisions are still made secretly by the hierarchy, as if secrecy were a divine mark. Everything operates as though the hierarchy received the decisions to be made directly from heaven in prayer. The arguments presented are decorative, because the decision is made not on the basis of the arguments but through a secret divine revelation, and secrecy is still the soul of church governance. Lay participation is minimal and hot issues are eliminated in advance. In organizing a diocesan synod in Santiago, Chile, the faithful were emphatically assured that they could freely express their opinions. Thousands of groups were formed to have discussions and make proposals, but on the eve of the synod a secret Roman instruction arrived prohibiting discussion of priestly celibacy, contraception, and women's ordination—though these matters were the very things that they wanted to discuss.

In addition, lay people are asked to offer reflections on big ideas: pastoral concerns, preferential options, with everything so vague and general that there is no application in practice. All serious practical matters are resolved secretly by the bishop or pastor. Thus, disillusionment sets in after any diocesan synod or assembly because in practice it is business as usual.

Canon 212 reads, "The Christian faithful are free to make known their needs, especially spiritual ones, and their desires to the pastors of the Church." In practice, anyone who does so is likely to be excluded and treated as a rebel. The faithful can only give opinions that are in tune with those of authorities. The code does not offer any guarantee or defense for those who sincerely express their needs and desires, and so many people who have something to say remain silent. That same canon then says,

> In accord with the knowledge, competence, and preeminence which they possess, the Christian faithful have the right and even at times a duty to manifest to the sacred pastors their opinion on matters which pertain to the good of the Church, and they have a right to make their opinion known to the other Christian faithful, with due regard for the integrity of faith and morals and reverence towards their pastors, and with consideration for the common good and the dignity of persons.

What constitutes "knowledge, competence, and preeminence" is not stated. It seems that the multitude of ordinary Christians are excluded and that only some elites can speak, even though the ones most in need are the masses or conscious minorities of the dominated peoples. Even though the political thrust of our age is toward seeking means of expression for the poor so that they can raise their voice in society, there does not seem to be such a concern in the church for the poor to be heard by their pastors. Yet according to the gospel, the poor should have more of a right to speak than elites with little awareness of the problems of the great masses.

It is not surprising that real participation by the faithful is so limited, because the same thing is true about the participation of the clergy, and especially the bishops. Bishops meetings or Roman synods have been increasingly manipulated. Bishops no longer have any significant initiative; their only function is to carry out orders from Rome, whether issued formally or only by way of suggestion: any suggestion constitutes an order, with the nuncios monitoring activities. If that is how bishops are treated, it is no wonder that the same thing happens to lay people.

This point of participation raises the issue of the extraordinary growth of the Roman Curia, primarily during the twentieth century. The pope used to have a small group of cardinals and some secretaries; today the Curia numbers many thousands. When that happens, the Curia begins to follow the laws of any large administration. Sometimes it is stronger than the pope, and can impose its demands on him or prevent his will from being carried out, as happens in any bureaucracy. Theoretically the Curia is at the service of the pope, but often it is the other way around. Can we know what happens in each case? Can Petrine power be said to extend to the whole Curia and to all decisions by all its officials? Of course the pope signs, but does he always know the scope of what he is signing? That would be surprising, because it does not happen in any other bureaucracy. Between the pope and the church is an administration that limits the expression of the people of God. The pope hears only what the Curia has decided he should hear; anything else is excluded. Thus, the pope generally makes decisions in keeping with what the Curia wants.

Indeed, by the very fact that it is anonymous, no administration can be evangelical or seek gospel solutions. A bureaucracy has only one end: to stay in power, hold on to its employees, and increase the power of the institution through all available means. That is true of all bureaucracies, so why should a religious bureaucracy be different?

There is a solution: restore to the local churches whatever they could solve by themselves—issues of catechesis and teaching, sacraments, dispensations for priests and religious, episcopal appointments—which make up at least 90% of canon law. Social problems would best be dealt with by bishops assemblies meeting in Rome for issues that are worldwide, and on each continent for local problems. The pope could exercise his Petrine privilege with a few dozen aides, and leave the church's everyday work to the local churches. There is no reason to keep the present system in place, except for the fact that the bureaucracy is fighting tooth and nail to preserve itself.

The new Code of Canon Law opened a path by recognizing lay people's right of association. In the old code, all associations were under the clergy. However, Catholics are so accustomed to dependence that they have not really taken advantage of freedom of association. In practice, associations not led by clergy or religious are not well received. Intellectuals are able to take advantage because they have greater personal autonomy, but among the people there is not enough maturity and they are not being trained for freedom. Christian base communities could facilitate the emergence of the people, but they remain dependent on the pastor. The sacralization of the priest is still so strong that whenever he is present, he is inevitably in charge. If pastors were to acknowledge the legitimate autonomy of the base communities these could acquire their own personality, but that does not often happen. As a rule, base communities are mini-parishes carrying out parish activities, and soon become self-enclosed and isolated from the neighborhood.

* * *

Participation of the people of God in church governance brings up a central issue that many theologians, observers, and analysts believe is the core of the problem and the key to its solution: choice of bishops. Appointment of bishops by the pope alone is the basis for the present centralized Roman system. There will be no relevant changes in the church without starting with a radical change in the system whereby the pope, i.e., the curial administration, chooses bishops. Some cases have been quite blatant and can only be explained by a resolute intention to break the unity of the episcopacy or to break an episcopal or ecclesial tradition in a particular diocese. Such impositions have been so clear that the injuries caused remain years later.

Such appointments run counter to the ancient tradition of the church.

Pope Celestine I (422-432) stated the rule: "Let no one be given as a bishop to those who do not want him. Let the desire and consensus of the clergy, and of the people and prominent men be sought. Someone should be chosen from another church only when no one worthy to be consecrated can be found in the city for which a bishop is being sought (and we do not think that can happen)."[5]

For a thousand years the Roman Curia has battled perseveringly to have the pope appoint all bishops, destroying all contrary customs. Until the mid-nineteenth century the pope appointed few bishops, but shortly after Vatican I the Curia fought to have all episcopal appointments centralized in Rome. The weapon for this battle was the 1917 Code of Canon Law, drawn up by Cardinal Gaspari with decisive help from Eugenio Pacelli, the future Pius XII, who devoted his best years to drafting this code. The soul of the code is the article limiting episcopal appointments to the pope (i.e., the Curia, because the pope is not in a position to appreciate the qualities of the candidates). After 1917 Rome struggled to have the code applied in all countries. It has been shown that the reason for signing the 1934 concordat with Hitler was to have the German bishops appointed by Rome. The Curia reached an agreement with Hitler and accordingly demobilized the German church and removed all means for combating the Nazi regime. German Catholics were forced to submit in order to defend the code. Tens of thousands of activist Catholics were killed as a result of their militancy, and got no help from the hierarchy, which had to remain silent in keeping with the concordat, because the Roman Curia, then represented by Eugenio Pacelli (later Pius XII), was seeking greater power.[6]

The Curia knows that appointment of bishops is the basis of the entire centralization system, and it chooses as bishops people who submit to it unconditionally and are willing to act as bishops in this manner. If bishops were chosen by the local churches everything would change. These bishops would feel accountable to the churches that chose them; they would be representatives of their people, with its good qualities and flaws. They would bring into the church the world's problems as they are felt locally, concretely rather than abstractly. The key to the rapprochement of the church to the world is the selection of bishops. Election of bishops by local churches would inevitably be a first step toward decentralizing power in the church, and that is just what the Curia fears most. That is why the basic issue for the future of the people of God is appointment of bishops.

Perhaps at some other time bishops chosen by Rome were better than those elected locally, but would that be true today? What system for episcopal appointment is best suited to the demands of our time? For us the principle is: which bishops will be most inclined to defend the cause of the poor and the oppressed, to make the gospel option for the meek and humble, even by sacrificing chances for temporal power and grandeur?

In the past century bishops appointed by Rome have not been better than others. In Germany, for example, the result was a disaster: the German church was ready to battle Nazism, but it was not allowed to do so by a Roman policy primarily pursuing Roman power. The first bishops appointed under the concordat were the ones who were weakest against Nazism. Was that an isolated instance?

In Latin America, Rome admittedly appointed a series of bishops who later led Medellín. But these bishops were fought, undercut, and replaced by others who did the exact opposite. All the bishops who were the "holy fathers" of Latin America were reprimanded, warned, punished, undermined, or simply removed. Some think that in recent years Rome has been focusing even more on appointing bishops who are good agents of Roman centralization, good administrators according to the Code of Canon Law. Their aim is at best to administer, also utilizing up-to-date marketing. Certainly there are exceptions because nuncios can make mistakes, as they themselves recognize.[7]

In the recent past Rome sought alliance with any government claiming to be Catholic no matter how oppressive, and that was its basis for choosing bishops, e.g., the Roman Curia made an alliance with Pinochet. Such are the demands of the current system: the Vatican state cannot openly criticize any state with which it has diplomatic representation. So where does that leave the bishops? They keep quiet so as not to upset diplomacy.

We can therefore conclude that the current system does not help the poor at all. Today the Roman Curia's major concern is evidently not the poor but the power of the church, particularly power acquired through agreements with governments and economic elites. In Europe it does not matter much because everything is set and is not going to change. But in the Third World, where the government is the greatest enemy of the poor, it does have repercussions. It prevents the church from being able to speak, just as Pacelli prevented the German bishops from speaking out against Nazism when there was still time. The Vatican bishop wants to preserve the status quo and hence a condition for being a bishop is never having had conflict with the authorities, no matter how oppressive, and having good relations with the powers that be, even when they violate human rights.

Certainly under another way of choosing bishops, the clergy and people could choose incompetent bishops. But that is less likely to happen under a new system than under the old one, given that the present system is clearly a disaster. That is why the issue of selection of bishops will be the decisive test on which the next papacy can be judged from the outset.

Let it not be asserted that the church is not democratic. The aim is not to propose that bishops should be chosen the way governors are. There is a broad consensus that the current method of choosing the national representation of civil society does not work well and needs to be corrected. The point is not to bring into the church methods from civil society that have been shown to be flawed, but to start from the church's own experience.

The bishop of Rome is not appointed by his predecessor. Why can't other bishops be elected? There are various ways to prepare and hold an election. The most important thing is that the process be open and transparent: the people must know who the candidates are and must be able to present candidates. Exploration can be done before the appointment, and the merits of each candidate examined. There can also be a group of electors: just as there are cardinals for the pope there can be "cardinals" in each diocese. Finally, the election would be submitted for the consent of the Holy See in case there are objections, and to place the new bishop-elect in communion with episcopal collegiality.[8]

All stages of the process have to be open and clear, not secret. The secrecy to which the Curia seems so attached is not suited to the mindset of an established and developed people. Secrecy is the weapon of all dictatorships, who zealously practice and defend it. Secrecy was not instituted by Jesus. It was introduced in imitation of dictatorial methods. That is why another test for checking the direction of the new pope will be the elimination of secrecy.[9]

PARTICIPATION OF THE PEOPLE OF GOD IN THE MAGISTERIUM

Jesus sends the Spirit to all his followers, not just to the Twelve and their successors. It is not the role of the hierarchy to give the word of God to the people—they receive it directly. As Vatican II recognized:

> The whole body of the faithful who have received an anointing which comes from the holy one (see 1 Jn 2:20 and 27) cannot be mistaken in belief. It shows this characteristic through the entire people's supernatural sense of the faith, when "from the bishops to the last of the faithful," it manifests a universal consensus in matters of faith and morals.[10]

Revelation does not come from the hierarchy. The people—including the hierarchy—receive God's revelation from their parents and from the educators or witnesses they encounter in the course of their life. The people transmit the faith; the hierarchy steps in only in specific cases. Most believers have never even had contact with a bishop. They often do not even understand the sermon given by the bishop when he occasionally comes for confirmation. God's word circulates in a vast network with no input from the magisterium.

In some instances the people maintain the truth of revelation better than the hierarchy. Newman showed how illiterate Egyptian monks and lay people kept the faith of Nicea better than most of the bishops, who had fallen into semi-Arianism or full-fledged Arianism. In Latin America at Medellín and Puebla the bishops recognized that they had heard the cry of the poor. The poor taught them that church is primarily of the poor and should make an option for the poor in order to become a church of the poor.[11] It was the people who taught the bishops that this message is the heart of Christianity, which is more important than particular dogmas.

History shows that dogmas defined by the magisterium were prepared by a long history in the Christian people. When that was not the case and the hierarchy took initiatives, as at Trent, it acted too quickly and caused an irreparable schism through lack of patience and dialogue. Had the hierarchy at Trent listened to lay people it would not have attacked Protestants so uncompromisingly; it would have sought points of agreement rather than issuing final condemnations. Today the theologians and even the hierarchy recognize that the various doctrines were compatible, and that it was the conciliar theologians who wanted them to be incompatible. When the magisterium rushes in, it makes mistakes.[12]

Especially since the papacy of Pius IX, the hierarchy has continually multiplied documents, statements, condemnations, warnings, and instructions. This can only be explained as an unconscious will to power. The Curia feels threatened, and reacts by raising up documents as a barrier to defend Catholics from contamination by the world.[13] There may also be a more trivial reason: the sheer multiplication of Vatican agencies, which generate documents in print or on the internet to demonstrate their efficiency. Far from thereby increasing credibility, one senses that credibility decreases as the number of new documents (e.g., of the Congregation for the Doctrine of the Faith) rises.

What is expected in the people of God is that statements about faith and morals will not be made without knowing what people feel at the grassroots level. Certainly consultations are made now, but since they are done secretly no one knows who was consulted. It is not wise for the hierarchy to rush to formulate a final ruling against the opposition of a large majority—or even of a significant qualified minority. Since many people now study psychology and sociology, it is obvious that popes and bishops do not receive particular revelations informing them that a particular teaching is true or false. Unless there is adequate consultation, one may fear that the authority will mistake a personal intuition or a prejudice that they have had from childhood or the seminary with an inspiration from the Holy Spirit. Sometimes a bishop is heard to say that he went off to pray many hours and that he came out of prayer with the light, knowing what was true. Such prayer is quite suspect. Any psychologist knows that the danger of illusion is very large, especially when one is praying by oneself, and that it is easy to confuse one's personal feelings with God's will.[14]

When the pope decides by himself against everyone or against a broad majority, he may be right, but he may also be confusing his personal conviction with divine revelation. How will history judge Paul VI's condemnation of artificial contraception? Judging by the results, it was massively rejected by the Christian people, especially women. The pope was very hesitant, but in the end he opted for a traditional solution against a significant portion of the bishops and clergy, and against the judgment of lay experts in biology and medicine. It was one of the most mistaken decisions of the twentieth century, because since then millions of women have decided to leave the church and have stopped teaching religion to their children.[15] What can the church do without women? Not a thing, because it is women who build the future.

There is another angle by which the people of God are involved in the magisterium, namely reception. In principle the reception of a church document does not change its value or make it true or not.[16] But few statements of the magisterium are to be qualified as infallible or irrevocable truths, and even then there is still the matter of interpretation, which can vary widely over the centuries. As with other statements, time may show that they were not so firm as it seemed. In that case, reception may be quite significant.

Truth does not exist by itself or on paper or in statements: it only begins to exist when it is accepted in human minds. To become truth it must be accepted, and that is where the people come in. The people do not respond automatically. In practice, reception is a slow and gradual process. Reception may be fast or slow, or simply not occur. Everything is received in a varying historic context and hence the meaning or scope of dogmas or morality or practices varies over time. Some dogmas are forgotten whereas others reemerge. For example, many aspects of biblical and patristic ecclesiology were forgotten for centuries, and reemerged in the twentieth century. For centuries, Chalcedon was interpreted in a spiritualizing manner that limited the humanity of Jesus to something outside of history. Today that council is understood differently.

Juridically, reception adds nothing to a document of the magisterium, but in practice it determines whether the document really exists or not. The reception of Vatican II is still the object of great controversy because of the sometimes opposite interpretations given. In terms of the issue here, a huge effort has been made over twenty years to have the doctrine of the people of God fall into oblivion, and that has almost been achieved.

Each sector of the church has its own kind of reception: Roman Curia, bishops, clergy, different social groups. Some issues are accepted with difficulty, and others arouse resistance. Until Vatican II resistance was more passive. Today those resistances are being expressed in a way that frightens authorities. Some members of the people can influence members of the hierarchy directly: the pastor may be influenced by his cook, the bishop by a secretary's opinion, or the pope may be struck by an observation made by the sisters around him.

The people of God practices discernment. Some documents are accepted immediately and incorporated into the Catholic life of the people, while others run up against a conscious or unconscious barrier: reception does not take place. Theologians are increasingly acknowledging the importance of reception, because it is the manifestation of the people of God.

The need for reception is a reminder that the hierarchy is not an independent body, but part of the people of God. If it does not express the sense of the people, it will meet massive resistance from the people. Some church documents are never applied and fall into oblivion, e.g., the decrees of the Biblical Commission under Pius X. They have disappeared, although in their time they caused a great deal of damage, halted biblical studies for decades, and eliminated outstanding Bible scholars. The same is true of the doctrine of monogenism in *Humani Generis* (1950). Everyone kept silent, but monogenism gradually disappeared and today this doctrine is forgotten.

Reception is an expression of the participation of the Christian people in the leadership of the church, even if not desired by the hierarchy. Ultimately if the people do not accept something, there is no one who can force it to accept what it rejects. And the people are a manifestation of the Spirit of God just as much as the hierarchy is.

Thus, the people have agency. The point is not to pit the people against the hierarchy, but to situate the hierarchy where it belongs, within the people. They live together, and influence one another, albeit to a different extent in different times. Today there is an immense aspiration for more explicit, conscious, and effective participation. Contrary to earlier times, most Catholics are literate. Many millions have finished high school and university. All these people have freed themselves from the mindset of subordination of ancient peoples. They can think and can see what happens in the church, and they detest secrecy. They want to think for themselves and they do not accept passively what another human being says, even one with authority, if they do not know the arguments for such assertions.

RELATIONSHIP BETWEEN CLERGY AND PEOPLE

The clergy as a caste separate from the members of the people of God goes back a long time, with some signs as far back as the second century. Integration into the Roman empire (Constantine to Theodosius) was a decisive step; the Council of Trent was another. Trent could have been interpreted various ways, but Pius V gave the decisive impulse toward creating a uniform clerical class worldwide, strictly subject to Rome, with no local autonomy. The spirituality of the French school finished the job with seminaries set up in the seventeenth century, which helped shape the clerical mindset.[17]

The medieval clergy, which Trent sought to reform, was more a response to medieval culture than to a theoretical model of priest. There was no clear model of a priest, and the various reforms of the clergy did not establish any model. Indeed, that helps explain the low regard for them. Monks, and later the mendicants, had some prestige, but the medieval clergy ministered not so much to the official church as to popular religiosity with its miracles, saints, and penitents. They did not preach or teach, but subordinated the sacraments to the interests of popular religiosity, and often their lives were hardly edifying. Because many came out of poverty, entering the clergy meant privilege and hence there were many vocations. Their training was not systematic.

Trent sought to correct all this, but what emerged was no better for the people of God than what had preceded. The program amounted to disciplining popular religiosity by integrating it into the doctrinal and sacramental system of the official church. Superstition had to be eliminated and everything else regulated. The clergy was charged with applying the Tridentine reforms; in practice that meant rationalizing traditional life, but no deeper change.

The new clergy learned an abstract catechism, distant from both the Bible and popular religion, thereby dividing the religion professed from the one practiced. A cleric was to be primarily a minister at the altar: he had to be the person set apart for worship, separated from the people to care for the things of God. Separation from the world was strongly emphasized. The clergy were the church's police, assuring that all the baptized frequented the sacraments, learned the catechism, and obeyed canon law. As mediators of the new religion defined after Trent by Roman orthodoxy, priests represented the authority of God and church.

The hierarchy decided on the Tridentine reforms without consulting the people. Traditions and customs were condemned without any kind of dialogue. The hierarchy and clergy emerging from Trent began an authoritarian church practice, applying very demanding discipline in doctrine, sacraments, morality, and parish life, with no exceptions. This period gave rise to the authoritarian, patriarchal style, closed to any dialogue, that created the clerical mindset for the following centuries.

Alberigo's description of the French episcopacy can be applied to the Tridentine clergy as a whole:

> When examining the Catholic episcopacy in the seventeenth century, one finds that it is primarily a rather rarified "order" (in the medieval sense of *ordo*) with limited involvement in the life of the faithful. The insufficient spiritual motivation of the episcopal office, combined with excessive functions of authority, led many bishops to fall into line with the social and economic characteristics of the dominant group, i.e., the aristocracy and haute bourgeoisie. Declining dynamism and aversion to risk placed the episcopacy on the side of protecting order in society, obviously in the name of guarding orthodox faith.[18]

The Tridentine reform did not allow for any dialogue with the people. They submitted, at least externally, because they had no choice. As it happened, the Tridentine reform coincided with the advent of the absolute monarchies, which sought legitimacy in religion, and thus offered political and police support to the authoritarian restoration of the clergy. The de facto alliance between the two authoritarianisms (clergy and kings) was often made explicit. The upshot was a radical distinction between a purely passive people and a clergy with all the power, concentrated in the hands of the bishop or the pastor.

This reform was not without resistance, at least internally. For example, annual confession was obligatory and a person who did not go to confession was reported to the police. Even so, St. Alfonsus Liguori estimated that most confessions were sacrilegious. Parishioners went to confession out of fear, but they said only what they wanted. When the French Revolution did away with police enforcement of the Sunday mass obligation, attendance dropped from 95% to 20% within a few months. This latter figure had been the normal average in the Middle Ages. Apparently, most people had attended under compulsion, and certainly with rage in their hearts.

Over the course of the eighteenth century the intellectual elites struggled to break free from clerical domination. In the following centuries, it was the population of the cities, and finally after 1950, the rural population also freed itself. The clergy resisted, issued condemnations, and did everything to maintain their control over populations. They saw those who became emancipated as enemies of God and of the church. The desertion of the masses was said to be due to the influence of the church's enemies. That does not explain why the people listened to them and did not resist them. The clergy was unable to understand that it was its own authoritarianism that was driving more and more people away.

Society changed, but the church did not. It continued to leave power in the hands of pastors who were supposed to administer a seventeenth-century system that the people no longer accepted. Unfortunately, this system of one person making all the decisions, which came from the age of absolute monarchy, has shaped the clergy, and remains in place to this day.

* * *

A purely imposed religious system would not last. Support from the state, the police, custom, and social pressure are persuasive, but would not be enough to assure fidelity from Catholics. Hence, the clergy made use of two methods, probably unconsciously. They closed their eyes to a portion of medieval abuses, i.e., popular traditions. However, the clergy was well aware that people cannot be guided by sheer constraint. They needed to convince the people that it was a good idea to submit voluntarily to the church's clerical system, that doing so was for their own good. This was where clerical power came in.

This was a strategy of persuasion. The approach was smooth, soft, easy—

but ultimately inexorable. The appeal was to those arguments that can arouse human passions and religious feelings. The beauty of commitment to serving Christ was pointed out; serving Christ was identified with submission to the system, because the clergy interprets and communicates God's will. Appeal was made to God's will, to adoration, and to submission to God's sovereignty. Fear was aroused: what could be more serious than offending God? An appeal was made to compassion for Jesus, the danger of ingratitude, the need to repair injuries done to him, to his need for co-workers. The heroism of those who followed the path with complete dedication was invoked. But it was all intended to bring about obedience to the system.

The clergy used all means of seduction and fear, attacking and frightening, a psychological pressure that gradually came to approach brainwashing. The sacrament of confession, "spiritual direction," and simple parish catechism were all employed. People were expected to entrust themselves completely to their "spiritual director," who was able to use methods from psychology, to God's (i.e., the church's) greater glory.

This strategy was aimed first at children and adolescents, who are easier to manipulate. Hence, in the post-Tridentine church a significant amount of time was devoted to working with them, on the grounds that Jesus had asked that the children be allowed to come near—even though when calling disciples Jesus had appealed to adults. Pastoral power was also aimed primarily at women, who were not as well educated as men. They put up less intellectual resistance and the clergy hoped to influence their husbands through sensitive arguments in the hands of women, and so most of those attending the parish church were women.

Over time, the scope of pastoral power kept declining. Women were admitted to universities and no longer let themselves be manipulated by clerical power. The popular milieus resisted, and young people moved away from their clerical teachers. Despite declining results, clerical manipulation lasted until the mid-twentieth century. At that point there began the revolt against Catholic education as the expression of this clerical power that, despite appearances of meekness, manipulated minds and feelings to bring about submission to the clergy. Today in Europe and in the middle classes of the Third World where Catholic schools still exist, this revolt is increasing.

The clergy became unable to exercise its traditional power and went into crisis because it lost its traditional means of action. There is no need to blame the outside world or a lack of spiritual formation for clerical insecurity. The reason is simple: the previously effective means of action had become largely ineffective. Those who sense that they are losing their effectiveness go into crisis.

The Jesuits were the great leaders of the post-Tridentine church, and directly or indirectly the great shapers of the clergy. Almost all male and female orders adopted their constitutions, or at least their spirit, and sought to operate like the Jesuits. Their spirituality was adopted by dioceses, and became part of the mindset of the secular clergy, though they never imitated their masters perfectly. Focus on adolescents and women, direction of conscience and the confessional, use of psychology, the appeal to total submission to the church embodied in the priests and the pope—all of this was common to the Jesuits and the post-Tridentine church.

We know that the Society of Jesus has changed a great deal, prompting a sharp reaction from the Holy See, which had taken its unconditional support for granted. In the eighteenth century when the pope forced the Jesuits to abandon the reductions in Paraguay they obeyed: they preferred to see the Indians massacred than disobey the pope. That was then—today they would not abandon the Indians, and would no doubt prefer to die with them, if it came to that.

Today it is organizations like Opus Dei and the Legionaries of Christ that enthusiastically exercise clerical power without scruples. They use psychology, which is now more developed, and they are willing to work with business people and advertising agencies. They have been educated in the environment of the twentieth century, when fascisms gained power. The fascist mindset is not yet dead, but lives in some ecclesiastical circles. These members of the hierarchy cannot see the burning coals that they are piling on the head of the church, which will have to pay a high price for such inappropriate methods.

Moreover, many priests have realized that this clerical power based on seduction, full of apparent sweetness and meekness, typical of mellifluous ecclesiastical language, loaded with adjectives, made up of manipulation of feelings and emotions, was not only disastrous but immoral, and went into crisis. They realized that the methods they were taught are obsolete, and they lost a sense of who they were. Significantly, those who left were the very ones who had the best human training and were most sensitive to the outside world. More than the numbers, it is the quality of those who left that should draw attention, though officially the hierarchy refuses to see the evidence. What is involved is the entire clerical strategy since the foundation of the clerical model in the seventeenth century.

Instead of the call to freedom, a call to the path of the gospel with the freedom of Jesus, so-called "evangelization" is set up as manipulation of people when they are weakest: children, adolescents, uneducated women, the sick, the oppressed minorities, etc. Priests who have seen the problem have sought other ways of being in the world, but they have not been supported by the hierarchy, when they were not simply condemned (worker priests). Their problem is clerical power, the dominant model imposed in seminaries since the seventeenth century.

We know that many priests applied themselves unenthusiastically to the model that had been imposed on them. They did so out of obedience, because they had been imbued with the spirituality of sheer obedience. "Anyone who follows the pope's orders is safe" was the justification. They left the responsibility with the hierarchy and acted without personal responsibility. Many sought to salvage their natural humanity in the niches allowed them by the imposed model of priestly life. With this system of compensation, they held out. But the spirituality of obedience was the great excuse: whenever they had to close their hearts and manipulate people, they excused it as obedience. They prayed to God for the grace of being able to obey, even though their hearts violently inclined the other way.

If this was all comprehensible (although not acceptable) in the seventeenth century, it is not in the twenty-first.

* * *

The priestly model set up in the seventeenth century tended to exacerbate the separation between clergy and people. Visible signs of separation proliferated: different clothes, a house set apart, noninvolvement of priests in manual labor, trade, or profane activities. A priest is set aside solely for sacred activities. He has his own language, he cannot appear in public gathering places: theaters, stadiums, circuses, beaches, movie theaters. He cannot see profane shows; his speech must be very reserved. Everything in the church maintains the separation: a space reserved for the priest and another for the people, and no one can cross the line, unless absolutely necessary (sacristan or cleaning woman). The confessional exemplifies this separation: priest and penitent cannot see or recognize one another. It is not a dialogue between persons, but between sin and absolution.

As justification for such separation, seventeenth-century books of priestly spirituality offer the separation between the sacred and the profane—just what Jesus came to eliminate. The priest is the man of the sacred: his realm is the sacred world, the church building, administering the sacraments. His world is full of sacred objects: the material of the sacraments, images, sacred books. The mass is seen in continuity with Old Testament sacrifice. Celebrating mass is the priest's work. One day at a priests' retreat, the cardinal who ordained me said that if a priest celebrates mass and prays the breviary, he has fulfilled his obligation. Actually that is his priesthood: maintaining the sacred functions. Anything else is optional, and may be dangerous; it is not what makes him a priest.

These priestly activities are completely inaccessible to lay people; they mark a radical separation. They are two entirely separate ways of life, because there is no communication between the profane and the sacred.

For over three centuries an edifice was erected to assure the priest's isolation at any cost. The theology of the sacrament of orders meant that priests were metaphysically different from lay people. The purpose of priestly training was to separate the priest from the outside world. Candidates studied scholastic philosophy and theology, which were incomprehensible to people outside and made them incapable of understanding other people's thinking.

Seminaries were set up for isolation, like a self-sufficient monastery. Students had everything on hand, and had no need to leave. They were well protected against any worldly contact that could contaminate them.

A priest could not dialogue but only announce the truth entrusted to him, assuming that others could understand. Thus the missionaries in colonial times addressed the Indians in Portuguese, which they could not understand, to explain to them that they had to submit to the soldiers of the priest, who was the great master of the Order of Christ and had a delegation from the pope to issue orders to them.

In addition, the law of celibacy was applied. The origins of celibacy lay in the sacred.[19] Because the priest is set apart for sacred functions, he cannot be contaminated with sexual acts. That was the primitive reason, and it remains in place to this day, although other reasons have been added. The basis is the opposition between sex and the sacred. This makes the separation between cleric and lay person all the greater, for celibacy is a very emphatic symbolic separation. It means separation from all women and from married men. Among many peoples, marriage signifies entry into the world of adults; by not marrying, the priest remains outside the world.

Celibacy also gives priests a feeling of moral superiority. Because they are celibates, priests feel holier, more heroic, morally superior, and that gives them moral authority to define moral values in all matters. Celibacy is a kind of barrier separating saints from sinners. If a priest acknowledges that he is a sinner, it is a sign of humility, yet another proof of his moral superiority, unlike lay people who are essentially sinners.

Hence the conviction among the people that marriage is synonymous with sin. Uneducated people think that this is why priests do not marry. Marriage is allowed for lay people, who are sinners by definition, but it is still sin, albeit tolerated. This belief still exists.

All of this is fully in line with the model of priesthood stemming from the seventeenth century, but as soon as doubts over the relevance of this model arise, everything comes into question. That is why the loss of the priest's identity has become a chronic problem in the church today.

* * *

Often enough it happens that a new pastor arrives, dismisses the people who were working with the previous pastor, dismantles what has been done, rejects plans made, dismisses what has been done, and says that from now on things are going to work differently. He starts over because he thinks that what has been done was wrong. Where does this leave the lay people?

The Code of Canon Law does not offer any legal remedy against arbitrary actions by the clergy in the event of conflict. It piously recommends that the clergy should be charitable and just, and apply all the virtues, but if they do not, the only remedy is patience and offering one's suffering to God. The clergy enjoy impunity; they can only be punished if they disobey their superior, bishop, or the pope; no tribunal can find them guilty for offending a lay person.

Of course, the code uses subtle terminology to assure an appearance of a right of defense for lay people, but in practice it is inoperative. The priest is always right, and in practice lay people must accept the priest's explanation. Of course a lay person can go to the bishop, but a bishop is unlikely to agree with a lay person against a priest; caste solidarity always prevails. Likewise, a bishop is very unlikely to agree with a nun against a priest, a woman against a man. The system is patriarchal. Somewhere in the world I imagine there must be an exception, but it only confirms the rule.

Yet that practice is no longer accepted without objection. True, the poor are still treated that way in society, but they do not accept it—and that is all the more true of those who are not economically poor. Why should it be different in the church? Today in the West there has arisen an entire legal structure—influenced by Christianity, but not necessarily by the clergy—which consists of creating and imposing on society a system of laws to defend those below from the abuses of power by those on top. Canon law is about the norms that those on top impose on those below. In the Christian conception, right has to do with laws and norms protecting those below from the abuses of those on top, and it offers them means of defense. In the church the "rule of law" still does not exist, because there are no rules protecting lay people from the abuses of the clergy. The assumption is that the clergy do not commit abuses; they make the laws and are above them.

Vatican II said nice things about communion in the church. Afterwards the hierarchy, led by Cardinal Ratzinger, sought to replace the theology of the people of God with that of communion. Unfortunately, communion is only words, because there are no structures to assure that communion will really exist. Communion is not possible unless there are laws and tribunals assuring the defense of equal rights for all members. There is no point in appealing to people's virtue, because sin and injustice are always there, and there is no communion if the victims always have to resign themselves.

Regarding communion, *Novo Millennio Ineunte* asks: "How can we forget in the first place those *specific services to communion* which are *the Petrine ministry* and, closely related to it, *episcopal collegiality?*" (44). Obviously, communion really means subordination to the Petrine ministry and to the body of bishops identified with it.

This structure of inequality leads to misgivings among many clergy, and they try to correct the faults of the laws in their practice, establishing just relations with lay people. The problem is that it all depends on the priest's goodwill. Another one can come by later and undo everything.

* * *

The great period of commitment to the poor has come and gone. The priests from that period have died or are over seventy. A new generation of priests has arrived, but it is still too early to write about it. In broad terms, it can be said that they have not been trained to be the presence of the gospel in the midst of the world. They have been trained to work in the parish, and they only feel at ease there. Certainly a parish can keep a priest busy all the time—that is not the issue. The issue is the overall direction of the church: staying in parishes and making them ever more lively, or giving witness to Jesus Christ in the world? Is the aim to make Catholics a disciplined flock, small and self-confident, unperturbed in conscience, and happy with traditions—or to make the people an active presence in the midst of the peoples?

The temptation to perpetuate or renew the traditional role of the clergy will remain great. The ruling class will continue to offer it a privileged position in society, with the impression that it is important, while in practice disregarding what it says. The ruling class likes priests who do not talk, or who talk but say nothing. Because it has little legitimacy in society, the ruling class needs the moral and religious support of the clergy, the bishops at the state level, and the priest at the municipal level. Priests will be invited to social ceremonies, not to offer a prophetic word, but to legitimize and support those presiding.

Priests will also continue to enjoy charismatic prestige as sacred persons. Such leadership can be good and useful, if it is really at the service of the poor. Sometimes it is indispensable because people are sometimes so crushed that only a strong appeal from strong leaders can awaken them from their lethargy. However, the danger is always that the masses will be kept as perpetual minors and not learn to judge and act on their own.

Yet such paternalism may be the only course to take in particular situations. Sometimes people are so poor that their problem is not one of participation in society or the church, but eating, shelter, work, security, being able to study, getting some peace where conditions are almost impossible. In such situations, society is no help; neither politicians nor experts can step in effectively. They can solve problems theoretically in their offices, but not in the midst of the people. The priest may be the only person who is in a position to be accepted and recognized as a person to be trusted. If the priest does not act, a Protestant pastor may do so. As a transitory situation, this may be a necessary way for the priesthood to be exercised, because in some cases no other form of participation may be possible.

Others use their sacred power to increase the church's prestige or power, and thus the people are treated as children. If the clergy consciously or unconsciously has tended to treat the people as children for fifteen centuries, no one should be surprised if the same pastoral situation continues. Moral exhortations to priests to overcome this situation are useless, because the problem is structural rather than moral. The moral dispositions of priests are probably better than in the past, but the problem is not one of virtue. Moral exhortations are no more effective than priests' retreats.

The primary requirement for structural reform is to define the relationship between clergy and people in terms of rights. Goodwill is not enough; the rights of lay people must be defined at all levels. There is no communion unless rights are defined. A number of church documents give one the impression that the concept of "communion" serves precisely to make the concept of rights expendable. Communion means a spontaneous harmony of good feelings, thereby maintaining the fiction that no one is on top and that everyone is brother and sister. But only if everyone has rights can they be brother and sister.

Such rights must be guaranteed by legal procedures. Currently there are no such procedures to guarantee even the few rights conceded in canon law. Without independent church courts, communion is mystification, as is a theology of communion with no definition of rights and courts to support such rights. That is quite evident to lay people.

In any case, priests need not be afraid of losing their position; their people want them out in front. But taking their place in the midst of the people is not a matter of whim. They must be clear about the route they take, in order to make their presence most fruitful.

Conclusion

Ignacio Ellacuría clearly stated the issue of the church of the poor, that is, of the people of God in Latin America:

> The real and fundamental problem is not to be seen in a contrast between a Church structured with a historical body of its own and an unstructured, spiritual Church. It is between a Church which, as a social and political power, connives with other social and political powers and this same Church which, as the people of God who are unified by the Spirit and have become a historical body, is directly at the service of God's reign: a Church that follows Jesus.
>
> In this Church that follows Jesus there are bishops, perhaps episcopal conferences, and even a general conference of bishops such as met at Medellín. There are religious congregations, parishes, pastoral letters, and so on. This Church has always been alive and has contributed and is now contributing to the liberation of the oppressed.
>
> But there is the other aspect of the Church: the worldly, secular Church that conforms to the powers and dynamism of a world of sin. This Church lives on side by side with the people of God. When the institutional Church is rejected, it is this worldly Church that is being rejected, and rightly so.[1]

It is worth noting that he uses the expression "people of God" only when speaking of the church of the poor, and does not seem to be able to bring himself to use the same expression when he speaks of the church that is captive to the powers of the world. Indeed, only the church of the poor can think of itself as people of God. When attention turns from the poor, the expression "people of God" becomes insignificant and empty. It is the poor who live as people; or at least only they are in a position to be people of God. Others may be the faithful, "lay people," isolated individuals, each contributing to his or her individual salvation.

The church must choose, take a stance, between these two directions; not to take a stance is tantamount to taking one. If it remains silent, that is a sign that it has chosen alliance with the powers.

That is why the expression "people of God" is so important. It means an option, the Medellín option. If you are with the powers that be you cannot have concern for a people. You do not need the people; the people hold you back. You simply want to be yourself, as presented by the neoliberal model. The powerful regard the people as constraining their individual freedom, the freedom of the power, which is a dependence on the will to power.

We must not have the illusion of thinking that the whole church could opt for the direction of the poor. It suffices that this church of the poor can continue to exist. These two directions have existed since the start of Christianity, and they are going to remain to the end of the world. The challenge is never to be discouraged and to keep struggling for the permanent conversion of the church, precisely because we know that this struggle will last until the end of time.

What the next papacy could be expected to do would be to bring the church closer as people of God: a church of the poor. To that end, would it be too much to expect someone with John XXIII's view of the world?

Notes

INTRODUCTION

¹ Cf. José Comblin, *O tempo da ação* (Petropolis, Brazil: Vozes, 1982); *A força da palavra* (Petropolis, Brazil: Vozes, 1986); *Vocação para a liberdade* (São Paulo: Paulus, 1999).

1. THE PEOPLE OF GOD AT VATICAN II

¹Yves Congar, O.P., "The Church: The People of God," in *Concilium*, vol. I (*The Church and Mankind*) (New York: Paulist Press, 1965), pp. 12-13.

²See commentary by Grillmeier in *Lexikon für Theologie und Kirche. Das zweite Vatikanische Konzil* (Freiburg, Switzerland: Herder, 1966), vol. I, pp. 176-209.

³Congar, art. cit., p. 11.

⁴Giuseppe Alberigo, "La condition chrétienne après Vatican II," in *La réception de Vatican II* (Paris: Cerf, 1985), pp. 33-35.

⁵It is worth noting that since 1985 a strange silence has surrounded this topic, as if the people of God had disappeared from the council and been replaced by that of communion. Cf. Ricardo Blasquez, *La Iglesia del Concilio Vaticano II* (Salamanca: Sígueme, 1991).

⁶Cf. Medard Kehl, S.J., *¿Adónde va la Iglesia? Un diagnóstico de nuestro tiempo* (Santander, Spain: Sal Terrae, 1997), p. 66.

⁷Kehl, *¿Adónde va la Iglesia?*, pp. 68-70.

⁸Cf. René Luneau and Patrick Michel (eds.), *Nem todos os caminhos levam a Roma* (Petropolis, Brazil: Vozes, 1999), pp. 287-387 (*Tous le chèmins ne mènent pas a Rome* [Paris: Albin Michiel, 1995]).

⁹Charles Journet, *L'Église du Verbe Incarné* (Bruges, Belgium: Desclée, 1955). Note that the book appeared on the eve of Vatican II.

¹⁰Cf. Benoît-Dominique de la Soujeole, *Le sacrement de la communion* (Paris: Cerf, 1998), pp. 17-25.

¹¹Ghislain Lafont, *Histoire théologique de l'Eglise catholique* (Paris: Cerf, 1994), interprets the twelfth and thirteenth centuries as a premature modernity, which did not develop until later, because the church took a negative stance toward its expansion starting in the fourteenth century. Hence modernity developed outside the church, which resisted it. Vatican II gave up this useless struggle, which had no true Christian basis, and began a rapprochement, but the last twenty-five years have seen a return to the battle against modernity (pp. 143-211).

¹²Cf. Xavier Léon-Dufour (ed.), *Vocabulaire de théologie biblique* (Paris: Cerf, 1962), "people," pp. 815-824 (*Dictionary of Biblical Theology* [New York: Desclée de Brouwer, 1967]).

[13]Cf. Joachim Jeremias, *Teologia do Novo Testamento* (São Paulo: Paulus, 1980), pp. 245-377 (*New Testament Theology* [Philadelphia: Westminster, 1971]).

[14]Cf. L. Cerfaux, *La théologie de l'Église suivant saint Paul* (Paris: Cerf, 1965). (*The Church in the Theology of St. Paul* [Nashville: Thomas Nelson, 1959]).

[15]This doctrine received official status in the encyclical *Redemptoris Missio*. For example, "The missionary thrust . . . belongs to the very nature of the Christian life. . . ." (1) and "missionary activity is a matter for all Christians" (2).

[16]Cf. "subsistit in," Benoît-Dominique de la Soujeole, *Le sacrement de la communion* (Paris: Cerf, 1998), pp. 83f. The Congregation for the Doctrine of the Faith gave an official interpretation of the "subsistit in" in the statement *Mysterium Ecclesiae* (June 24, 1973), (AAS 65 [1973], pp. 396-406), and returned to the issue in a commentary on Leonardo Boff's book, *Igreja, carisma e poder* (*Church, Charism and Power* in 1985 [AAS 77 (1985) pp. 758-759]).

[17]Cf. Ghislain Lafont, *Imaginer l'Église* (Paris: Cerf, 1995), pp. 51-61.

[18]Lafont, *Imaginer,* pp. 87-14.

[19]Cf. Giuseppe Alberigo, "The People of God in the Experience of Faith," *Concilium* (196) (Edinburgh: T & T Clark, 1984), p. 33.

[20]Alberigo, "The People of God," p. 27.

[21]Alberigo, "The People of God," n. 11, p. 33.

[22]Encyclical *Ad sinarum gentes*, AAS 47 (1955) pp. 8-9. Cited by Lafont, *Imaginer*, p. 81.

[23]This theme has been studied a great deal under the title of the spiritualization of worship. Spiritualization here actually refers to the application of sacred vocabulary to the profane, normal, everyday life of Christians led and inspired by the Holy Spirit. Because the Spirit is in all profane actions, they are all spiritual. Cf. L. Cefaux, *Le Chrétien dans la théologie paulinienne* (Paris: Cerf, 1962), pp. 255-265; K. H. Schelkle, *Teologia do Novo Testamento*, vol. 5 (São Paulo: Loyola, 1979), pp. 179-184.

[24]Cf. G. Alberigo, *A Igreja na história* (São Paulo: Paulinas, 1999), pp. 28f.

2. HISTORY OF THE IDEA OF PEOPLE OF GOD

[1]Actually the author is unknown and must have written in the late fourth or early fifth century in the East. His several works include a famous book on the celestial hierarchy and another on the ecclesiastical hierarchy.

[2]Ghislain Lafont, *Imaginer l'Église* (Paris: Cerf, 1995), pp. 21-29; *Historie théologique de l'Eglise Catholic* (Paris: Cerf, 1994), pp. 91-94.

[3]Cf. the classic work by Alois Dempf, *Sacrum Imperium* (Darmstadt, 1929, new ed. 1954); Robert Folz, *La idée d'empire en Occident du Ve au XIVe siécle* (Paris: Aubier, 1953).

[4]Folz, *La idée*, pp. 87-101.

[5]Lafont, *Imaginer*, pp. 60-73.

[6]Lafont concludes carefully, "It may be that the conflicts between the pope and the emperor little by little contributed to placing the issue of papal primacy in terms that are not proper to it, and where a political mystique of the One outweighs the data from theology and tradition on Peter and the early church in Rome." *Histoire théologique*, p. 120; see also pp. 115-120, 135ff.

[7]A good summary of Catholic teaching on the bishop of Rome as successor of Peter

may be found in J. M. R. Tillard, *Église d'Églises* (Paris: Cerf, 1987), pp. 323-398. See also Tillard, *L'eveque de Rome* (Paris: Cerf, 1984).

[8]Cf. Charles Petit-Dutaillis, *Les communes Françaises* (Paris: Albin Michel, 1947, 1970).

[9]Cf. G. Alberigo, *A Igreja na história* (São Paulo: Paulinas, 1999), pp. 245-268.

[10]For an overview of European history seen as a struggle between two representations of the world and the church, see Fr. Heer, *Europäische Geistesgeschichte* (Stuttgart: Kohlhammer, 1957).

[11]On the formation of the consciousness of people in the West, cf. Fr. Heer, *La democracia en el mundo moderno* (Madrid: Rialp, 1955) pp. 19-55.

[12]Cf. C. Violante, "Hérésies urbaines et hérésies rurales en Italie du 11e au 13 siècle," in Jacques LeGoff (ed.), *Hérésies et sociétés dans l'Europe pré-industrielle. 11e-13e siécle* (Paris: Le Haye, 1968), pp. 171-198; H. Grundmann, "Hérésies savantes et hérésies populaires au Moyen Âge," in ibid., pp. 209-215.

[13]Cf. Raymond Delatouche, *La chrétienté médievale* (Paris: Téqui, 1989), pp. 83-100.

[14]On the lay movement in the Middle Ages, cf. the basic work by Georges de Lagarde, *La Naissance de l'esprit laïque au déclin du Moyen Âge* (Louvain-Paris: Nauwelaerts, 1958), 6 vols.

[15]Cf. E. Benz, *Ecclesia spiritualis, Kirchenidee und Geschichtstheologie des franzikanishcen Reformation* (Stuttgart: Kohlmammer, 1934).

[16]On Joachim of Fiori and his heirs up to our own times, see the monumental work of Henri de Lubac, *La postérité spirituelle de Joachim de Flore* (Paris: Lethielleux, 1979), 2 vols. Also Henry Mottu, *La manfiestation de l'Ésprit selon Joachim de Flore* (Paris: Neufchâtel, 1977). Frei Carlos Josafat compares Joachim to Aquinas in *Tomás de Aquino e a Nova Era do Espírito* (São Paulo: Loyola, 1998).

[17]Cf. Cahiers de Fanjeaux, *Franciscains d'Oc. Les Spirituels ca 1280-1324* (Paris: Privat, 1975).

[18]On the great debates among the Franciscans until the mid-fourteenth century, cf. Gordon Leff, *Heresy in the Later Middle Ages* (New York: Barnes & Noble, 1967), vol. 1, pp. 51-190.

[19]The history of the Franciscans was a tragedy, one of the most significant phases in Christian history. The two tendencies were central to the history of the fourteenth and fifteenth centuries. As of the sixteenth century, Rome established the hierarchical system so radically that it was impossible to jeopardize complete homogeneity. The Franciscan movement was disciplined, and little room was left for maneuvering. Cf. Leff, *Heresy.*

[20]Cf. Alberigo, *A Igreja na história*, p. 20.

[21]On Wycliffe, cf. Leff, *Heresy*, vol. 2, pp. 494-558.

[22]Cf. Alberigo, *A Igreja na história*, pp. 114-142.

[23]Cf. Josef Macek, *¿Herejía o revolución? El movimiento husita* (Madrid, 1967).

[24]Cf. Alberigo, *A Igreja na história*, pp. 132-142.

[25]Cf. Pierre Chaunu, *Les temps des réforms* (Paris: Fayard, 1975), pp. 293-368.

[26]Cf. Alberigo, *A Igreja na história*, pp. 199-220.

[27]The "reductions" in Paraguay are significant: they were successful in transforming the Guarani people—but everything depended on the priests. When the priests were expelled by the decision of the king of Spain with the consent of the pope, nothing was left. There were no lay people prepared to give it continuity. It all depended on the Jesuits. We know that today the Jesuits have changed radically, especially after the leadership of Father Pedro Arrupe; some even call him the second founding father. Unfortunately, the model that the Jesuits used for four hundred years seems to be used

in an even more extreme fashion through institutions like Opus Dei and the Legionaires of Christ, and some others. The Jesuits were neophytes by comparison.

²⁸Alberigo, *A Igreja na história*, pp. 199-219.

²⁹Cf. Ernst Bloch, *Thomas Münzer, théologien de la révolution* (Paris: 1964, orig. 1921).

³⁰Cf. John Cogley (ed.), *Religion in America* (New York: Meridian, 1958); Thomas O'Dea, *The Sociology of Religion* (Englewood Cliffs, NJ: Prentice-Hall, 1966).

³¹That is how it is explained in the encyclopedia. Cf. Albert Soboul, *L'Encyclopédie: Textes choisis* (Paris: 1984), pp. 296-299.

³²See, for example, Paul Hazard, *La pensée européene au XVIIIe siècle* (Paris: 1946), vol. 1, pp. 48-174.

³³The church defended, against all evidence, the literal interpretation of the miracles in the Bible until the mid-twentieth century. It was easy for the bourgeoisie— an explanation of Genesis chapter 1 was enough to cause students to lose their faith. Cf. A. Desqueyrat, *Le civilisé peut-il croire* (Paris: Desclée de Brouwer, 1963).

³⁴I can speak from experience because that was how I was educated.

³⁵Cf. Émile Poulat, *Catholicism, démocratie et socialisme* (Tournai, Belgium: Casterman, 1977), pp. 255-333, especially pp. 315ff.

³⁶J.B. Metz, *The Emergent Church: The Future of Christianity in a Post-bourgeois World* (New York: Crossroad, 1981).

³⁷Cf. Henri Desroche, *Socialismes et sociologie religieuse* (Paris: Cujas, 1965), pp. 117-143.

³⁸Cf. René Cost, *Les chrétiens et la lutte des classes* (Paris: S.O.S., 1975); Jean Delmarle, *Classes et lutte des classes* (Paris: Ed. Ouvrières, 1973); Jean Guichard, *Église, lutte des classes et stratégies politiques* (Paris: Cerf, 1972). In Latin America the issue was debated within Christians for Socialism.

³⁹Cf. Jean Frisque, "L'écclésiologie du XXe siècle," in *Bilan de la théologie au XXe siécle* (Tournai-Paris: Casterman, 1970, pp. 431-441; José Comblin, *Teologia da ação* (São Paulo: Herder, 1967).

⁴⁰Cf. J. Frisque, "Lécclésiologue du XXe siècle," pp. 436, 442-453.

⁴¹Cf. Émile Poulat, *Église contre bourgeoisie* (Tournai, Belgium: Casterman, 1977); Pierre Pierrard, *L'Église et les ouvriers en France (1840-1940)* (Paris: Hachette, 1984); Henri Rollet, *L'action soicale des catholiques en France (1871-1914)* (Bruges: Desclée de Brouwer, 1958), 2 vols.

3. PEOPLE OF GOD IN LATIN AMERICA

¹Here is an example of the Curia's police methods. Romero was condemning the crimes of the military against the people and even the clergy. The Vatican sent Cardinal Quarracino as apostolic visitor, the archbishop of Buenos Aires who was friendly with leaders of the Argentine military dictatorship, generals who tortured and killed as many as 30,000. Quarracino recommended that Romero be removed and replaced by someone else.

²On the impact of Vatican II in Latin America, cf. Gustavo Gutiérrez, "Le rapport entre l'Eglise et les pauvres, vu d'Amérique latine," in G. Alberigo and J. P. Joussa, *La réception de Vatican II*, pp. 229-257, and Segundo Galilea, "Medellín et Puebla comme application du Concile," pp. 85-103.

³On these meetings, cf. Paul Gauthier, "Consolez mon peuple," in *Le Concile et l'Église des pauvres* (Paris: Cerf, 1965), pp. 208-213, 277-283; quotation by Bishop

Himmer in Ignacio Ellacuría, *Conversión de la Iglesia al Reino de Dios* (Santander, Spain: Sal Terrae, 1984).

[4]See, for example, the use of the word "church" in Gustavo Gutiérrez, *A Theology of Liberation* (Maryknoll, NY: Orbis, 1988; first Spanish publication, Lima: 1971), the book that launched liberation theology.

[5]Gutiérrez, *Theology of Liberation*, pp. 34-46, Medellín Conclusions, Pastoral de las élites.

[6]Gutiérrez, *Theology of Liberation*, p. 174; Boff, *Igreja: carisma e poder* (São Paulo: Ática, 1994), p. 223 (*Church: Charism and Power: Liberation Theology and the Institutional Church* [New York: Crossroad, 1985]).

[7]For an excellent presentation of the church of the poor, see Jon Sobrino, *The True Church and the Poor* (Maryknoll, NY: Orbis, 1984), pp. 84-159. Also Ignacio Ellacuría, *Conversión de la Iglesia al Reino de Dios*, pp. 56-79, 93-100, 153-178.

[8]See Lercaro's magnificent speech, in Paul Gauthier, "Consolez mon peuple," pp. 198-203.

[9]Jon Sobrino, *The True Church*.

[10]Cf. Sobrino, *The True Church*, pp. 91-92. Ignacio Ellacuría, "The Church of the Poor, Historical Sacrament of Liberation," in Ignacio Ellacuría, S.J., and Jon Sobrino, S.J. (eds.), *Mysterium Liberationis: Fundamental Concepts of Liberation Theology* (Maryknoll, NY: Orbis Books, 1993), pp. 543-563.

[11]Sobrino, *The True Church*, pp. 86ff.

[12]Puebla documents from John Eagleson and Philip Sharper (eds.), *Puebla and Beyond: Documentation and Commentary* (Maryknoll, NY: Orbis Books, 1979), paragraph numbers from conclusions.

[13]Cf. Juan Carlos Scannone, "Theology, Popular Culture, and Discernment," in Rosino Gibellini, *Frontiers of Theology in Latin America* (Maryknoll, NY: Orbis Books, 1979).

[14]On the Sucre Conference (November 15 to 23, 1972) cf. Enrique Dussel, *De Medellín a Puebla. Una Década de sangre y esperanza* (Mexico City: Edicol, 1979), pp. 268-296. However, he does not mention what happened in great secrecy, the nuncio's involvement in the election and the assembly's capitulation to the order from the nunciature. No one knew the identity of the authority who had picked the names for the new CELAM board.

[15]See a commentary in Gustavo Gutiérrez, "Sobre el documento de consulta para Puebla," in *La fuerza histórica de los pobres* (Lima: CEP, 1979), pp. 183-236 (*The Power of the Poor in History* [Maryknoll, NY: Orbis Books, 1983]).

[16]On Vekemans, see Dussel, *De Medellín a Puebla*, pp. 275-280. All of Cardinal Ratzinger's arguments in the Roman instructions were in Vekemans' writings.

[17]The best commentary by a liberation theologian was Juan-Luis Segundo, *Theology and the Church: A Response to Cardinal Ratzinger and a Warning to the Whole Church* (Minneapolis: Winston Press, 1985).

[18]Cf. Enrique Dussel, *Las metáforas teológicas de Marx* (Estella, Spain: Verbo Divino, 1993); Michel Henry, *Marx* (Paris: Gallimard, 1976) 2 vols.

4. REVERSAL AT THE 1985 SYNOD

[1]The cardinal systematically devalues the human element in the church, thereby contradicting the council's intentions. See the observations of Gustave Thils, *En*

dialogue avec l'"Entretien sur la foi" (Louvain-la-Neuve, Belgium: Université catholique de Louvain, 1986), pp. 49-52.

²Cardinal Joseph Ratzinger/Vittorio Messori, *Entretien sur la foi* (Paris: Fayard, 1985) , p. 52; *The Ratzinger Report* (San Francisco: Ignatius Press, 1985).

³*Synod extraordinaire. Célébration de Vatican II* (Paris: Cerf, 1986), p. 9 n. 1.

⁴The American theologian Joseph Kommonchak writes, "On the basis of the Final Report, one could never think that 'People of God' had been the title of an entire chapter of *Lumen Gentium*, that it had been one of the overarching themes of the Council's ecclesiology, and that it had been introduced precisely as an organizing principle of the true mystery of the church in the time between the Ascension and the Parousia," cf. *Synode extraordinaire* p. 20.

⁵*Synode extraordinaire*, p. 21, n. 13 p. 559, and p. 554.

⁶*Synode extraordinaire*, p. 345.

⁷*Synode extraordinaire*, p. 559; *Christifideles Laici*, no. 19 and 18e.

⁸For example, Benoît-Dominique de La Soujeole, *Le sacrement de la communion* (Paris: Editions Universitaires de Fribourg-Cerf, 1998); Walter Kasper, *La théologie et l'Eglise* (Paris: Cerf, 1999; original publication, 1987); Jerome Hamer, *The Church Is a Communion* (London: Geoffrey Chapman, 1964).

⁹*Christifideles Laici* says clearly that communion refers to the invisible mystery of the church: such communion is the very mystery of the church (18e); "The reality of the Church as Communion is, then, the integrating aspect, indeed the central content of the 'mystery'" (19d).

¹⁰Cf. Cleto Caliman: "The category People of God better expresses the community and social dynamism that should propel the church in the world" ("Visão eclesiológica do Sínodo," in José Ernanne Pinheiro (ed.), *O Sínodo e os leigos* (São Paulo: Loyola, 1987), p. 91. He is talking about the 1987 synod which would lead to the publication of *Christifideles Laici*. Fr. Caliman is very charitable and kindly attributes to the synod what the pope forgot to mention in the apostolic exhortation. Caliman notes, "The ecclesiology of the people of God helps us to understand that the world is part of the very definition of the church" (p. 90).

¹¹Avery Dulles has some useful ideas on ecclesiologies of communion.

¹²Cf. Cleto Caliman, "The category People of God serves precisely to fulfill the function of drawing language on the church closer to the conflictive reality in which the lay Christian lives and for which the category of 'communion' is scarcely apt" (p. 90).

¹³This is the concept used by canon law, and the canonical concept easily makes its way into theological or pastoral usage. Canon 96: "By baptism one is incorporated into the Church of Christ and constituted a person in it, with the duties and the rights which, in accordance with each one's status, are proper to Christians, in so far as they are in ecclesiastical communion and unless a lawfully issued sanction intervenes." Canon 205: "Those baptized are in full communion with the Catholic Church here on earth who are joined with Christ in his visible body, through the bonds of profession of faith, the sacraments and ecclesiastical governance." Canon 209 §1: "Christ's faithful are bound to preserve their communion with the Church at all times, even in their external actions."

5. THE CHURCH AS PEOPLE

¹Cf. Hans Küng, *Qu'est-ce que l'Eglise?* (Paris: DDB, 1972), p. 87.

²Cf. *Synode extraordinaire. Célébration de Vatican II* (Paris: Cerf, 1986), p. 481.

[3]Cf. Medard Kehn, S. J., *¿Adónde va la Iglesia? Un diagnóstico de nuestro tiempo* (Santander, Spain: Sal Terrae, 1997); Ricardo Mariano, *Neopentecostais: Sociología do novo pentecostalismo no Brasil* (São Paulo: Loyola, 1999).

[4]Among the many books demonstrating the effects of social breakdown and the destruction of solidarity in the most advanced nations, cf. Francis Fukuyama, *The Great Disruption* (New York: Simon and Schuster, 2000); Christopher Lasch, *The Culture of Narciscism* (New York: Norton, 1979); *The Revolt of the Elites and the Betrayal of Democracy* (New York: Norton, 1995); Allan Bloom, *The Closing of the American Mind* (New York: Simon and Schuster, 1987).

[5]There is a contrary mystical tradition which idealizes the solitary life, e.g., along the lines of the *Imitation of Christ* of Thomas à Kempis. It is hard to agree that this tradition is Christian. It may express advice from traditional wisdom, but it is not grounded in the gospels. Some moments of solitude are necessary to prepare for moments of communion, but they are always secondary.

[6]These issues are being examined in works on urban pastoral work. Cf. José Comblin, *Pastoral Urbana* (Petropolis, Brazil: Vozes, 2000, second edition).

[7]Enrique Dussel defines the Latin American people as follows: "A 'people' is the 'communal bloc' of a nation's oppressed. A people consists of the dominated classes (the working or industrial class, the campesino class, and so on). But it is also constituted of any human group that is non-capitalistic or that performs class practices only sporadically (marginal groups, ethnic groups, tribal groups, and so on). The entire 'bloc'—in Gramsci's sense—constitutes the people: a people is the historic 'subject' or agent of the social formation of a given country or nation" (*Ethics and Community* [Maryknoll, NY: Orbis Books, 1988], pp. 81-82).

[8]Cf. Pedro Ribeiro de Oliveira, "Que signifie analytiquement 'people'?" in *Concilium*, no. 196, pp. 131, 142.

[9]Cf. Octavio Ianni, *A formação do Estado populista na América Latina* (Rio de Janeiro: Civilização Brasileira, 1975); *O colapso do populismo no Brasil* (Rio de Janeiro: Civilização Brasileira, 1968).

[10]Cited by Gustavo Gutiérrez, in "Le rapport entre l'Eglise et les pauvres, vu d'Amérique latine," in G. Alberigo and J. P. Joussa, *La réception de Vatican II*, p. 234.

[11]See almost the entire work of Juan Luis Segundo, or the works of Jon Sobrino, *Jesus in Latin America* (Maryknoll, NY: Orbis Books, 1987), *Jesus the Liberator: A Historical-Theological View* (Maryknoll, NY: Orbis Books, 1994).

[12]On martyrs in Latin America, cf. José Marins et al., *Martiro: Memória perigosa na América Latina hoje* (São Paulo: Paulus, 1984); various authors, *A práxis do martírio ontem e hoje* (São Paulo, Paulus, 1980).

[13]On the meaning of martyrdom in Latin America, cf. Jon Sobrino, *Witnesses to the Kingdom* (Maryknoll, NY: Orbis Books, 2003); "Spirituality and the Following of Jesus," in Ignacio Ellacuría, S.J., and Jon Sobrino S. J. (eds.), *Mysterium Liberationis: Fundamental Concepts of Liberation Theology* (Maryknoll, NY: Orbis Books, 1993), pp. 677-701.

[14]Something must be said about the sad way the archdiocese treats the grave of Archbishop Oscar Romero, hidden in a crypt like a storeroom. Is this a sign of the rejection of the martyr bishop? Why? The hierarchy is rejecting the people's canonization!

[15]It is shocking that even today the bishops of Argentina have said nothing about the martyrdom of Angelelli. They accept or pretend to accept the version of the military who say that his death was due to a traffic accident, which is contradicted by witnesses.

[16]See nos. 400-402 of the working document which spoke of sufferings and

persecutions, though it was not clear whether it referred to the poor or to the persecutions that killed the martyrs. Even such a weak allusion disappeared from the final document.

[17]There is much talk of inculturation, even in Roman documents. But it goes no further than talk, because any real inculturation is strictly prohibited.

[18]Cf. J. Comblin, *Called to Freedom: The Changing Context of Liberation Theology* (Maryknoll, NY: Orbis Books, 1998), pp. 64 ff.

[19]This subculture has been described by anthropologists a number of times. See the still valuable works of Oscar Lewis, *Five Families: Mexican Case Studies in the Culture of Poverty* (New York: Basic Books, 1961); *The Children of Sánchez: Autobiography of a Mexican Family* (New York: Random House, 1965); *La Vida: A Puerto Rican Family in the Culture of Poverty* (San Juan and New York: Vintage Books, 1965); Larissa Lomnitz, *Networks and Marginality: Life in a Mexican Shantytown* (New York: Academic Press, 1977).

[20]Romanization came through the first plenary Latin American council held in Rome in 1899. Roman attacks had already changed the churches in Latin America, e.g., around 1870, the "religious question" in Brazil. Cf. Joseph Komonchak, "La réalisation de l'Eglise en un lieu," in G. Alberigo and J. P. Jossua (eds.), *La réception de Vatican II* (Paris: Cerf, 1985), pp. 110-113.

[21]The worst thing is that what they call evangelization consists of forcing peoples to enter into this Roman subculture.

[22]The best way to prevent change is to praise and exalt what has changed since the council. Actually the changes thus far have been insignificant, because essentially nothing has changed. But exalting these changes sets the stage for recommending a pause now.

6. THE PEOPLE AS ACTOR

[1]Cf. Jorge Castañeda, *Utopia Unarmed: The Latin American Left after the Cold War* (New York: Knopf, 1993); Daniel Camacho, "Los movimientos populares," in Pedro Vuskovic et al., *América Latina hoy* (Mexico, Siglo XXI, 1990). On Central America, Phillip Berryman, *The Religious Roots of Rebellion: Christians in Central American Revolutions* (Maryknoll, NY: Orbis Books, 1984).

[2]Cf. Franz Hinkelammert, *El grito del sujeto* (San Jose, Costa Rica: DEI, 1998).

[3]Cf. Friedrich Heer, *Europäische Geistesgeschichte* (Stuttgart: Kohlhammner, 1957).

[4]"Sancta mater ecclesia no solum est ex clericis, sed etiam ex laicis," from the play *Antequam essent clerici*, cited in G. de Lagarde, *La naissance de l'esprit laique au déclin du moyen âge*, vol. I (Louvain-Paris: Secteur social de la scolastique, 1956), p. 207.

[5]Lagarde, *La naissance*, vol. II, pp. 51-85, 106-120, 131-138.

[6]Jean Comby, *Para ler a história da Igreja*, vol. II (São Paulo: Loyola, 1994), p. 105 (Lamenais); vol. I, p. 171 (Boniface VIII).

[7]The popes claimed imperial dignity and sought to play the role that the emperor had played in antiquity. Cf. Robert Folz, *L'idée d'empire en Occident du Ve au VIXe siècle* (Paris: Aubier, 1953), pp. 87-101.

[8]Comby, *Para ler a história*, vol. I, p. 136.

[9]Folz, *L'idée d'empire*, pp. 196, 101-106.

[10]Translation from *Five Contemporary Accounts of the Coronation of Charlemagne.*

As reproduced in *The Coronation of Charlemagne: What Did It Signify?*, trans. and ed. Richard E. Sullivan (Boston: D.C. Heath and Company, 1959), pp. 2-3.

[11]Maurice Duverger, *Constitutions et documents politiques* (Paris: PUF, 1957), p. 3.

[12]Cf. Jena Touchard, *Histoire des idées politiques* (Paris: PUF, 1959), vol. II, pp. 501-507.

[13]John Milbank's *Theology and Social Theory: Beyond Secular Reason* (Oxford: Blackwell, 1990) deserves thoughtful attention.

[14]Cf. José Maria Mardones, *Postmodernidad y cristianismo* (Santander, Spain: Sal Terrae, 1988), pp. 59-80; Luis González-Carvajal, *Ideas y creencias del hombre actual* (Santander, Spain: Sal Terrae, 1991), pp. 153-179.

[15]Statement of George W. Bush, March 29, 2001.

[16]Cf. Lewis Mumford, *La cité a travers l'histoire* (Paris: Seuil, 1964), pp. 312-400 (*The City in History* [New York: Harcourt, Brace and World, 1961]). The struggles of Savonarola in Florence were emblematic. Cf. Donald Weinstein, *Savonarola and Florence: Prophetism and Patriotism in the Renaissance* (Princeton, NJ: Princeton University Press, 1970).

[17]The best representation of the spirit of Swiss cantons is the national hero, St. Nicolas of Flue. Cf. Charles Journet, *Saint Nicolas de Flue* (Neuchatel, France: La Baconnière, 1966).

[18]Cf. José Ignacio González Faus, *La autoridad de la verdad: Momentos oscuros del Magisterio Eclesiástico* (Barcelona: Herder, 1996), pp. 131 and 140.

[19]Ghislain Lafont, *Historie théologique de l'Église catholique* (Paris: Cerf, 1994), pp. 83-97; *Imaginer l'Église catholique* (Paris: Cerf, 1995), pp. 51-59; Gerald R. Arbuckle, *Refundar la Iglesia* (Santander, Spain: Sal Terrae, 1998), pp. 103-148 (*Refounding the Church: Dissent for Leadership* [Maryknoll, NY: Orbis Books, 1993]).

[20]Cf. G. Alberigo, *A Igreja na história* (São Paulo: Paulinos, 1999), pp. 269-306.

[21]Friedrich Heer, *Europa, Mutter der Revolutionen* (Stuttgart: W. Kohlhammer, 1964), p. 1028.

[22]Cf. J. M. R. Tillard, *Église d'Églises. L'ecclésiologie de communion* (Paris: Cerf, 1987). There are two ecclesiologies of communion. Tillard's is an ecclesiology of communion between churches; another more contemporary one is a communion of individuals or souls.

[23]Concern about a pastoral approach to the city is beginning but still very timid, because the diocesan structure is so strong that it absorbs all energy. Cf. Alberto Antoniazzi and Cleto Caliman (eds.), *A presença da Igreja na cidade* (Petropolis, Brazil: Vozes, 1994); Lucia Maria M. Bogus and Luiz Eduardo W. Wanderley (org.), *A luta pela cidade em São Paulo* (São Paulo: Cortez, 1992); José Comblin, *Viver na cidade. Pistas para uma pastoral urbana* (São Paulo: Paulus, 1996); *Pastoral urbana* (Petrópolis, Brazil: Vozes, 1999).

[24]Cf. Yves Congar and B. D. Dupuy (eds.), *L'Épiscopat et l'Église universelle* (Paris: Cerf, 1964); Tillard, *Église d'Églises*; *L'Église locale* (Paris: Cerf, 1995).

7. PEOPLE OF THE POOR

[1]Cf. Gustavo Gutiérrez, *The Power of the Poor in History* (Maryknoll, NY: Orbis Books, 1983), pp. 125-165; Ronaldo Muñoz, *Nueva conciencia de la Iglesia en América Latina* (Santiago: Universidad Nueva, 1973), pp. 390-407; David Regan,

Igreja para a libertação. Retrato pastoral da Igreja no Brasil (São Paulo: Paulinas, 1986), pp. 153-182.

[2]Some examples of the vast literature on CEBs: Marcello Azevedo, *Basic Ecclesial Communities in Brazil* (Washington, D.C.: Georgetown University Press, 1987); Faustino Luiz Couto Teixeira, *Comunidades eclesiais de base: Bases teológicas* (Petropolis, Brazil: Vozes, 1988); "As CEBs no Brasil: Cidadania em proceso," in *REB* fasc. 211 (1993), pp. 596-615; Carmen Cinira Macedo, *Tempo de Gênesis. O povo das comunidades eclesiais de base* (São Paulo: Brasiliense, 1986); José Marins, *A comunidade eclesial de base* (São Paulo: Salesianos, n.d.); *Comunidade Eclesial de Base na América Latina* (São Paulo: Paulinas, 1977); *Comunidades eclesiais de base: foco de evangelização* (São Paulo: Paulinas, 1980); Domingos Barbé and Emmanuel Rebuma, *Retrato de uma comunidade de base* (Petropolis, Brazil: Vozes, 1970); David Regan, *Igreja para a libertação* (São Paulo: Paulinas, 1986), pp. 43-111.

[3]This diagnosis might not be equally valid everywhere in Brazil. My direct experience shows that this is the case in the Northeast and São Paulo. In Rio de Janeiro, Rio Grande do Sul, Paraná, Minas Gerais, etc., the communities might be more independent of the clergy, less parish-bound, and more devoted to the needs and struggle as they were in the past, until approximately 1985.

[4]Cf. M. Camisasca and M. Vitale (eds.), *I movimenti nella Chiesa negli anni 80* (Milan: Jaca Books, 1982); Antonio Alves de Melo, *A Evangelização no Brasil. Dimensões teológicas e desafios pastorais* (Rome: Gregoriana, 1996), pp. 222-232; "Classe média e opção preferencial pelos pobres," in *REB* 43 (1983), pp. 340-350; Salvatore Abbruzzese, "Comunione e liberazione," *Identité catholique et desqualification du monde* (Paris: Cerf, 1989).

[5]The bourgeoisies have always used this justification for denying help to the poor and being entirely free to get rich with a good conscience. Many adopt Benjamin Franklin's view of England during his time: "There is no country in the world where so many provisions are established for them; so many hospitals to receive them when they are sick and lame, founded and maintained by voluntary charities; so many almshouses for the aged of both sexes, together with a solemn law made by the rich to subject their estates to a heavy tax for the support of the poor. . . . In short, you offered a premium for the encouragement of idleness, and you should not now wonder that it has had its effect in the increase of poverty." Quoted by Gertrude Himmelfarb in *The Idea of Poverty: England in the Early Industrial Age* (New York: Alfred Knopf, 1984), p. 5.

[6]From the vast literature we cite only Robert Reich, *El trabajo de las naciones* (Buenos Aires: Vergara, 1993), pp. 247-255 (*The Work of Nations* [New York: Knopf, 1991]); John Kenneth Galbraith, *La cultura de satisfacción* (Buenos Aires: Emecé, 1992) pp. 51-60 (*The Culture of Contentment* [Boston: Houghton Mifflin, 1992]).

[7]Gustavo Gutiérrez, *Las Casas: In Search of the Poor of Jesus Christ* (Maryknoll, NY: Orbis Books, 1993).

[8]Cf. José Comblin, "Ricos e pobres nos Atos dos Apóstolos," in *Vida Pastoral*, no. 182, 2001, pp. 2-9.

[9]On the social makeup of the Pauline communities, cf. Wayne A. Meeks, *The Social World of the Apostle Paul* (New Haven: Yale University Press, 1983), pp. 51-73; Gerd Theissen, *Sociología da cristandade primitiva* (São Leopoldo: Sinodal, 1987), pp. 133-147 (*Sociology of Early Palestinian Christianity* [Philadelphia: Fortress, 1978]).

[10]One of the most common objections against Christians was precisely that they were communities of the poor. That was what Cecelius, an educated Roman, said in the dialogue with Minucius Felix, in *Octavius*: "Fellows who gather together illiterates

from the dregs of the populace and credulous women with the instability natural to their sex, and so organize a rabble of profane conspirators" (cf. Gustave Bardy, *La conversion au christianisme durante les premiers siècles* [Paris: Aubier, 1949], p. 229). In his dispute with Celsus, Origen encounters one objection made repeatedly: Christian communions are made up solely of ignorant people from the lower strata. Cf. Jean Danielou, *Origène* (Paris: 1948), pp. 109-138.

[11]Cf. José Comblin, *Paulo: trabalho e missão* (São Paulo: FTD, 1991).

[12]Cf. Ricardo Mariano, *Neopentecostais: Sociologia do novo pentecostalismo no Brasil* (São Paulo: Loyola, 1999), pp. 147-186.

[13]Cf. Jean Gaudemet, *L'Église dans l'empire romain (Ive-Ve siècles)* (Paris: Sirey, 1958), pp. 316 ff.; 172-179 (privileges of clergy), 165-170.

[14]Cf. J. B. Metz, "Iglesia y pueblo o el precio de la ortodoxia," in Karl Rahner et al. (eds.), *Dios y la ciudad* (Madrid: Cristiandad, 1975), p. 119.

[15]Jean Gaudemet, *L'Église dans l'empire romain*, pp. 353 ff. A basic work on the development of charity as aid to the poor is Michel Mollat (ed.), *Études sur l'histoire de la pauvreté (Moyen Âge-XVIe siècle)* (Paris: Sorbonne, 1974), two vols., esp. pp. 563-822.

[16]Cf. Octavio Paz, *El laberinto de la soledad* (Mexico City: Fondo de Cultura Económica, 1994, orig. 1950) (*The Labyrinth of Solitude* [New York: Grove Weidenfeld, 1962]).

[17]Cf. José Ignacio González Faus, *La libertad de la palabra en la Iglesia y en la teología. Antología comentada* (Santander, Spain: Sal Terrae, 1985) (*Where the Spirit Breathes* [Maryknoll, NY: Orbis Books, 1989]).

[18]From the abundant literature we select Gordon Leff, *Heresy in the Later Middle Ages* (Manchester: Manchester University Press, 1967); Jacques LeGoff (ed.), *Hérésies et sociétés dans l'Europe industrielle 11e-18e siècles* (Paris-La Haye: Mouton, 1968).

[19]Cf. José Ignacio González Faus, *Vicarios de Cristo: Los pobres en la teología y espiritualidad cristianas* (Madrid: Trotta, 1991).

[20]Michel Mollat, *Les pauvres au moyen âge* (Paris: Hachette, 1978), pp. 147-164.

[21]See comments by Metz in *Iglesia y pueblo o el precio de la ortodoxia* (pp. 130-134).

[22]Georges Baudot, *La pugna franciscana por México* (Mexico City: Alianza Editorial Mexicana, 1990), pp. 13-36; Christian Duverger, *La conversion des Indiens de Nouvelle Espagne* (Paris: Seuil, 1987), pp. 29-43. For an old document, see Fray Gerónimo de Mendieta, *Historia eclesiástica indiana* (Mexico City: Porruá, 1971), pp. 196-230.

[23]González Faus, *Vicarios de Cristo,* p. 243.

[24]See González Faus, *Vicarios de Cristo,* pp. 246-251, for comments on the reception of Bossuet's well-known sermon. Bossuet's place in literature is like that of Father Viera in Portuguese literature.

[25]González Faus, *Vicarios de Cristo,* p. 247.

[26]I feel compelled to quote here a well-known passage from Peguy written in the early twentieth century: "Our socialism was—and was not—nothing less than a religion of temporal salvation. To this day it is nothing less than that. We wanted nothing less than the temporal salvation of humankind by healing the working class world, by healing work, and the world of work, by restoring work and the dignity of work." See "Notre Jeunesse" (1910), in the Pléiade edition of *Oeuvres en prose. 1909-1914* (Paris: Gallimard, 1957), p. 592.

[27]José Ignacio González Faus, *Memoria de Jesús, Memoria del pueblo* (Santander, Spain: Sal Terrae, 1984), pp. 9.

[28]E. Isambert, *Cristianisme et classe ouvrière* (Paris: 1961), pp. 288 ff.

[29]Medellín conclusions, document on poverty, par. 8, translation in Alfred T. Hennelly (ed.), *Liberation Theology: A Documentary History* (Maryknoll, NY: Orbis Books, 1990), p. 116.

[30]"The Puebla Final Document" is found in John Eagleson and Philip Sharper (eds.), *Puebla and Beyond: Documentation and Commentary* (Maryknoll, NY: Orbis Books, 1979).

[31]Puebla 8.

[32]Of course the people is made up of saints and sinners; that is true of all peoples, including the people of God. The people is people of God precisely because it is en route: from sin to salvation.

[33]Gustavo Gutiérrez, "The Irruption of the Poor in Latin America and the Christian Communities of the Common People," in Sergio Torres (ed.), *The Challenge of Basic Christian Communities* (Maryknoll, NY: Orbis Books, 1982), p. 111.

[34]C. Violante, "Héresies urbaines e héresies rurales en Italie du 11e au 13e siècle," in Jacques LeGoff, *Héresies et sociétés*, pp. 171-197.

[35]G. D. H. Cole, *A History of Socialist Thought. I. The Forerunners (1789-1850)*.

[36]Cited in González Faus, *Memoria de Jesús*, p. 100.

[37]Cf. Pierre Pierrard, *L'Église et les ouvriers en France (1840-1940)* (Paris: Hachette, 1984), p. 139.

[38]Cf. Pierrard, *L'Église et les ouvriers en France*, pp. 145ff.

[39]With his deep sensitivity for the people, Charles Peguy saw this very clearly: "All the Church's difficulties stem from the point; all its real, profound, popular difficulties: from the fact that in spite of some so-called works among the working-class, under the cloak of some so-called social workers, and a few so-called Catholic workers, the factory is closed to the Church and the Church to the factory; that in the modern world, it too has suffered a modernization, has become the religion, almost solely the religion of the rich, and is no longer, if I may so express it, socially the communion of the faithful. The whole weakness, and perhaps one ought to say the growing weakness of the Church in the modern world does not come, as people think, from the fact that Science has constructed systems against religion which are said to be invincible, or that Science has discovered arguments against religion said to be victorious, but from the fact that what remains of the Christian world is lacking to-day, profoundly lacking, in charity. It is not arguments that are wanting. It is charity.

"That is the reason why the Church in the modern world . . . is no longer a people socially, an immense people, an immense race; that Christianity is no longer the religion, socially, of the depths, a people's religion, a religion of the people, a common religion, of a whole people, temporal, eternal, a religion rooted in the temporal depths themselves, the religion of a race, of a whole temporal race, an eternal race; and that it is only a religion of the bourgeois, of the rich, a superior sort of religion for the upper, superior, classes of society, of the nation, a miserable sort of refined religion for refined people" (Charles Peguy, *Temporal and Eternal* [London: Harvill Press, 1958], pp. 64-66).

[40]Cf. Pierrard, *L'Église et les ouvriers en France*, p. 177.

[41]Protestantism was more open to accepting socialism, and hence the presence of Christians (especially Lutherans) in socialist movements was stronger and those movements were not antireligious. Cf. Tieje Brattinga, *Theologie van het socialisme* (Bolsward, Holland: Het Witte Boekhuis, 1980). The greatest theologian who spoke of socialism was Paul Tillich.

[42]This issue was uppermost in the documents of Christians for socialism. Cf. the final document of the Congress of Christians for Socialism held in Santiago in 1972,

which reads: "The revolutionary process in Latin America is in full swing. Many Christians are committed to it, but most, held back by mental inertia and categories imbued with bourgeois ideology, view it with fear and insist on traveling along reformist and modernizing paths that are impossible. There is only one all-encompassing Latin American process. We Christians do not have our own political path to offer, nor do we want one."

[43]*Los Cristianos y la Revolución* (Santiago, Chile: Quimantú, 1972), p. 176; Pablo Richard, *Cristianos por el socialisimo: Historia y documentación* (Salamanca, Spain: Sígueme, 1976), pp. 22, 33.

[44]Juan Hernandez Pico, "The Experience of Nicaragua's Revolutionary Christians," in Torres, *The Challenge of Basic Christian Communities*, p. 68.

[45]Gustavo Gutiérrez, "The Irruption of the Poor in Latin America and the Christian Communities of the Common People," in Torres, *The Challenge of Basic Christian Communities,* p. 108.

[46]In Torres, *The Challenge of Basic Christian Communities*, p. 6.

[47]The group at the UCA (Central American University) in El Salvador, Ignacio Ellacuría, Jon Sobrino, and J.I. González Faus, have developed this most fully.

8. THE PEOPLE WITHIN OTHER PEOPLES

[1]The Vatican state reflects a contradiction. It claims that the pope and his aides are above and outside of all peoples (i.e., a people alongside other peoples) and yet the Roman church claims that it is the only embodiment of the universal church, because other churches are set within particular peoples.

[2]Cf. Yves Congar, *Un peuple messianique* (Paris: Cerf, 1975).

[3]See, for example, the document of the French bishops, *Proposer la foi dans la societé actuelle: Lettre aux catholiques de France* (Paris: Cerf, 1999).

[4]Marcel Gauchet, *The Disenchantment of the World: A Political History of Religion* (Princeton, NJ: Princeton University Press, 1998; original French, 1985).

[5]Cf. Ghislain Lafont, *Historie théologique de l'Eglise catholique* (Paris: Cerf, 1995), pp. 47-69.

[6]Cf. Hélène Ahrweiler, *L'idééologie politique de l'empire byzantin* (Paris: PUF, 1975), pp. 36-59.

[7]Friedrich Heer, *Europäische Geistesgeschichte* (Stuttgart: Kohlhammer, 1957), pp. 80-90.

[8]See Paulo Suess's suggestively titled book *A conquista espiritual da América espanhola* (Petropolis, Brazil: Vozes, 1992).

[9]See an introduction in David J. Bosch, *Dynamique de la mission chrétienne* (Paris: Karthala, 1995), pp. 599-612; David J. Bosch, *Transforming Mission* (Maryknoll, NY: Orbis Books, 1991); Paulo Suess, "Inculturación," in I. Ellacuria and Jon Sobrino (eds.), *Mysterium liberationis* (Madrid: Trotta, 1990), vol. II, pp. 377-422.

[10]E.g., V. Neckbrouck, *Paradoxes de l'inculturation* (Leuven, Belgium: Peeters, 1994).

[11]Cf. Diego Irrarázaval, "Nadie ve el reino, si no nace de nuevo," in Paulo Suess (ed.), *Os confins do mundo no meio de nós* (São Paulo: Paulinas, 2000).

[12]For the preceding pages, cf. Jean Gaudemet, *L'Eglise dans l'empire roman Ive-Ve* (Paris: Sirtey, 1958), pp. 511-581.

[13]From a vast literature, Raymond Delatouche, *La chrétienté médiévale: Un modèle de développement* (Paris: Tequi, 1989).

[14]One may visit any large ecclesiastical library and find tons of books read only by those attending seminaries or convents that are of little use for the church's dialogue with the world.

[15]For examples, just examine Brazilian and Latin American literature from colonial times to the present.

9. ACTION OF THE PEOPLE OF GOD IN THE WORLD

[1]Inaugural address (January 28, 1979), 3, 7.

[2]Efforts to have a motion of support for Archbishop Romero, who had received death threats, were unsuccessful. A group of friendly bishops wrote and signed one.

[3]Cf. "Dom Hélder, bispo do Terceiro Milênio," in Zildo Rocha (ed.), *Hélder, o Dom: Uma vida que marcou os rumos da Igreja no Brasil* (Petropolis, Brazil: Vozes, 1999), pp. 91-94.

[4]Cf. Dom Marcelo Carvalheira, "Momentos históricos e desdobramentos da Ação Católica brasileira," in *REB*, fasc. 169, vol. 43 (1983), pp. 10-28; Scott Mainwaring, "A JOC e o surgimento da Igreja na Base (1958-1970)," in *REB*, fasc. 169, vol. 43 (1983), pp. 29-92.

[5]Cf. Cardinal Joseph Cardign, *Leigos nas linhas da frente* (São Paulo: Paulinas, 1967).

[6]Pedro A. Ribeiro de Oliveira, *Religão e dominação de classe* (Petropolis, Brazil: Vozes, 1985), pp. 297-305.

[7]Cf. Phillip Berryman, *Stubborn Hope: Religion, Politics, and Revolution in Central America* (Maryknoll, NY: Orbis Books, 1994), pp. 23-62. See Ignacio Ellacuria, *Escritos teológicos* (San Salvador: UCA, 2000), pp. 603-849.

[8]Cf. homily at the mass of beatification of Friar Joseph Kalinowski and Brother Adam Chmielowski, founder of the Albertines, in Krakow on June 22, 1983. See *Documentation catholique*, n. 1857, year 65, vol. LXXX, no. 15, col. 809. The pope said that for them the insurrection was "a stage toward sanctity, which is lifelong heroism."

[9]See my book, *Called for Freedom: The Changing Context of Liberation Theology* (Maryknoll, NY: Orbis Books, 1998).

10. PEOPLE OF GOD AND THE CHURCH INSTITUTION

[1]Cf. Medard Kehl, *¿Adónde va la Iglesia? Un diagnóstico de nuestro tiempo* (Santander, Spain: Sal Terrae, 1997), pp. 17-24; Herman J. Pottmeyer, "Vers une nouvelle phase de réception de Vatican II. Vingt ans d'herméneutique du Concile," in G. Alberigo and J. P. Jossua (eds.), *La réception de Vatican II* (Paris: Cerf, 1985), pp. 43-46.

[2]Cf. G. Alberigo, "La condition chrétienne après Vatican II," in Alberigo and Joussa, *La réception de Vatican II*, p. 29. John XXIII looked far ahead and discerned long-range changes in the churches. Most of the bishops did not understand it.

[3]Cf., for example, the ecclesiology of Jean-Marie Tillard, *Église d'Églises: L'écclesiologie de communion* (Paris: Cerf, 1987); *L'Église locale. Ecclésiologie de communion et catholicité* (Paris: Cerf, 1995); or of Walter Kasper, *La théologie et l'Église* (Paris: Cerf, 1990).

[4]Pius IX once exclaimed: "I am tradition." See Yves Congar, "La réception comme réalité ecclésiologique," in *Concilium*, no. 77 (1972), pp. 771-72.

[5]*Letter to the Bishops of Vienna*, PL 50, 434. A great deal of documentation can be found in José I. González Faus, "Ningún obispo impuesto," in *San Celestino, papa: Las elecciones episcopales en la historia de la Iglesia* (Santander, Spain: Sal Terrae, 1992).

[6]Cf. John Cornwell, *Hitler's Pope* (New York: Viking, 1999).

[7]In Brazil mistakes have been made because it is a big country and it is impossible to monitor everything. The situation is different elsewhere in Latin America.

[8]Cf. Ghislain Lafont, *Imaginer l'Église* (Paris: Cerf, 1995), pp. 217-224; Tillard, *L'Église locale* (Paris: Cerf, 1995), pp. 228-241.

[9]Cf. Gerald Arbuckle, *Refounding the Church: Dissent for Leadership* (London: Geoffrey Chapman, 1993).

[10]*Lumen Gentium* 12, citing St. Augustine, *De prædestinatione Sanctorum*, 14, 25; PL 44, 980.

[11]Cf. Jon Sobrino, "L'authorité doctrinae du peuple de Dieu en Amérique Latine," in *Concilium*, no. 200 (1985), pp. 73-82.

[12]On the errors of the magisterium, cf. José Ignacio González Faus, *La autoridad de la verdad* (Barcelona: Herder, 1996).

[13]On the expansion of the magisterium of the hierarchy, cf. Yves Congar, *Église et Paupauté* (Paris: Cerf, 1994), pp. 283-315; Alberigo, *A Igreja na história* (São Paulo: Paulinas, 1999), pp. 269-306.

[14]Just before the 1976 military coup in Argentina, General Videla went to mass in San Miguel, near the military neighborhood. He came out of mass as though he had had a revelation, and told an aide, "Now I know what I have to do." He thought God had given him revelation and that it was his mission to carry out a coup—which in fact happened shortly afterward.

[15]Cf. Congar, "La réception comme réalité ecclésiologique."

[16]Cf. Alberigo, *A Igreja na história*, pp. 221-244.

[17]Most seminaries around the world have been run by Sulpicians, Vincentians, and Eudists, and they shaped the mindset and external behavior of priests until Vatican II.

[18]Alberigo, *A Igreja na história*, pp. 243ff.

[19]Cf. R. Gryson, *Les origines du célibat ecclésiastique du premier au septième siècle* (Gembloux, France: Duculot, 1979); "Dix ans de recherches sur les origines du célibat ecclésiastique," in *Revue Théologique de Louvain*, 11 (1980), pp. 157-185.

CONCLUSION

[1]Quoted by Jon Sobrino, *The True Church and the Poor* (Maryknoll, NY: Orbis Books, 1984), p. 123.

Index